Vibrant Learning

PRAISE FOR VIBRANT LEARNING

"*Vibrant Learning* brings a refreshing, inclusive, and comprehensive approach to content area teaching and learning. The authors provide the foundations for learning, including theory, history, and standards. These include the Common Core Standards as well as the professional standards for reading, literacy, English, mathematics, science, and social studies. The authors address and establish the importance of assessment and the tools of assessment, vocabulary instruction and learning, comprehension, fluency, writing, discussion, questioning, integration of the arts, and motivation in the well-designed chapters of this important book. The strategies for teaching these important and integrated areas play an integral part in the total picture of content area development and learning for teachers at all levels of instruction." —**Dr. Rona F. Flippo**, professor of education, University of Massachusetts Boston

"This remarkable book should be read and re-read by every educator; there are numerous lessons to be learned by teachers at all levels! Students in my Content Area Reading class raved that the complex concepts were easy to understand as a result of the excellent writing and beautiful visuals. The authors' vast teaching experiences paired with a conversational writing style makes this book come alive." —**Abigail New**, adjunct professor, Rollins College; classroom teacher, Orange County Public Schools

"*Vibrant Learning* illuminates the process of integrating content areas from theory to practice. The textbook is extremely helpful for both pre-service and in-service teachers who want to implement elements of instruction and assessment that deepen learning for all students." —**James A. Telese**, professor of mathematics education, University of Texas Rio Grande Valley

"I hope you and your students find *Vibrant Learning: An Integrative Approach to Teaching Content Area Disciplines* as enjoyable as I have discovered. The text begins with a very readable discussion of five progressive learning theorists, and connects these through each chapter to model teaching ideas and activities. Each chapter begins with an interesting vignette and concludes with a theory to practice section." —**Alan Zollman**, PhD, past president, School Science and Mathematics Association; past vice president, Research Council on School Mathematics; faculty emeritus, Department of Mathematics Sciences at Northern Illinois University; Secondary Mathematics Education at Indiana University Southeast

Vibrant Learning

An Integrative Approach to Teaching Content Area Disciplines

Debra K. Wellman, Cathy Y. Kim,
Lynn Columba, and Alden J. Moe

ROWMAN & LITTLEFIELD
Lanham • Boulder • New York • London

Published by Rowman & Littlefield
A wholly owned subsidiary of The Rowman & Littlefield Publishing Group, Inc.
4501 Forbes Boulevard, Suite 200, Lanham, Maryland 20706
www.rowman.com

Unit A, Whitacre Mews, 26-34 Stannary Street, London SE11 4AB

British Library Cataloguing in Publication Information Available

Library of Congress Cataloging-in-Publication Data

Names: Wellman, Debra K., author. | Kim, Cathy Y., author. | Columba, Lynn, author. |
Moe, Alden J., author.
Title: Vibrant learning : an integrative approach to teaching content area disciplines /
Debra K. Wellman, Cathy Y. Kim, Lynn Columba and Alden J. Moe.
Description: Lanham, Maryland : Rowman & Littlefield, [2018] |
Includes bibliographical references and index.
Identifiers: LCCN 2018005303 (print) | LCCN 2018022472 (ebook) |
ISBN 9781475842371 (Electronic) | ISBN 9781475842357 (cloth : alk. paper) |
ISBN 9781475842364 (pbk. : alk. paper)
Subjects: LCSH: Content area reading. | Interdisciplinary approach in education.
Classification: LCC LB1050.455 (ebook) | LCC LB1050.455 .W54 2018 (print) |
DDC 372.47/6—dc23
LC record available at https://lccn.loc.gov/2018005303

This book is dedicated to our students
and colleagues who touch our hearts and
inspire us to teach with vibrancy.

Contents

Preface

Content area instruction is a term usually attributed to secondary discipline-based subjects like mathematics, social studies, and science. This book was written to support content area teachers, who are often characterized by an unapologetic passion for their discipline and subject matter, to infuse and weave literacy—reading, writing, listening, speaking, and viewing—to make learning more *vibrant*.

What does vibrant learning mean? Close your eyes for a minute and think about the word. For the four of us, vibrancy moves us to a creative space where active learning is essential. In vibrant classrooms, students are engaged in wondering and questioning, and their curiosities generate excitement and energy. They are challenged to think analytically, solve problems, and transfer knowledge into action. In vibrant classrooms, teachers ignite creativity and imagination through their knowledge and pedagogy. They masterfully deliver an equal dose of support and gentle nudging as they teach, guide, and challenge. In vibrant classrooms, learning is recursive and messy, slowly and steadily transforming students (and teachers).

This book, written *by* teachers *for* teachers, is packed with classroom-tested strategies for vibrant learning. These strategies, ones we have used with our own students and in our college teacher preparation programs, are meant to facilitate students to construct meaning from experiences and texts. Our hope for the readers of this text is to provide helpful ideas for teaching your discipline, a deeper understanding of the importance of a literate environment, and inspiration to create a learning space that is truly vibrant.

Acknowledgments

Debra, Lynn, and Cathy would like to acknowledge Alden J. Moe, their mutual friend and colleague who brought this collaboration together. As a brilliant scholar, intuitive teacher, and generous mentor, you have been a steadfast influence in our academic careers as well as our lives. Thank you, Al.

Merging Constructivist, Sociocultural, and Collaborative Theories

Vibrant Learning

I hear and I forget. I see and I remember. I do and I understand.

—Confucius

Impact of a Teacher

Few teachers ever get to see the impact they have on their students. This story begins with serendipity putting me in a hospital emergency room with my husband whose foot had an encounter with the lawn mower and an unknown cussing machine of a man behind the curtain of his shared room.

The quiet of my husband's hospital room was disrupted when the man behind the curtain began blurting obscenities about the hospital's inability to contact his mom and his refusal of stitches in his head until his mom came to the hospital. It went something like this:

Man: How long have I f*%#ing been here?

Police Officer: We are going on forty minutes.

Man: Why haven't you f*%#ing called my G#* D*%# mom?

Security Guard: The number you gave us doesn't work.

These small outbursts of profanity-laced conversations typically followed seven to ten minutes of absolute silence. About the third time this conversation was repeated, the young man let out a key detail that caught my attention.

Man: Why don't you f*%#ing call my mom?

Police Officer: Well, the number you gave us doesn't work.

Man: What the f*%# does that mean? Sh*#!

Security Guard: You gave us too many numbers.

Man: That's f*%#ing impossible. I've know my G#* D%#* phone number since I was a kid.

Security Guard: Well, why don't you give it to us again. Maybe you've sobered up enough to remember the right number.

Man: It's 555-321-90210 (*90210* was a popular TV teen drama show that aired in the 1990s.)

Police Officer: That is *still* too many numbers.

I looked at the nurse attending my husband's injuries and asked if she could reveal the name of the person behind the curtain. The young man said "321" and that was the phone exchange for the small town I taught in. She moved to the other side of the curtain that was once again eerily quiet. She came back and whispered his name to me. Sure enough, Chris was in my seventh-grade class about ten years ago—I loved this kid. He had a hard life, and although I wasn't privy to the details, I knew that he wasn't allowed to be at home in the evenings and a local bartender had taken him in under his wing and allowed him to stay in the back room where he could do homework or play pool during the cold winter months.

The cussing conversation started up again.

I told my husband I was going around the curtain to go talk to Chris. Just as things escalated, I peered around the curtain.

Me: Chris?

Chris: (Chris looks up, sees me, and in the sweetest, most cherub-sounding voice you can imagine, slowly says . . .) Ms. Wellman? Chris tries to get up with outstretched arms to give me a hug. Both the security officer and the policeman set him back down. I take a few steps closer.

Me: Chris, what happened? Are you okay?

Chris again tries to get up to hug me, and I assure the officers that it is fine. Chris throws his arms around me and gives me a big bear hug. He begins to explain what has transpired that evening that led him to be in the hospital with a gash in his head.

I glance up and notice both the police officer and the hospital security guard staring at the two of us with their mouths gaped open. Chris turns to the security guard and police officer.

Chris: This is Ms. Wellman, my favorite teacher. Then turning and facing me, he starts, Ms. Wellman, this is . . . [he realizes he doesn't know either of the officers' names and pauses] a police officer and a hospital security guard.

We all laugh. Both men reach out to shake my hand. Not one single cuss word has come out of Chris's mouth since I entered the room, and his demeanor is tender and warm toward me.

Chris: They tell me I need stitches. (He tilts his head so I can see the wound.) Do I?

Me: Yes, it looks like you'll need three to five stitches.

Chris turns to the hospital security guard.

Chris: You can call the doctor. If Ms. Wellman says I need stitches, you can stitch me up.

A few moments later, I decide to head back to my husband's side of the curtain. I tell Chris it was nice to see him and I wish him well. The three men on the other side of the curtain continue to converse, but Chris does not utter another bad word.

This is one of the impacts of being a teacher.

THEORETICAL FOUNDATIONS OF VIBRANT LEARNING

Isaac Newton has been credited as saying, "If I have seen farther, it is from standing on the shoulders of giants." In teacher education, this comment has become a metaphor for building on the research and work of other great teachers and researchers. An entire course could be taught on the theories of those that have come before us, but that is not the purpose of this text. Table 1.1 presents theorists and their ideas that have influenced what some educators call active or hands-on learning. Vibrant learning, a term that better defines the lively, exuberant learning that happens in classrooms that are pulsating with energy, is what this book strives to support. By merging the constructivist, sociocultural, and collaborative perspectives of teaching, the vibrancy that emerges in classrooms creates students motivated to learn in the various content areas they encounter throughout their middle grade and high school years.

Constructivist Theories

Constructivist theory is based on the understanding that learning is deeper and more meaningful when students are able to "construct" new ideas and concepts under the guidance of a "more knowledgeable other," which could be a teacher, parent, or peer. According to Richardson (1997), "It suggests that individuals create their own new understandings, based upon the inter-action of what they already know and believe, and the phenomena or ideas with which they come into contact" (p. 3). Unfortunately, constructivism has been broadly defined and used to describe unguided or minimally guided in-structional approaches where students determine what they want to learn and are motivated to explore a topic until they understand it. Kirschner, Sweller, and Clark (2006) make the point that "these approaches ignore both the structures that constitute human cognitive architecture and evidence from em-pirical studies over the past half-century that consistently indicate that min-imally guided instruction is less effective and less efficient than instructional approaches that place a strong emphasis on guidance of the student learning process" (p. 75).

Our definition of constructivist teaching does not imply support of minim-ally guided instruction. The authors of this text believe that teachers are an essential component of the learning process that not only provide support for student learning but also guide students to situations that allow them to have "a-ha" moments. Each of the authors of this text have witnessed moments when our students have enjoyed the thrill of discovering how something works or when a concept comes into focus and a student understands it for

Table 1.1. Theories underpinning constructivist, sociocultural, collaborative perspectives.

Theorist	Theory	Ideas	Seminal Works
Jean Piaget	Cognitive Theory, Schema Theory	Child-centered learning through active discovery. The mechanism of learning is the process of equilibration. Cognitive structure assimilates and accommodates to create new knowledge.	*The Child's Conception of the World* (1928) *Origins of Intelligence in the Child* (1936) *The Origins of Intelligence in Children* (1952)
Jerome Bruner	Discovery Learning, Constructivism	Discovery leads the child "to learn varieties of problem solving, of transforming information for better use, helps him to learn how to go about the very task of learning" (1966, p. 87).	*The Process of Education* (1960) *Toward a Theory of Instruction* (1966) *Actual Minds, Possible Worlds* (1986) *The Narrative Construction of Reality* (1991)
John Dewey	Pragmatism, Experiential Education, Collaboration	Ideas are instruments or tools to make sense of the world. The optimal way to learn is through experience and participation. Education is a social and interactive process.	*Democracy and Education: An Introduction to the Philosophy of Education* (1916) *How We Think: A Restatement of the Relation of Reflective Thinking to the Educative Process* (1933) *Experience and Education* (1938)
Lev Vygotsky	Zone of Proximal Development, Scaffolding, Sociocultural Theory, Language Development, Play, Collaboration	The optimal learning takes place between the child's independent level and the potential level with the assistance of a more knowledgable other (teacher or peer). New knowledge is dependent on prior knowledge. Play has an important role in children's development. There is an explicit connection between language and thought.	*Mind in Society: The Development of Higher Psychological Processes* (1978) *Thought and Language* (1986) (original work published in 1934) *Thinking and Speech* (1987)

Theorist	Theory	Ideas	Seminal Works
Louise Rosenblatt	Transactional Theory	The meaning-making process takes place among the text, the reader, and the context. It is the reader that transforms the text into a set of meaningful symbols.	*Literature as Exploration* (1938) *The Reader, the Text, the Poem: The Transactional Theory of the Literary Work* (1978) *Making Meaning with Texts: Selected Essays* (2005)

the first time. These moments provide a "teacher high" that we hope you get to experience often in your career.

We like to think of our collaborative learning approach as the "sweet spot" in a spectrum of teaching approaches. On one end of the spectrum lie "unguided" approaches, where students are allowed to wander from topic to topic that interests them, to the other end of the spectrum and equally troubling "direct instructional" approaches, where teachers are given a script and students are expected to respond with a single "right" answer. Yet teaching without a script or creating innovative lessons can be overwhelming to "new" teachers. As Loughran and Russell (1997) argue, teacher education can only be the starting point for the development of constructivist-oriented teaching, since no teacher preparation program could fully "equip" a teacher with all the skills and understandings necessary to teach. This text is designed to provide you with the theory and the essential tools you will need to be successful as you begin your teaching career.

Piaget (1928, 1936) is credited with being the first psychologist to study the ways in which children think. Prior to his research, children were not studied because it was thought that children and adults thought in similar ways, adults were just able to do it better. Piaget's work on developmental stages had a profound impact on teachers' understanding of young children and the way in which they learn.

One of the most important learning theories that Piaget (1928) pioneered was *schema theory*. He originally described schema as categories of knowledge that help us interpret the world. Bartlett's (1932) research extended the understanding of schema when he noticed that on recall, people would substitute something familiar in place of a word or concept they did not understand when retelling a story. Schema theory conflicted with the predominate learning theory of the 1940s through the 1970s—Skinner's (1938, 1961, 1964, 1968) behaviorist theory proposed that behavior (learning) could be controlled by a stimulus that would produce the correct response. According

to Watson (1913), psychology as the behaviorist views it is a "purely objective experimental branch of natural science. Its theoretical goal is the
prediction and control of behavior" (p. 158). This way of thinking dominated
psychology until the cognitive psychology movement emerged that studied
how actual children think and learn.

Anderson (1977) is credited with bringing schema theory to the field of
education. Anderson explained how *what we already know* (schema) has an
impact on our understanding of new information. Schema theory provides
us with an explanation of how we organize and integrate information in our
minds. Smith (1988) calls this cognitive structure or system of knowledge
"a summary of our past experiences" that endows us with "a *theory* of what
the world is like, a theory that is the basis for all our perceptions and understanding of the world, the root of all learning, the source of hopes and fears,
motives and expectations, reasoning and creativity" (p. 7). We use what we
already know to make sense of new information, new knowledge, or new
experience. Spiro (1980) refers to this as "the constructive orientation, with
its attendant emphasis on the importance of what one already knows in determining what one will come to know" (p. 2). In this process, the cognitive
structure or system of knowledge is dynamic and constantly changing—
adding, deleting, merging, separating, modifying, relabeling, shifting, and
more—what we know and how we organize what we know.

Bruner (1960) is considered to be one of the founding fathers of constructivist theory. Piaget was a strong influence on Bruner's concept that learners
construct new ideas or concepts based on what they already know. In Bruner's
opinion, learning is an active process, not a passive one. When a child learns a
new concept, he attaches the new material to already learned concepts.

An example would be to think about the different understandings of the
following short poem "Lightning Bugs" by Debra Wellman.

In the warmth of a summer night,
As the day begins its goodbye,
It appears as though the stars
Have descended from the sky.

My watchful eyes are focused
As I stalk the twinkling light,
My hands reach out to the darkness
And I capture him when he's bright.

A child growing up in the Midwest who has been catching lightning bugs
throughout her childhood has developed a schema, or a category of understanding about lightning bugs that a child growing up west of the Rocky
Mountains, where there are no lightning bugs would not have developed

(figure 1.1). The difference in each child's schema about lightning bugs would enhance or hinder their understanding this poem.

Bruner's conception of categories of knowledge is a significant emphasis in how he believed teachers should instruct students for optimal learning. Bruner (1966) theorized that there were six features to a child's intellectual growth: "1) a predisposition to learn; 2) the structure of the knowledge; 3) modes of representation including visual, words, and symbols; 4) interaction with the 'tutor'; 5) development of language; 6) and effective sequencing" (pp. 5–6).

When you introduce a new concept to your students, you will want to know what they already understand about the topic by activating their prior knowledge, or in other words activating their schema. Sometimes this may require a teacher to "unteach" or repair schema that is incorrect. For example, a young science student may think the moon and sun is the same round object in the sky, the only difference is that the object looks different during the day versus the night. Misconceptions that have been committed to memory are very difficult to unteach and can hinder student learning. This is especially true if the teacher does not realize the student's misconceptions.

By understanding the theories of Piaget and Bruner, you will see the purpose for activating prior knowledge at the start of a lesson. (More on this topic is presented in chapter 6.) Finding out what your students already know about the topic, along with what they *think* they know about the topic, allows a teacher to plan for instruction. Only then can you develop a sequence of lessons that build one upon another to improve student learning. Bruner (1960) emphasized the importance of personalizing or making the material relevant to the students, followed by structuring and sequencing the material

Figure 1.1   Lightning bug. iStock illustration ID: 619244050. Credit: Nauma.

to build on past knowledge and reinforcing what students are learning through appropriate pace and motivation.

Sociocultural Theories

In the last decade, researchers have begun to investigate the importance of discussion and group dynamics on learning. This is not a new concept; the basic tenet of Socrates' teaching was that knowledge comes through logic, interactive dialogue, contemplation, and reflection. Recent interest in discussion-based instruction stems from better understanding that humans are social creatures, and allowing students to work together enhances their learning. Teachers also need to think about and plan for helping students from diverse backgrounds learn to work together by understanding and showing respect to one other. We expect that in your undergraduate teacher education program you took courses that discussed the importance of how language and culture are connected (e.g., Nieto, 2017) and how teachers must work toward socially just classrooms.

Dewey (1938) contends that learning is a socially constructed process. He believed students would thrive in learning environments that allowed students the ability to experience and interact with the concepts. Mathematics manipulatives allow students to play with various fractional pieces of the whole so that they gain a deeper understanding of the concepts of fractions. Genuine learning takes place through connected experiences that Dewey called "educative" (p. 25). These educative experiences enhance a child's education, but not all experiences are educative; some experiences may be miseducative and detract from a child's education. For example, completing a series of worksheets may negatively affect a child's opinion of or love of reading. A teacher we once observed asked a student, "What is reading?" and the child replied, "It is being able to answer the questions at the end of the story." Imagine what the same child would say if she were given beautiful trade books to read and then engaged in conversations with others about her reading.

Dewey's (1938) progressive movement suggests that students' learning should take place in a relaxed atmosphere with the freedom to explore some topics more deeply if it is of interest to the student. Authentic learning experiences include social interactions such as discussions and debates with their peers, or sociocultural learning experiences such as group activities. Students participating in educative experiences are engaged in authentic learning that is grounded in real-life experiences. Teachers teaching the skills involved in writing business and personal letters should avoid made-up or contrived reasons to write letters. Instead, an authentic learning experience would be to write *real* business letters about *real* concerns and *actually* mail the letters. When assignments or projects are authentic, students are more enthusiastic about them.

Vygotsky (1978) extends our constructivist framework to include sociocultural perspectives by addressing the importance of language in learning. The role of language in the development of thought is considered one of the key components of Vygotsky's theory. He stressed that learning was constructed from verbal interactions between students or between students and their teacher. In these interactions, the gap between what the learner knows and what their "more knowledgeable other" knows is called the *zone of proximal development* (Vygotsky, 1978, p. 86).

The zone of proximal development is "the distance between the actual developmental level as determined by independent problem solving and the level of potential development as determined through problem solving under adult guidance or in collaboration with more capable peers" (Vygotsky, 1978, p. 86). Scaffolding is the process of filling in the gap between what the learner understands and what the more knowledgable other knows. As students participate in discussions, they are scaffolding, or helping their peers to build new understandings by extending their current views, or schemata (Bruner, 1960). Through scaffolding, students learn by attaching new concepts to their existing knowledge, allowing them to tackle material beyond their individual abilities. When we allow students the opportunity to discuss, we provide the opportunity to apply Vygotsky's theory to actual classroom practice. In language arts classrooms where students are encouraged to read authentic literature, teachers encourage students to choose texts that are more challenging because they know the discussions with their peers and others will enable them to comprehend texts they once thought were too difficult for their students. Scaffolding through peer interactions, like group work activities, have a similar effect in the content areas.

Rosenblatt's (1978) theory of reading described the actual reading process as transactional. She claimed that students do more than simply read the words; they make connections to their own lived experiences and interpret the author's words in personal and meaningful ways. Instead of the old way of checking for comprehension by regurgitating correct answers at the end of the story, students participate in discussions with each other where readers debate perceptions, ask pertinent questions for clarification, and share interesting concepts. In addition, multiple "meanings" or interpretations that readers create from their reading are accepted and acknowledged.

In many traditional classrooms, good grades are earned by locating correct answers and interpreting stories in the same way the answer key suggests. The sociocultural perspective encourages students to take risks in their learning. Students are encouraged to predict, make assumptions, and share their own interpretations—all of which are higher-order thinking skills. As students transact with the text and their peers, they create thought-provoking questions that may lead to deep discussions and debates. They are vibrant learners. "The constructivist position argues for giving students opportunities to read and respond personally to literature" (McMahon & Goatly, 1995, p. 23). This perspective has the potential to shift focus from students answering the questions the textbook may pose to empowering students with the ability to generate their own questions. By introducing growing minds to authentic problems and situations that challenge their own thinking about issues, we are beginning to create critical thinkers. When the characters in the stories struggle with real-life situations, readers can empathize with them and learn from their experiences. As teachers, when we create vibrant learning environments, we are doing more than just teaching reading, art, science, music, social studies, or mathematics; we are creating future citizens and thoughtful leaders.

Collaborative Theories

Significant learning does not take place when students are passive listeners. Hamilton Holt, former president of Rollins College (1925–1949), had never served as a professor when he was invited to serve as president of this small, liberal arts college in central Florida. He came to Rollins from years of serving as a former journal editor. Through his experiences, he felt *real* learning happened when he met and discussed ideas with small groups of intelligent colleagues. Holt stated "that my colleagues in the editorial room, who never thought of teaching me anything, taught me everything, while my professors at Yale and Columbia, who were paid to teach me, taught me virtually nothing" (Ratjar & Ratjar, 2009, p. 86). He shared his concerns openly with the Rollins professors and requested that there would be "no more lectures."

> I objected to the lecture system. I agreed with the young man who described it as a process whereby the content of the professor's notebook are transferred by means of a fountain pen to the student's notebook without having passed the mind of either. (Woolf, 1947, p. 116)

Holt proposed a two-hour conference course that would allow small groups of students to meet with a faculty member in a casual classroom setting (Ratjar & Ratjar, 2009). President Holt's 1926 "conference plan" was perhaps the first version of a "flipped classroom." Holt wanted the students to participate in small group interactions, with the faculty member serving more as a coach who would guide their instruction. The faculty unanimously adopted this fresh approach and set Rollins on a path of distinction for curricular innovation (Ratjar & Ratjar, 2009).

In 1931, Holt invited prominent members of the education community to Rollins for a symposium to think about education around the novel idea of *what the students desired*, a concept that was highly controversial. He asked his friend, John Dewey, to serve as the host, and prominent scholars from "Columbia, Sarah Lawrence, Vanderbilt, and Cornell touched on subject[s] as diverse as the meaning of liberal arts and what effort should be taken to bridge the gap between practical concerns and traditional subject matter" (Chambliss, 2009).

In a vibrant classroom environment, we want our students to be active participants and not passive observers. Providing opportunities for students to collaborate and discuss what they are learning with their peers has multiple positive outcomes.

- More students have a chance to voice their opinions.
- Quiet or reluctant speakers are more likely to share with small groups of peers.
- Intimate discussions allow students to make deeper connections with the text and their own lived experiences.
- Interactions with peers enhance social skills.

Collaborative techniques designed to get students to work together and solve complex problems have a multitude of purposes. We know

- student motivation increases when they are involved in solving real-world problems.
- students need practice learning how to negotiate and work together in teams.
- students enjoy working with their friends; in fact, they are able to get to the problem at hand more readily.
- students see a purpose to the end product (letter, proposal, etc.) rather than simply a grade.

VIBRANT LEARNING

The theories presented in this chapter shift our understanding of how students learn. As we move away from passive teaching techniques to active learning and to encourage more active learning, we move from linear to multidimensional and from isolated to social. The constructivist theory, based on the ideas of Piaget, Anderson, and Bruner, established the notion that students create their own knowledge rather than being passive consumers who receive knowledge. The collaborative and sociocultural perspectives based on ideas generated by Dewey, Vygotsky, and Rosenblatt support teaching and learning through social interactions.

Richardson's (2003) five distinct characteristics of constructivist-oriented pedagogy sums up nicely many of the ideas presented in this chapter:

- attention to the individual and respect for the students' backgrounds and developing understanding of and beliefs about elements of the domain (this could also be described as student centered)
- facilitation of group dialogue that explores an element of the domain with the purpose of leading to the creation and shared understanding of a topic
- planned and often unplanned introduction of formal domain knowledge into the conversation through direct instruction, reference to text, exploration of a website, or some other means
- provision of opportunities for students to determine, challenge, change, or add to existing beliefs and understandings through engagement in tasks that are structured for this purpose
- development of the students' meta-awareness of their own understandings and learning processes (p. 1626).

Vibrant learning unites constructivist, collaborative, and sociocultural theories into a dynamic learning environment. Teachers embracing this vibrant learning approach have moved away from the idea of transmitting or pouring knowledge into their students' heads to the more progressive notion of providing the platform, such as discussions, lab experiments, and hands-on activities, for students to be able to construct knowledge. Learning in such authentic contexts results in deeper understanding of concepts and motivation to learn. An added benefit is that vibrant learning transcends all content areas, and research is showing higher achievement benefits all students in all subjects when they are truly engaged in learning.

Finally, and perhaps most importantly, the teacher's ability to create a *community of learners* in secondary classrooms is essential for learning. For many future teachers, who have been educated in a competitive, achievement oriented, and grade-based approach, to think about teaching and learning as a community activity is foreign and, perhaps, unnerving. Developing a strong community of learners is a crucial element of a vibrant classroom that takes a great deal of up-front work by the teacher and students. Creating this positive work culture begins with building rapport between the teacher and the students, but also includes building rapport among the students who will be expected to learn together, to help each other, and support one another. You will learn more on this topic in chapter 12 on motivation.

THEORY TO PRACTICE

While Gordon (2009) noted that "constructivist teaching practices are becoming more prevalent in teacher education programs and public schools across the nation" (p. 40), we understand the ease in which teachers might resort back to the *transmission of knowledge* techniques from yesteryear. We hope that by utilizing this text, you will build a repertoire of pedagogical skills designed to help your students *collaborate* and enjoy their membership in a community of learners, to embrace a *constructivist* approach of learning by doing, and to appreciate the diversity of ideas found in *sociocultural* classrooms that will enhance students' understanding of content area concepts as well as our broader world.

For those of you using this book in an undergraduate or graduate content area literacy course, we hope that your professor will design the curriculum and create the learning environment based on these theories so that you can experience the powerful learning that can occur when they are in practice. Once you have experienced the positive environment of being a member of a community of learners, you will have the basic tools you need to establish this environment for your own students.

If you are already a practicing teacher, we are excited that this professional development book has found its way into your hands. This book is designed to provide you with a myriad of ideas so that you, too, can join your students by taking risks and experimenting with learning strategies that are more active than you have previously experienced. If you are using this book as a faculty book club, you are experiencing a collaborative learning experience.

The four authors of this text hope that our love for our students and respect for those of you who have decided to become teachers is embraced in each chapter of this book. We teach our classes from these perspectives, we wrote this book from these perspectives, and we anticipate that you will have a more rewarding teaching experience if you are able to implement these ideas and create a positive classroom atmosphere in the content area for which you have a passion.

REFERENCES

Anderson, R. C. (1977). The notion of schemata and the educational enterprise: General discussion of the conference. In R. C. Anderson, R. J. Spiro & W. E. Montague (Eds.), *Schooling and the acquisition of knowledge*. Hillsdale, NJ: Erlbaum.

Bartlett, F. C. (1932). *Remembering*. Cambridge: Cambridge University Press.

Bruner, J. S. (1960). *The process of education*. Cambridge, MA: Harvard University Press.

Bruner, J. S. (1966). *Toward a theory of instruction*. Cambridge, MA: The Belknap Press of Harvard University Press.

Chambliss, J. C. (2009). "Hamilton Holt," golden personalities: Notable people of Rollins and Winter Park. Summer. http://lib.rollins.edu/olin/oldsite/archives/golden/Holt.htm.

Dewey, J. (1938). *Experience and education*. New York: Collier Books.

Gordon, M. (2009). Toward a pragmatic discourse of constructivism: Reflections of lessons from practice. *Educational Studies, 45*(1), 39–58.

Kirschner, P. A., Sweller, J. & Clark, R. E. (2006). Why minimal guidance during instruction does not work: An analysis of the failure of constructivist, discovery, problem-based, experiential, and inquiry-based teaching. *Educational Psychologist, 41*(2), 75–86.

Loughran, J. J., & Russell, T. (Eds.). (1997). *Teaching about teaching: Purpose, passion and pedagogy in teacher education*. New York: Routledge.

McMahon, S. I. & Goatley, V. J. (1995). Fifth graders helping peers discuss texts in student-led groups. *Journal of Educational Research, 89*(1), 23–34.

Nieto, S. (2017). *Language, culture, and teaching: Critical perspectives* (3rd ed.) New York: Routledge.

Piaget, J. (1928). *The child's conception of the world*. London: Routledge.

Piaget, J. (1936). *Origins of intelligence in the child*. London: Routledge & Kegan Paul.

Ratjar, G., & Ratjar, S. (2009). A different breed of college president: Hamilton Holt's nonconformist belief set Rollins on a path to excellence. *Winter Park Magazine*, June, p. 86.

Richardson, V. (1997). Constructivist teaching and teacher education: Theory and practice. *Constructivist teacher education: Building a world of new understandings*, 3–14.

Richardson, V. (2003). Constructivist pedagogy. *The Teachers College Record, 105*(9), 1623–40.

Rosenblatt, L. (1938, 1978). *The reader, the text, and the poem*. Carbondale, IL: Southern Illinois University Press.

Skinner, B. F. (1938). *The behavior of organisms: An experimental analysis*. New York: Appleton Century Company.

Skinner, B. F. (1961). *Cumulative record*. New York: Appleton Century Crofts.

Skinner, B. F. (1964). *Science and human behavior*. New York: Simon & Schuster.

Skinner, B. F. (1968). *The technology of teaching*. New York: Appleton-Century-Crofts.

Slyman, Earnest. (2010). "Lightning bugs." *Poems that make you laugh*. www.smashwords.com.

Smith, Frank. (1988). *Understanding reading* (4th ed.). Hillsdale, NJ: Lawrence Erlbaum Associates.

Spiro, R. J. (1980). *Schema theory and reading comprehension: New directions* (Tech. Rep. 191). Urbana: Center for the Study of Reading, University of Illinois.

Vygotsky, L. S. (1978). *Mind in society: The development of higher psychological processes*. Cambridge, MA: Harvard University Press.

Watson, J. B. (1913). Psychology as the behaviorist views it. *Psychological Review, 20*(2), 158–77.

Woolf, S. J. (1947). Dr. Holt looks at education and youth. *New York Times*, August 17, 1947; ProQuest Historical Newspapers: *New York Times*, p. 116.

2

It Is *Not* Either/Or; It Is *And*

Integration

There is, it seems, more concern about whether children learn the mechanics of reading and writing than grow to love reading and writing; learn about democracy than have practice in democracy; hear about knowledge . . . rather than gain experience in personally constructing knowledge . . . see the world narrowly, simple and ordered, rather than broad complex and uncertainly.

—Vitto Perrone, "Letter to Teachers"

Teaching Social Studies

I remember distinctly the meeting with my principal prior to my fifth year of teaching when he informed me that the next year I was going to be teaching seventh-grade social studies. I hated social studies. I was not qualified to teach social studies. I did not *want* to teach social studies. I was not happy, and my principal knew it. A week later he called me back to his office, and I was sure he was going to change my teaching assignment—which he did. Not only was I going to teach social studies, I now had the gifted section of students for social studies. I cried. I pleaded. I begged. And then I taught seventh-grade social studies to four groups of seventh-graders, one being the gifted group.

In the second or third week of school that year I had an "a-ha!" moment. "Teaching social studies was like teaching language arts except I had specific content." As a language arts teacher (code for reading teacher), I was used to a middle grade language arts basal (a compilation of stories and workbooks designed to teach reading) that would jump from one week with a story about pirates, to the next week with a story about ballerinas, and the following week to a story about rats taking over the world (*Rats of NIHM*). The social studies textbook laid out the history of the United States in an orderly fashion, beginning with the exploration of the "new lands," followed by settling the wilderness, then creating a new government, and ending somewhere around the New Deal.

17

As a social studies teacher with a reading background, I was able to bridge some of what I had considered to be the "boring textbook approach of teaching dates and facts" by supplementing the textbook with novels written about people who lived in those times. For example, when we studied the Revolutionary War, I read a chapter or two from *Johnny Tremain* each day at the start of class, and when Paul Revere was mentioned in the text, I supplemented the lesson that day with Longfellow's poem "Paul Revere's Ride."

Later in the year when we were studying about the Holocaust, I was able to get a class set of Lois Lowry's *Number the Stars*. A friend of mine invited her aunt, a Holocaust survivor, to come to my class to talk to my students. One of my students asked if she had been "tattooed." I still have a strong memory of the "audible gasp" from my students when she rolled up her sleeve and showed the students the numbers on her arm.

I fell in love with social studies—and I think many of my students did, too.

In the real world, outside of school, we do not compartmentalize our thinking as simply English, mathematics, science, social studies, music, art, and more. Life is always multidimensional; topics are naturally connected to each other in a myriad of ways. This chapter explores making classrooms a place where students examine topics in the content areas from multiple perspectives—historical, cultural, sociological, economical, political, technological, anthropological, and others—to fully understand concepts.

THEORETICAL FOUNDATIONS OF INTEGRATION

Integration is not a new concept; it has been in the educational vernacular for decades, if not longer. John Dewey's ideas on pragmatism (linking theory and practice) and experiential learning (linking ideas and experience) have influenced much of the progressive education we attempt to practice. Many of the ideals of progressive education, including the focus on process over product, integrated curriculum, and social responsibility and democracy, trace their roots to Dewey. While integrated learning, based on Dewey's ideas from the nineteenth century, is found in practice in some of today's educational contexts and realities, it is also true that much of teaching curriculum and learning in middle and high schools is still fragmented by subject areas and isolated in topics.

Middle and high schools are where various content specialists (i.e., teachers) and interests (i.e., students) congregate, making it an optimal zone for wondrous connections to take place. When students see and feel these connections, they may have those "a-ha" moments, and in those moments, the most genuine, authentic, and lasting learning occurs.

Hamston and Murdoch (1996) present a rationale for an integrated curriculum:

- It loosens the pressure created by rigid timetables and a stop-start curriculum, assisting teachers and students to use and manage their time more productively.
- It assists student and teachers to develop more efficient means of gathering, organizing, and processing the information increasingly available to us on a global as well as a local level.
- It helps us deal with curriculum that is "bulging at the seams" and challenges teachers to develop ways in which students can reorganize and bring the pieces together.
- It focuses on the "big ideas" rather than trivializing the content of programs.
- It makes more sense to the child's (and teacher's) day by providing a flow of learning rather than a stop-start approach.
- It develops a sense of community.
- It caters more successfully for individual differences—for the interests and needs of the learner.
- It encourages students to consider how they learn while developing important concepts and understandings.
- It provides genuine and rich contexts for developing a range of skills and understandings.

Integration presented in this chapter will come in a number of different but intersecting ways: integrating literacy and language processes, using age-appropriate and content-friendly literature, and connecting content area subjects.

LITERACY AS THE CONNECTING AGENT

Whether delivering lectures, facilitating discussions, conducting experiments, assigning textbook reading, or requiring lab reports, one cannot imagine a content class without one or more of the literacies—reading, writing, listening, speaking, and viewing. And there are many more ways in which content learning can be enhanced through integration of these language processes. For example, science teachers will benefit from the use of mind maps to help students understand processes such as photosynthesis. Mathematics teachers will be able to help their students understand word problems by incorporating sequential order vocabulary such as *before, after, then,* and others. Social studies teachers will find their students understand historical periods better when their students engage in writing about the periods.

In the early grades of elementary schools (K–2), teachers spend a majority of their time teaching children the fundamentals of learning to read. Third grade is typically viewed as the year reading instruction transitions from "learning to read" to "reading to learn." By the time students are in the middle grades, literacy strategies *support* learning in all content areas. By the time students are in high school, literacy skills propel and deepen learning. The following are brief descriptions of the five areas that make up literacy instruction and support content area learning.

Reading. Students read materials provided by the teacher to develop understanding. Many students will not be reading at their grade level, and you may need to deliver explicit instruction on skills and strategies for comprehension. You will need to support their learning with ancillary or supplemental texts to help them organize the concepts and learn the new technical vocabulary. (See chapter 6 for instructional strategies in promoting comprehension skills.)

Writing. Reading helps us take in knowledge; writing makes it our own. Teachers should provide students with multiple opportunities to organize their thoughts, create meaning, and communicate their knowledge through writing. There is strong research evidence that links writing and reading—improvement in writing skills improves reading skills; improvement in reading skills improves writing skills (Calkins, 1994; Harste, 2013; Sadoski & Paivio, 2013). (See chapter 8 for instructional strategies in promoting writing skills.)

Listening. Students learn by listening to their teachers as they explain concepts and ideas, particularly in content area classrooms. This area of literacy is often overlooked as something that does not need to be taught; perhaps some teachers have also assumed this is an area that cannot be improved. However, once listening skills are taught in classrooms, they may have transferability and provide a positive effect on students' communication skills outside of school as well. (See chapter 7 for instructional strategies in promoting listening skills.)

Speaking. Students need opportunities to discuss and learn from their peers. In fact, we cannot imagine how learning can take place in any classroom without students talking, conversing, engaging in discourse, debating, and presenting ideas. However, school can be a place where the silence, and hence a perception of order, is privileged over talk. (See chapter 7 for instructional strategies in promoting speaking skills.)

Viewing. Students today, more than in the past, rely on viewing or visual representations as a form of learning. Movie clips, web searches, YouTube videos, and other media all provide a means of delivering concepts to students. According to Moline (2011), "Visual information literacy is about making meaning with a mix of visual elements—lines, boxes, outline-drawings, arrows, labels, numbers, and so on" (p. 11). Flipping through the pages of a content area textbook, you will see how much content is represented through a "mix of visual elements" such as charts, graphs, illustrations, signs, sketches, diagrams, outlines, and more. Students in the content areas must be able to construct meaning through these visual representations, both in creating understanding and in demonstrating their evolving understandings. (See chapter 11 for using the arts as a way to promote learning.)

These five essential literacy components are the foundation for teaching any subject and any concept. Since students learn differently, it is essential that students have experiences in all of these literacy elements. Combining these elements can produce remarkable improvements in student learning.

THE IMPACT OF LITERATURE

In all content areas, age-appropriate and content-friendly literature added to the curriculum can be valuable in helping students understand concepts, even complex ones. While literature is a vital component in an English class, teachers in other disciplines have long advocated the use of literature as a means for teaching and supplementing the curriculum. In an integrated curriculum, the use of authentic literature helps students to build on previous experiences, including the experiences of characters in books, thus making learning more personal and meaningful. With the wealth of quality authentic literature available, it is becoming increasingly easy to develop and enhance content area concepts through stories, poems, biographies, journals, and so forth. The use of literature to develop content area concepts is encouraged by experts for the following reasons:

- It builds on the positive reaction that most students have to hearing and reading both familiar and new stories.
- It integrates learning in a variety of curriculum areas.
- It humanizes mathematics, science, and social studies in the eyes of children and parents.
- It challenges the stereotype of mathematics as a sterile, noncreative subject that is unrelated to the arts.
- It provides an alternative vehicle for communicating about mathematics, science, and social studies.
- It stimulates interest, enjoyment, and confidence in children (Lawrence, Hope, Small & Martin, 1996).

According to Spann (1992), perhaps the most powerful reason for using literature to teach content areas is that literature speaks to the heart of young adults. This type of instruction helps students realize the variety of situations in which people or book characters are faced with authentic problems they must resolve. Stories about people—both famous and ordinary—and their experiences—both remarkable and dull—are sources of deep connection that readers can make with an added sense of humanity.

Selecting Quality Literature for Content Areas

In selecting literature for a content area classroom, three types of books that Columba, Kim, and Moe (2009) offer might be a start: content explicit, content implicit, and content invisible. *Content explicit* books are written to inform and to teach the concepts presented; all expository texts fall in this category. An example of a content explicit text would be Jim Murphy's informational book *An American Plague: The True and Terrifying Story of the Yellow Fever Epidemic of 1793* (2003), written to inform the reader about the yellow fever epidemic in Philadelphia. The same story is told in a fictionalized account in Laurie Halse Anderson's *Fever 1793* (2000), in which the epidemic plays a backdrop to the main character's story of trial and survival, making this a content implicit book. *Content implicit* books are typically found in narrative stories where concepts are included but are not central to the story. *Content invisible* books are those texts that may not have any visible or apparent connection to content area concepts but can be used as a springboard for extending the conceptual learning.

Any book, whether content explicit, implicit, or invisible, has the power to transform learning in the hands of a good teacher who is committed to bridging worthy concepts through the beautiful words of a writer. Words recreated by master writers in good books, in fiction and in nonfiction and in a range of genres, will open new ways to learn in students.

So, what makes a book good? Certainly, this is a complex and perhaps even an impossible question to answer. What is good according to one reader may not be good to another; what we consider good literature may vary slightly or greatly according to what we find engaging, appropriate, or relevant. A good place to start when choosing books is with yourself and your colleagues. According to Columba, Kim, and Moe (2009), questions teachers should ask themselves when selecting books are:

- Is the book engaging to the reader?
- Is the book age appropriate?
- Is the book too difficult? Too simplistic?
- Does the book contribute to the balance of our collection?
- Does the book include meaningful and relevant concepts? (pp. 30–31)

The research in the field of adolescent literature also provides some guidelines created by experts. Typically, the selection criterion for adolescent literature varies according to the genre; each genre has its own particular qualities that make a book a good representative of the particular category. For example, a good informational book should have compelling details as well as an attractive format and design (Tunnel & Jacobs, 2007). A historical fiction selection, if being used to supplement the social studies content area, would need to have the historical events and details represented accurately in addition to compelling story lines and characters.

Another way to rely on professional opinions as we select good books is to use the guidelines drafted by experts in various professional organizations in a given field. For example, Donovan and Smolkin (2002) published criteria for selecting trade books for science instruction in the International Reading [now Literacy] Association's journal, *The Reading Teacher*. Likewise, Hellwig, Monroe, and Jacobs (2000) have an article in *Teaching Children Mathematics*, published by the National Council of Teachers of Mathematics, about selecting trade books for mathematics instruction. Annual lists have also become trusted resources for teachers looking to deliver a range of content area concepts through quality children's literature (table 2.1). The National Council for the Social Studies, for example, publishes its annual list of "Notable Trade Books for Young People" in its journal *Social Education.* Certainly, these and other professional insights into the selection process are important and useful to consider.

Once you begin to look for quality literature with the potential to enhance your content area, you may be surprised by the variety of options available. And once you begin to incorporate whether they are novels or informational texts, you will see how they transform students' engagement with topics and concepts.

THE POWER OF THE (RIGHT) PICTURE BOOK: YES, IN SECONDARY CLASSROOMS

As a content area teacher, be open to the power of picture books. Resist the temptation to dismiss them based on the format. In addition to the practical reasons, mainly due to their short lengths, you may be compelled to use them based on their sophisticated presentation of complex topics.

In picture books, both the text and the illustrations contribute to the understanding of the story. Because of their short length, often simple plots, and minimal number of words, many teachers thought picture books were only appropriate for elementary students. If picture books were used in middle or high school classrooms, they were typically used as remediation for struggling readers or English language learners.

Table 2.1. Notable book lists in the content areas.

Content Area	Sponsoring Organization	Description	Resource Link
Social Studies	National Council for the Social Studies with Children's Book Council	In the May/June issue of *Social Education*, the Notable Social Studies Trade Books for Young People shares K–12 books that emphasize human relations, represent a diversity of groups and are sensitive to a broad range of cultural experiences, present an original theme or a fresh slant on a traditional topic, are easily readable and of high literary quality, and have a pleasing format and, when appropriate, illustrations that enrich the text.	http://www.socialstudies.org/notable
Social Studies	International Literacy Association	The Notable Books for a Global Society selects twenty-five outstanding trade books for enhancing student understanding of people and cultures throughout the world. The committee reviews books representing all genres intended for students K–12.	http://clrsig.org/nbgs.php
Social Studies	National Council for the Social Studies	The Carter G. Woodson Book Awards recognize the most distinguished social science books appropriate for young readers that depict ethnicity in the United States.	http://www.socialstudies.org/awards/woodson/winners

Content Area	Sponsoring Organization	Description	Resource Link
Science	National Science Teachers Association with Children's Book Council	The Outstanding Science Trade Books for Students K–12 is created with the belief that reading science trade books is the perfect way for students to build literacy skills while learning science content. The list is also published in the March issue of NSTA's K–12 journals.	http://www.nsta.org/ publications/ostb/
Science	American Association for the Advancement of Science	The *Science Book & Films* (SB&F) is an online global critical review journal devoted exclusively to print and nonprint materials in all of the sciences for all age groups (K–college, teaching and general audience).	http://www.sbfonline.com
Mathematics	Ohio Resource Center	The *Mathematics Bookshelf* presents K–12 books in Number, Measurement, Geometry, Algebra, Data, and Multiple Strands.	http://ohiorc.org/for/math/ bookshelf/default.aspx
All Content Areas	National Council of Teachers of English	The Orbis Pictus Award for Outstanding Nonfiction for Children was established for promoting and recognizing excellence in the writing of nonfiction for children.	http://www.ncte.org/ awards/orbispictus
All Content Areas	Association for Library Service to Children	The Robert F. Sibert Informational Book Medal is awarded annually to the most distinguished informational book published in the United States in English during the preceding year.	http://www.ala.org/ alsc/awardsgrants/ bookmedia/sibertmedal
All Content Areas	Young Adult Library Services Association	The YALSA Award for Excellence in Nonfiction honors the best nonfiction book published for young adults (ages 12–18).	http://www.ala.org/yalsa/ nonfiction-award

During the last thirty years, there has been an emergence of "sophisticated picture books" (Miller, 1988), and the audience has expanded to include older readers (Giorgis, 1999). Authors and illustrators have begun to use picture books to tackle complex topics, some that would be entirely inappropriate for young readers (Lott, 2001). Although a text may *look* like a picture book, it might not be intended, or even appropriate, for a young audience (Pearson, 2005). The use of picture books in the middle grades as supplementary or complementary resources can increase student engagement and learning for even the most sophisticated student. The idea of using picture books in classrooms should now include a vision of a secondary teacher sharing a read-aloud that might cover topics such as gang violence, eating disorders, or even gay and lesbian relationships and/or marriage.

Picture books in the secondary classroom also present concerns to teachers of that age group. First, many worry that their classes may be perceived by administration as not having the proper level of vigor (Beckman & Diamond, 1984). Once viability has been addressed, teachers also worry that their students' attitudes might be negative toward picture books. Giorgis (1999) cautions teachers about being apologetic about using a picture book for fear students would perceive it as being "read down to." Beckman and Diamond (1984) insist the way to address this issue is to listen to their students' concerns. When met with skepticism from students, try opening the discussion to include a debate over the notion that a good story could be accompanied and/or supported by illustrations. Allowing students to compare and contrast (e.g., critique) a picture book for content compared to their textbook may turn up surprising results. Kane (2007) suggests that "once their concerns have been recognized, students are free to stay tuned, their maturity and dignity intact" (p. 103). If a teacher respects picture books and firmly believes that the book will enhance learning, students will too.

Veteran teachers who use picture books as a means of instruction note that students relax and return to a state of childhood during a read-aloud. Reiker (2010) observed high school social studies students' reactions when being read a picture book such as *Rose Blanche* by Innocenti (1985), *The Firekeeper's Son* by Park (2004), and *Tops & Bottoms* by Stevens (1995) by their teacher for the first time. At first students were quietly mocking the event, giggling or fidgeting as if uncomfortable. However, when the teacher continued to read, the students physically changed. Reiker noted "their demeanor relaxed, they nodded with approval and furrowed their brows when they did not like what was taking place. She noted smiles on the faces of students as the story was being read and thought perhaps this transported them back to positive experiences of being read to when they were children. At the close of the book, the students applauded and the discussion took on a vigor that the teacher had not seen previously" (p. 17).

Many notable books intended for older readers are in picture book format. Some of these picture books, unexpectedly sophisticated in language and concept, are much better suited for readers with more extensive prior knowledge and understanding of the world than those possessed by young children. For example, Graeme Base's *The Eleventh Hour: A Curious Mystery* (1988) calls for readers with deductive skills and the ability to tune into minute details in order to solve the mystery that unfolds in the plot. Readers are asked to find clues of many types—pictures, numbers, words, and sentences—embedded in the illustrations as well as the text. They are also asked to keep track of the characters in their costumes, perhaps to account for their whereabouts during the various events in the story.

To further the argument, some picture books are not only less suitable for young children, they are *intended* for older readers and adults. There are many examples of such picture books. Tom Feelings's *The Middle Passage: White Ships/Black Cargo* (1995) records the transatlantic slave trade, depicting the suffering of African slaves. Both the illustrations and the content of Feelings's book show the brutal truths about the treatment of slaves. Similarly, Tatsuharu Kodama's *Shin's Tricycle* (1995) and Laurence Yep's *Hiroshima* (1995) document the horrors of the atomic bomb and its devastating impact on human life. Share these powerful picture books with students, and explicitly tell them that *they* are the intended readers.

Facilitating Book Clubs

Adults gather in bookstores, coffee shops, or someone's home to enjoy the camaraderie of discussing a good book. Book clubs are generally considered to be adult literacy events most likely because adults have the autonomy to choose any book they want, read the books independently, and then have the option to discuss and share their interpretations with other adults who have also read the book. Adults enjoy debating and sharing their perceptions and conclusions with each other.

Frank Smith (1988) challenges this idea that "clubs" are adult events by suggesting that children are inducted into a variety of informal "clubs" designed to help them acquire the literacy skills of adults. For example, the spoken language club invites infants into the organization and takes for granted that the child will learn to speak like the adult members. As children learn to speak, they are invited to join additional clubs such as the reading club or writing club where adults model the uses of reading and writing for the new members. By the time children are school age, many have already become members of the "literacy club" (Smith, 1988, p. 9).

Teachers emulate these learning experiences by creating book clubs within their classrooms. In the book club setting, students take on a new "role"; they are no longer expected to answer questions the teacher poses but instead are expected to generate their own questions, insights, and connections.

Wilhelm (1997) described "readers" as students engaged in the texts, while "nonreaders" used a variety of avoidance behaviors to get out of reading. During one class, Wilhelm (1997) overheard one of his nonreading students questioning a reading student about why he enjoyed reading. The reader responded, "You gotta BE the book," a comment that helps to define an engaged reader.

According to Guthrie (1996), "An engaged reader is motivated, involved, curious and has made links between their inner experience and the outer world of books" (p. 433). Teachers who are themselves "readers" understand how important and influential reading for enjoyment is in developing students' literacy. As another of Wilhelm's students clearly understands, "Most teachers must not read or they'd know how to teach reading and not ruin it for us" (p. 34). McMahon and Goatley (1995) state: "The constructivist position argues for giving students opportunities to read and respond personally to literature" (p. 23).

In the process of discussing a novel (speaking and listening), students engage in metacognition (talking about their own ways of thinking) and assist each other in making clearer meaning of the text. When students engage in book clubs for the first or second time, they may have trouble knowing what to discuss. The truth is that for many years, students have practiced answering questions their teachers have posed. Giving students the power to control the conversation may feel daunting to them at the start, but with a little encouragement, their conversations will flourish.

Integrating Across Disciplines

In simplest terms, integration takes place when two or more content areas are taught together in order to make explicit the multidimensional nature of concepts and to make connections between and among the concepts. According to Parker (2005), "The purpose is not to eliminate the individual disciplines but to use them in combination . . . to develop a more powerful understanding of a central idea, issue, person, or event" (pp. 452–53).

An integrated curriculum, as opposed to a fragmented curriculum, better facilitates conceptual learning. Beyond learning based on isolated dates, names, figures, and definitions, an integrated curriculum provides broader contexts for learning, often answering students' questions of "how" and "why." The interdisciplinary connections offer room for intellectual curiosities and natural wonderments about the world. Recall some of your own questions about the world. Few would have an answer grounded in a single discipline or a subject area.

In addition to making topical connections, content areas link naturally when they are presented as related *processes* instead of isolated topics and skills. Consider how often we have been presented with the perception that science is inquiry and mathematics is problem solving. Teachers' views of science as inquiry typically include the process of science, doing hands-on experiments, using kits, or involving students in activities (Bybee, Ferrini-Mundy & Loucks-Horsley, 1997). Understanding mathematics as problem solving is also often limited to acquiring some problem-solving strategies and developing application abilities with simple word problems (Hiebert et al., 1996; Meire, Hovde & Meire, 1996).

Despite many compelling arguments for integrating learning processes in science and mathematics, classroom instruction emphasizing connections remains an exception rather than the norm (Watanabe & Huntley, 1998; Ruiz, Thornton & Cuero, 2010). The American Association for the Advancement of Science (AAAS, 1989) states that proficiency in the mathematics and science disciplines requires extensive student experience using relevant and interconnected principles to solve problems, to communicate ideas, and to connect and generalize concepts. Other current scholarship in mathematics and science education (NCTM, 2000; NSTA, 2013) endorses similar interdisciplinary approaches in solving real-life problems that require the integration of multiple STEM (Science, Technology, Engineering, and Mathematics) concepts (Johnson, 2013). Why stop there? How do other content areas (history, philosophy, art) also help with solving real-world problems, or maybe more important, understanding the problems?

Without question, students need to be developing connections *between* content area topics to fully understand the world they live in. As a teacher of a specific content, you will enhance your own subject when you stretch to include perspectives from other content areas as you teach.

In practical terms, integration may take place in a single lesson, in a unit comprising a series of lessons over several days or weeks, or even in a yearlong integrated course. A teacher can accomplish integration by organizing learning experiences that incorporate topics of interest to students, such as the environment and technology and by helping students make connections across curricular areas (Freeman & Person, 1998). And as presented in this chapter, teachers can accomplish integration by incorporating literacy—reading, writing, speaking, listening, and viewing—and quality, age-appropriate literature.

To a certain degree, it would be accurate to say that there is no magic formula for creating the perfect lesson. You can carefully plan and create what seems to be the perfect lesson only to see it "flop." Likewise, you may begin to teach a lesson that you wish you had more time to prepare for only to see it flourish as students engage with the concept. And sometimes, the most memorable lessons spring spontaneously as you take advantage of a "teachable moment." Having said that, let us be clear: quality lessons do not just happen; they are carefully planned, taught, revised, retaught, and repeated as many times as necessary. As you begin to think like a teacher, you will need to organize your thoughts around the best way to teach the worthy concepts and important skills in your content area. In this section, we present what we consider to be necessary ingredients for good integrated lessons: content, skills, and instructional strategies.

As content teachers, you must have a thorough understanding of your content. Your students must sense the passion you have for your content and be inspired to learn because of that passion. While you may carry around much of the content in your head, you must also continue to be a learner in your field, as all fields continue to evolve.

When planning units of study and individual lessons, the content you know will direct you to the goals for learning you set for your students. After noting what the curriculum of your school/district/state determines that your students should know, you must ask yourself a series of additional questions:

- What is worthy of knowing?
- What big idea concepts would you like for your students to know?
- How are the concepts connected and interrelated?
- How do you plan to show the complexities and multidimensionalities of those interrelated concepts?

Next, you must identify the skills you are aiming to teach. What skills are necessary for your students to access and understand the content? Each discipline requires a different set of skills to make content accessible. For example, computational fluency is a skill necessary in mathematics whereas geography requires spatial processing skills for map reading. Science requires skills for careful observation and systematic collection of data. As discussed earlier, however, shift your disciplinary paradigm as you identify the skills you want to teach. Are there related skills or processes in other content areas that you might be able to integrate? For example, while engaging in a map reading activity in your social studies class, can you also tie in mathematics skills? Can you incorporate an inquiry activity that includes questions from other perspectives? For example, as students are learning about the sociological impact of the Dust Bowl, they can also investigate the science behind the agricultural practices that contributed to the Dust Bowl.

The following principles might help you to deliver your lesson with the most integrative power:

- Begin with students' genuine questions about the target concept. Provide opportunities for students to generate and compile questions. End with students' inquiries about the concept beyond what your class was able to explore as a learning community so that they can continue to learn on their own.
- Offer students choices among texts (when possible), perspectives, and products to both learn and to demonstrate their learning.
- You will have many disciplinary specialists in your school building and in the community. Do not hesitate to consult with these specialists to plan learning or to invite them to guest lecture or lead an activity.
- Challenge yourself to include as many different texts—textbooks, literature, websites, articles, and others—that present the target concept. The variety of texts will ensure the multiple perspectives you need to integrate learning.
- Challenge yourself to include as much reading, writing, listening, speaking, and viewing as possible in the learning experiences. Provide opportunities for students to present their evolving understanding in a multitude of ways, and offer time and space for peers to respond to each other in authentic ways.
- Ask students to make explicit the connections they are making between their prior knowledge and new learning.
- Ask students to make explicit the connections between the topics that the class is exploring together.

It is entirely possible to accomplish integrated learning by a single teacher in a particular class, lesson, or unit. However, imagine the potential power of integration when a group of content experts and specialists work together in grade-level teams or in a school building. Consider the following questions as you strive to promote collaborations for integrative learning:

- What are the big ideas or essential questions in your district or school curriculum or standards?
- What is your (content) part in teaching the big ideas?
- What are others' roles in their content?
- Where can you draw worthy connections?
- What can you and others do to make these connections explicit to students?
- What will you do in your class?
- What will others to do in their classes?
- Are the connections you and others make natural and conceptually rich?
- Will students use these connections to understand the big ideas and answer essential questions?

This type of collaboration is filled with tension; on one hand, a content specialist will have to insist on the disciplinary validity and perspective to do justice to that content, and on the other hand, the specialist will have to be open to other ways of knowing and making meaning that might be wildly different from one's own. All involved in this collaboration will have to agree that the more of the different perspectives students can use to see the same topic, the more fully they will understand that topic.

THEORY TO PRACTICE

Providing students with opportunities to see how subjects connect and inform one another is essential to an integrated curriculum. Historically, schools have been designed to departmentalize subjects, but there is evidence that integrating learning opportunities provides deeper learning in students as they see how subjects connect with each other. Students' learning in schools should (and can) mirror the complex, sophisticated, and multidimensional ways in which all topics in real life are interconnected.

Great works of literature, art, and other primary documents will support students in understanding your particular content area. Imagine students gaining an understanding of the zeitgeist of a particular time in history, or how a period in history impacted a scientific discovery, or a piece of literature that a famous painting or work of music depicts. This chapter described why integration facilitates more meaningful and powerful learning. In particular, we introduced you to ways to integrate whatever topic you are teaching using literacy skills and strategies to aid in comprehension. By utilizing a variety of quality texts, images, film clips, and online resources you are helping your students make natural connections between literate behaviors and your content area topics. Finally, we encourage you to seek collaborations with your faculty colleagues in order to create innovative and integrated vibrant learning opportunities.

REFERENCES

American Association for the Advancement of Science. (1989). *Science for all Americans: Project 2061*. Washington, DC.

Anderson, L. H. (2000). *Fever 1793*. New York: Simon & Schuster.

Base, G. (1988). *The eleventh hour: A curious mystery*. New York: Abrams.

Beckman, J. & Diamond, J. (1984 February). Junior high/middle school: Picture books in the classroom: The secret weapon for the creative teacher. *The English Journal, 73*(2), 102–4.

Buckley, M. (1992). Focus on research: We listen a book a day; we speak a book a week: Learning from Walter Loban. *Language Arts, 69,* 622–26.

Bybee, R. W., Ferrini-Mundy, J., & Loucks-Horsley, S. (1997). National standards and school science and mathematics. *School Science and Mathematics, 97*(7), 325–34.

Calkins, L. M. (1994). *The art of teaching writing.* Portsmouth, NH: Heinemann.

Columba, L., Kim, C. Y., & Moe, A. J. (2009). *The power of picture books in teaching math, science, and socials studies: Grades prek–8* (2nd ed.). Scottsdale, AZ: Holcomb Hathaway.

Donovan, C. A., & Smolkin, L. B. (2002). Considering genre, content, and visual features in the selection of trade books for science instruction. *The Reading Teacher, 55*(6), 502–20.

Feelings, T. (1995). *The middle passage: White ships/black cargo.* New York: Dial.

Freeman, E. B., & Person, D. G. (1998). *Connecting informational children's books with content area learning.* Boston: Allyn & Bacon.

Giorgis, C. (1999). The power of reading picture books aloud to secondary students. *The Clearing House: A Journal of Educational Strategies, Issues, and Ideas, 73*(1), 51–53.

Guthrie, J. (1996). Educational contexts for engagement in literacy. *The Reading Teacher, 49*(6), 432–45.

Hamston, J., & Murdoch, K. (1996). *Integrating socially: Planning integrated units of work for social education.* Portsmouth, NH: Heinemann.

Harste, J. C. (2013). Reading–writing connection. *The Encyclopedia of Applied Linguistics.*

Hellwig, S. J., Monroe, E. E. & Jacobs, J. S. (2000). Making informed choices: Selecting children's trade books for mathematics instruction. *Teaching Children Mathematics, 7*(3), 138–43.

Hiebert, J., Carpenter, T. P., Fennema, E., Fuson, K., Human, P., Murray, H., Olivier, A., & Wearne, D. (1996). Problem solving as a basis for reform in curriculum and instruction: The case of mathematics. *Educational Researcher, 25*(4), 12–18.

Innocenti, R. (1985). *Rose blanche.* Creative Editions.

Johnson, C. (2013). Conceptualizing integrated STEM education. *School Science and Mathematics Journal, 113*(8), 267–68.

Kane, S. (2007). *Literacy & learning in the content areas* (2nd ed.). Scottsdale, AZ: Holcomb Hathaway.

Kodama, T. (1995). *Shin's tricycle.* New York: Walker Books for Young Readers.

Lawrence, P. R., Hope, J., Small, M., & Martin, M. (1996). *Windows on math.* Warren, NJ: Optical Data Corporation.

Lott, C. (2001). Picture books in the high school English classroom. In Ericson, B. (Ed.), *Teaching reading in high school English classes* (139–54). Urbana, IL: National Council of Teachers of English.

McMahon S., & Goatley, V. (1995). Fifth graders helping peers discuss texts in student-led groups. *Journal of Educational Research, 89,* 23–24.

Meier, S. L., Hovde, R. L., & Meier, R. L. (1996), Problem solving: Teachers' perceptions, content area models, and interdisciplinary connections. *School Science and Mathematics, 96*, 230–37.

Miller, T. (1988). The place of picture books in middle-level classrooms. *Journal of Adolescent & Adult Literacy, 41*(5), 376–81.

Moline, S. (2011). *I see what you mean: Visual literacy k–8*. Portland, ME: Stenhouse Publishers.

Murphy, J. (2003). *An American plague: The true and terrifying story of the yellow fever epidemic of 1793*. New York: Clarion.

National Council of Teachers of Mathematics. (2000). *Principles and standards for school mathematics*. Reston, VA: Author.

National Science Teachers Association. (2013). NSTA position statement: The Next Generation Science Standards. Retrieved from http://www.nsta.org/docs/PositionStatement_NGSS.pdf.

Park, L. S. (2004). *The firekeeper's son*. New York: Clarion.

Parker, W. C. (2005). *Social studies in elementary education* (12th ed.). Columbus, OH: Pearson Merrill, Prentice-Hall.

Pearson, M. (2005). *Big ideas in small packages: Using picture books with older readers*. Santa Barbara, CA: Linworth.

Reiker, M. (2010). *The use of picture books in the high school classroom: A qualitative case study*. Master's level project.

Ruiz, E. C., Thornton, J., & Cuero, K. K. (2010). Integrating literature in mathematics: A teaching technique for mathematics teachers. *School Science and Mathematics, 110*(5), 235–37.

Sadoski, M., & Paivio, A. (2013). *Imagery and text: A dual coding theory of reading and writing*. New York: Routledge.

Smith, F. (1988). *Joining the literacy club: Further essays into education*. Portsmouth, NH: Heinemann.

Spann, M. B. (1992). *Literature-based multicultural activities: An integrated approach*. New York: Scholastic Professional Books.

Stevens, J. (1995). *Tops & Bottoms*. New York: HMH Books for Young Readers.

Tunnell, M. O., & Jacobs, J. S. (2007). *Children's literature, briefly*. (4th ed.). Upper Saddle River, NJ: Prentice Hall.

Watanabe, T., & Huntley, M. A. (1998). Connecting mathematics and science in undergraduate teacher education programs: Faculty voices from the Maryland collaborative for teacher preparation. *School Science and Mathematics, 98*(1), 19–25.

Wilhelm, J. (1997). *"You gotta BE the book": Teaching engaged and reflective reading with adolescents*. New York: Teachers College Press.

Yep, L. (1995). *Hiroshima: A novella*. New York: Scholastic.

3

Guiding Instruction

Standards

One looks back with appreciation to the brilliant teachers, but with gratitude to those who touched our human feelings. The curriculum is so much necessary raw material, but warmth is the vital element for the growing plant and for the soul of the child.

—Carl Jung

Ask Before Touching

This chapter is particularly difficult to think of a vignette that would add humor or insight to the topic of standards. In preparation for the following vignette, it has nothing to do with standards. However, one of the funniest things to happen during my middle-grade teaching days was one of the years I was assigned to teach Physical Education to seventy-five to ninety students each period (three homerooms at a time)! One day . . .

Eugene was always one of the last students out of the locker room and on his "spot" on the gym floor for attendance. I stood at the entrance of the gym with my clipboard in hand doing a preliminary role by noting the students who were not "dressed" for PE. My colleague was standing on my right telling me about something that happened earlier in the day.

Eugene came walking through the door, with wet hair, and came up to Mr. Reed and me.

"Do you have any shampoo?" he asked.

Mr. Reed calmly rubbed the top of Eugene's head and kindly told him to get to his seat.

"Why do you need shampoo?" I asked as he started to walk away from us.

"Because I was sitting on the toilet peeing and I dropped my wallet. When I leaned over to pick up my wallet, I peed all over my hair."

I will never forget Mr. Reed's face or how quickly he made it into the locker room to wash his hands! He and I still laugh about this with tears in our eyes!

In this age of accountability and high-stakes testing, discussions about academic standards seem especially timely as content area teachers in all grade levels (regardless of where they teach) must be prepared to navigate their way through them. Most teachers today follow curriculum developed according to standards, cite standards in their lesson plans, or teach to specific standards mandated by the "pacing guides" in their districts. Many are mindful of the various forms of testing that occur in the spring term of an academic year, if not vigilantly teaching their students using district-approved test-preparation materials. The extent to which a teacher is concerned about standards in their daily practice seems to rely heavily on her school district's level of adherence to standards. This chapter provides a brief historical perspective on standards, a compilation of relevant and influential standards currently available to teachers, and a list of principles that may help you meaningfully integrate standards in instruction for student learning.

HISTORICAL PERSPECTIVE ON STANDARDS IN EDUCATION

While standards for student learning at the district and state levels have been available for well over one hundred years, they have been sporadic, uneven, and inconsistent. A great deal of work began in the 1980s as teachers began to develop standards of instruction. The publication of *A Nation at Risk: The Imperative for Educational Reform* (1983) received much national attention because it outlined major shortcomings in American education. This publication was widely read and discussed by educators, parents, and policymakers. Perhaps the biggest push for standards began in 1989 when then President George H. W. Bush convened the nation's governors for the first national meeting on educational goals.

The major outcome of this conference was the promulgation of America 2000, which provided a list of six broadly stated goals that were expanded by the Clinton administration into The Goals 2000: Educate America Act (1994) with two additional goals; these eight goals covered (1) school readiness; (2) school completion; (3) student achievement and citizenship; (4) teacher education and professional development; (5) mathematics and science; (6) adult literacy and lifelong learning; (7) safe, disciplined, and alcohol- and drug-free schools; and (8) parental participation (Ravitch, 1995).

These broadly stated goals began a move for more specifically stated standards, with the National Council of Teachers of Mathematics being among the first to provide standards in mathematics grades K–12 in 1989. A move for greater testing of students was also implemented, with results that brought varying degrees of acceptance among teachers. The term *high-stakes testing* became associated with assessment at the elementary, middle school, and high school levels. Books like *Standardized Minds* (Sacks, 1999) and *The Case Against Standardized Testing: Raising the Scores, Ruining the Schools* (Kohn, 2000) presented arguments that were strongly against this type of testing, particularly at the K–8 levels.

Some, like Popham (2001), took a more moderate approach while arguing that testing was taking too much time from instruction and were against the use of student test scores as the primary measure of teacher effectiveness. Nevertheless, by 2000 almost every state in the nation had developed their own tests for grade-level assessment in grades three through twelve. It is important to keep this information in mind as you study the more recent developments of the professional associations during the 1990s and the recent work to develop common standards for the entire nation. Today, we have greater national consistency as to what benchmarks need to be reached at each grade level.

COMMON CORE STATE STANDARDS (CCSS): A COLLABORATIVE EFFORT

The most recent effort at establishing national standards came about through the collaboration of two influential national organizations. Here is how the *New York Times* (Dillon, 2010) reported it:

> A panel of educators convened by the nation's governors and the state school superintendents proposed a uniform set of academic standards on Wednesday, laying out their vision for what all the nation's public school children should learn in math and English, year by year, from kindergarten through high school graduation.
>
> The new proposals could transform American Education, replacing the patchwork of standards ranging from mediocre to world-class that have been written by local educators in every state. (p. 1)

In *Pathways to the Common Core: Accelerating Achievement* (Calkins, Ehrenworth, and Lehman, 2012), the authors are even more emphatic. They state:

> The Common Core State Standards (CCSS) are a big deal. Adopted by forty-five states so far, the standards represent the most sweeping reform of the K–12 curriculum that has ever occurred in this country. It is safe to say that across the entire history of American education, no single document will have played a more influential role over what is taught in our schools. (p. 1)

The Common Core State Standards (CCSS), developed by the Governors Association for Best Practices and the Council of Chief State School Officers in 2010, have been widely adopted and are now being used in forty-five states. As of this printing, Alaska, Indiana, Nebraska, South Carolina, Texas, and Virginia have chosen not to participate, and Minnesota has implemented everything with the exception of mathematics.

To a large degree, the development of the CCSS came about because of the proliferation of differences that occurred in the late 1980s and the early 1990s that led to much disparity in the K–12 academic standards across the nation at the state and local school district levels. The intention of the chief state school officers and the state governors was to provide teachers with "a consistent curriculum framework that can be used across the states" (Reutzel & Cooter, 2013, p. 14). Another announced objective of the effort was to better prepare high school graduates to enter the workforce or to enter college.

Contrary to some public perception, the federal government has not been a participant in the development of the CCSS standards. However, the U.S. Department of Education created the "Race to the Top" (2010) funding initiatives in which individual states that applied for federal funding were asked to adopt CCSS to enhance their funding prospects. The U.S. Department of Education has also created the What Works Clearinghouse (www.whatworks.ed), which provides helpful information regarding good instructional practices in English, mathematics, and science in working with all students, including English language learners and students with disabilities. There is a strong link between the CCSS and the What Works Clearinghouse in that many individuals and several professional organizations have participated in both efforts.

Space does not permit a complete listing of the CCSS; therefore, readers are referred to the website, www.corestandards.org. The links to the standards in English language arts and mathematics are provided in the tab "Read the Standards." In addition, you will notice a set of standards within the ELA standards that pertain specifically to content area teachers in grades six through twelve (in history/social studies, science, and technical subjects). Examine the standards in your grade level and in your content area. Think about the feasibility of the standards in your lesson or unit planning and in your daily instruction. Explore the standards in grade levels below and above your certification area. Think about whether they are consistent with what you are expected to teach.

Look for your state in the "Standards in Your State" tab. Click on the link to see how your state has implemented the CCSS. For example, Pennsylvania has modified the CCSS to create its own PA Core standards. While some of the standards are written using the same language, the PA Core ELA standards are organized and presented in a grade-level-friendly format. Select another state to see how your state's core standards may be similar or different. It is imperative that you become familiar with your state core standards. Most likely, the mandates you must address in curriculum, pacing, and testing come from the core standards at the state level.

CCSS English Language Arts Standards

The English language arts core standards (www.corestandards.org/ELA-Literacy) are grade-level specific and are published in three main sections. The first is the comprehensive reading, writing, speaking, listening, and language standards in grades K–12 sections. The next two sections are content area specific to grades six through twelve in history/social studies, science, and technical subjects where the focus is on content area understanding through reading and writing.

At each of the grade levels in the English language arts are four categories of standards: (1) key ideas and details; (2) craft and structure; (3) integration of knowledge and ideas; and (4) range of reading and level of text complexity. We will look at a portion of the high school standards and note the progression in grades seven through twelve for Reading: Informational Text. Under the heading "Integration of Knowledge and Ideas," the three standards at each grade level are shown in table 3.1.

The English language arts standards are not completely new. They do, however, emphasize the importance of the close reading and critical analysis of complex fiction and nonfiction texts. The standards also demonstrate the importance of gauging the relevance and the differences of information from standard text, digital text, and visual or multimedia sources.

CCSS Mathematics Standards

In mathematics there are two types of standards, those for mathematical *practice* and those for mathematical *content* (www.corestandards.org/Math). There are eight standards for mathematical practice that are the same for grades K–12. These standards "describe varieties of expertise that mathematics educators at all levels should seek to develop in their students" (NGACBP & CCSS, 2010, p. 6). These standards of mathematical practice indicate that teachers should strive to develop students who

1. make sense of problems and persevere in solving them
2. reason abstractly and quantitatively
3. construct viable arguments and critique the reasoning of others
4. model with mathematics
5. use appropriate tools strategically

Table 3.1. English language arts standards for reading: Information Text—Integration of Knowledge and Ideas.

Grade 7	Compare and contrast a text to an audio, video, or multimedia version of the text, analyzing each medium's portrayal of the subject (e.g., how the delivery of a speech affects the impact of the words).
	Trace and evaluate the argument and specific claims in a text, assessing whether the reasoning is sound and the evidence is relevant and sufficient to support the claims.
	Analyze how two or more authors writing about the same topic shape their presentations of key information by emphasizing different evidence or advancing different interpretations of facts.
Grade 8	Evaluate the advantages and disadvantages of using different mediums (e.g., print or digital text, video, multimedia) to present a particular topic or idea.
	Delineate and evaluate the argument and specific claims in a text, assessing whether the reasoning is sound and the evidence is relevant and sufficient; recognize when irrelevant evidence is introduced.
	Analyze a case in which two or more texts provide conflicting information on the same topic and identify where the texts disagree on matters of fact or interpretation.
Grades 9–10	Analyze various accounts of a subject told in different mediums (e.g., a person's life story in both print and multimedia), determining which details are emphasized in each account.
	Delineate and evaluate the argument and specific claims in a text, assessing whether the reasoning is valid and the evidence is relevant and sufficient; identify false statements and fallacious reasoning.
	Analyze seminal U.S. documents of historical and literary significance (e.g., Washington's Farewell Address, the Gettysburg Address, Roosevelt's Four Freedoms speech, King's "Letter from Birmingham Jail"), including how they address related themes and concepts.
Grades 11–12	Integrate and evaluate multiple sources of information presented in different media or formats (e.g., visually, quantitatively) as well as in words in order to address a question or solve a problem.
	Delineate and evaluate the reasoning in seminal U.S. texts, including the application of constitutional principles and use of legal reasoning (e.g., in U.S. Supreme Court majority opinions and dissents) and the premises, purposes, and arguments in works of public advocacy (e.g., *The Federalist*, presidential addresses).
	Analyze seventeenth-, eighteenth-, and nineteenth-century foundational U.S. documents of historical and literary significance (including the Declaration of Independence, the Preamble to the Constitution, the Bill of Rights, and Lincoln's Second Inaugural Address) for their themes, purposes, and rhetorical features.

Common Core State Standards Initiative (2017). Retrieved from http://www.corestandards.org/ELA-Literacy/.

6. attend to precision
7. look for and make use of structure
8. look for and express regularity in repeated reasoning.

These standards are a combination of the National Council of Teachers of Mathematics (NCTM) and National Research Council (NRC) process and proficiency standards, some of which we will examine when we look at standards developed by professional organizations.

The mathematical content standards vary from one grade level to another and show an increasing understanding of mathematical content. They "describe ways in which . . . students . . . increasingly ought to engage with the subject matter. . . . They are a balanced combination of procedure and understanding" (CCSS, 2010, p. 8).

In grades six through eight, there are five strands of *content* standards in each grade. There is reasonable continuity from grade to grade, but there is only one strand, geometry, that is found in all four grades. As the entire set of mathematics standards is too much to present in its entirety, let us sample just one area. These CCSS mathematics standards in geometry, shown progressively, are shown in table 3.2.

Grades nine through twelve are collectively listed as "High School" with content standards in (1) number and quantity; (2) algebra; (3) functions; (4) modeling; (5) geometry; and (6) statistics and probability. While sample pathways for courses are offered to high schools, the content standards do not mandate a sequence of courses, curriculum, pedagogy, or delivery of content.

For those who have examined geometry standards developed by the NCTM during the 1980s and 1990s, these CCSS look very similar, and they are, because the National Governor's Association (NGA) and the CCSS intended to build on the good work of the previous decade by the professional associations.

Table 3.2. CCSS mathematics standards in geometry.

Grade 6	Solve real-world mathematical problems involving area, surface area, and volume.
Grade 7	Draw, construct, and describe geometrical figures and describe the relationship between them. Solve real-life mathematical problems involving angle measure, area, surface area, and volume.
Grade 8	Understand congruence and similarity using physical models, transparencies, or geometry software. Understand and apply the Pythagorean Theorem. Solve real-world and mathematical problems involving volume of cylinders, cones, and spheres.

Retrieved from http://www.corestandards.org/Math/Practice/.

CCSS Anchor Standards

One of the rationales for the development of the CCSS is college and career readiness. Standards specific to this goal are presented in sets of College and Career Readiness (CCR) anchor standards that cover all grades, K–12. The CCR standards are the central goals toward which all grade-level standards are directed. A look at these standards show they all deal with aspects of language learning—reading, writing, speaking and listening, and language. They are to be covered in increasing degrees of complexity beginning in kindergarten. In achieving the anchor standards fully by grade twelve, it is expected that all students will have achieved college and career readiness. For a thorough discussion of each anchor standard and how they are to be applied at the middle school and high school levels, you are encouraged to examine *The Common Core: Teaching Students in Grades 6–12 to Meet the Reading Standards* (McLaughlin & Overturf, 2013).

NATIONAL ORGANIZATIONS' PROFESSIONAL STANDARDS

Several national organizations have led the way in developing and introducing standards in specific content areas. It must be emphasized that these are not federally mandated standards. Rather, the standards presented in this section are created by national professional organizations in the fields of mathematics, science, social studies, and English education. Note that the CCSS state that the CCSS "literacy standards in history/social studies, science, and technical subjects are meant to supplement content standards in those areas, not replace them" (Governors Association for Best Practices, Council of Chief State School Officers, 2010, http://www.corestandards.org/ELA-Literacy/).

The national professional organizations serve as tremendous resources to teachers and offer expert guidance that many teachers use as a valuable part of their professional development. Although states do not mandate that these standards be implemented, it is fair to say that many states use them to shape and inform their own state academic standards. Of particular interest in this text are the academic standards developed by the following national organizations in table 3.3. These national professional organizations offer more than standards. Each organization offers regional and national conferences that we encourage you to attend for your own professional development.

Table 3.3. National professional organizations.

Content Area	National Organization	Website
English Language Arts	International Literacy Association (ILA)	www.literacyworldwide.org
	National Council of Teachers of English (NCTE)	www.ncte.org
Mathematics	National Council of Teachers of Mathematics (NCTM)	www.nctm.org
Science	National Research Council (NRC)	www.nationalacademies.org/nrc
	National Science Teachers Association (NSTA)	www.nsta.org
Social Studies	National Council for the Social Studies (NCSS)	www.socialstudies.org

English Language Arts Standards from the International Literacy Association (ILA) and National Council of Teachers of English (NCTE)

Joint efforts by the ILA and the NCTE produced the Standards for the English Language Arts (www.ncte.org/standards), which were adopted by both organizations in 1996. These standards broadly address oral and written communications, and more specifically, reading, writing, speaking, and listening:

1. Students read a wide range of print and nonprint texts to build an understanding of texts, of themselves, and of the cultures of the United States and the world; to acquire new information; to respond to the needs and demands of society and the workplace; and for personal fulfillment. Among these texts are fiction and nonfiction, classic and contemporary works.
2. Students read a wide range of literature from many periods in many genres to build an understanding of the many dimensions (e.g., philosophical, ethical, aesthetic) of human experience.
3. Students apply a wide range of strategies to comprehend, interpret, evaluate, and appreciate texts. They draw on their prior experience, their interactions with other readers and writers, their knowledge of word meaning and of other texts, their word identification strategies, and their understanding of textual features (e.g., sound-letter correspondence, sentence structure, context, graphics).
4. Students adjust their use of spoken, written, and visual language (e.g., conventions, style, vocabulary) to communicate effectively with a variety of audiences and for different purposes.

5. Students employ a wide range of strategies as they write and use different writing process elements appropriately to communicate with different audiences for a variety of purposes.
6. Students apply knowledge of language structure, language conventions (e.g., spelling and punctuation), media techniques, figurative language, and genre to create, critique, and discuss print and nonprint texts.
7. Students conduct research on issues and interests by generating ideas and questions, and by posing problems. They gather, evaluate, and synthesize data from a variety of sources (e.g., print and nonprint texts, artifacts, people) to communicate their discoveries in ways that suit their purpose and audience.
8. Students use a variety of technological and informational resources (e.g., libraries, databases, computer networks, video) to gather and synthesize information and to create and communicate knowledge.
9. Students develop an understanding of and respect for diversity in language use, patterns, and dialects across cultures, ethnic groups, geographic regions, and social roles.
10. Students whose first language is not English make use of their first language to develop competency in the English language arts and to develop understanding of content across the curriculum.
11. Students participate as knowledgeable, reflective, creative, and critical members of a variety of literacy communities.
12. Students use spoken, written, and visual language to accomplish their own purposes (e.g., for learning, enjoyment, persuasion, and the exchange of information).

These standards are broad, but thorough. They cover areas believed to be crucial to the study of the English language arts by students at every grade level. The lessons in this text help students meet the NCTE/ILA standards in three ways. First, they expose the students to the quality literature necessary to develop the literacy skills described in the standards. Second, they include experiences in reading, writing, speaking, listening, viewing, and visually representing as outlined in standards 1–6 and 12. These language arts experiences help students learn the mathematics, science, and social studies concepts. Third, the lessons will help students apply a wide range of advanced reading comprehension strategies; for example, the strategies mentioned in standard 3.

Mathematics Standards from the National Council of Teachers of Mathematics (NCTM)

The mathematics standards (www.nctm.org/standards) have been available since 1989 as the Curriculum and Evaluation Standards for School Mathematics (NCTM, 1989) and were revised in 2000 as the Principles and Standards for School Mathematics (NCTM, 2000). Preceding the Standards, the Principles list basic concepts that are "fundamental to a high-quality mathematics education," including equity, curriculum, teaching, learning, and assessment. The standards for grades Pre-K–12 were designed to ensure that students become mathematically fluent and are able to demonstrate competence in the following ten areas of mathematics.

Strands 1–5 are *content* standards; Standards 6–10 are *process* standards:

1. Numbers and Operations
2. Algebra
3. Geometry
4. Measurement
5. Data Analysis and Probability
6. Problem Solving
7. Reasoning and Proof
8. Communication
9. Connections
10. Representation

These ten strands in the NCTM standards are to be used across grade levels Pre-K–12. Each strand varies in breadth and depth according to the grade level. For example, in a sixth-grade classroom, geometry may mean measuring angles in triangles, whereas in an eighth-grade classroom it includes the measurement of the volume of cylinders and cones.

Science Standards from the National Research Council (NRC) and the National Science Teachers Association (NSTA)

The Next Generation Science Standards (NGSS) released in April 2013 are based on the National Research Council's A Framework for K–12 Science Education (www.nextgenscience.org). The Disciplinary Core Ideas (content) included in the NGSS for high school include the following:

- Physical Science
- Life Science
- Earth and Space Science

- Engineering, Technology, and Applications of Science

Each of these Disciplinary Core Ideas is accompanied by Science and Engineering Practices and Crosscutting Concepts to represent the three dimensions necessary in science proficiency. The vision of science in the NGSS "rests on a view of science as both a body of knowledge and an evidence-based model and theory building enterprise that continually extends, refines, and revises knowledge" (www.nextgenscience.org). If you are a content area specialist in science, it will be worth your time to gain a fuller description of the three dimensions—content, practice, and crosscutting (concepts that are connected across disciplines)—from the NGSS's website: http://www.nextgenscience.org/three-dimensions.

"Integration" and "application" seem to be two major themes that are highlighted in the NGSS. In addition to advocating the integration of core concepts, they also attempt to integrate content and application reflecting how science and engineering is practiced in the real world. This vision of science proficiency is evident in the language of the standards; representing performance expectations, each standard begins with "Students who demonstrate understanding can . . . " For example, a middle school standard in Physical Science under Structure and Properties of Matter has three performances expectations:

- Develop models to describe the atomic number of simple molecules and extended structures.
- Gather and make sense of information to describe that synthetic materials come from natural resources and impact society.
- Develop a model that predicts and describes changes in particle motion, temperature, and state of a pure substance when thermal energy is added or removed.

Social Studies Standards from the National Council for the Social Studies (NCSS)

The NCSS published its curriculum standards (www.socialstudies.org/standards), Expectations of Excellence: Curriculum Standards for Social Studies, in 1994 to serve as a "curriculum alignment and development tool." A revised version was published in 2002 with a new title National Curriculum Standards for Social Studies, with ten interdisciplinary themes in social studies for grades Pre-K–12:

Theme 1: Culture
Theme 2: Time, Continuity, and Change

Theme 3: People, Places, and Environments
Theme 4: Individual Development and Identity
Theme 5: Individuals, Groups, and Institutions
Theme 6: Power, Authority, and Governance
Theme 7: Production, Distribution, and Consumption
Theme 8: Science, Technology, and Society
Theme 9: Global Connections
Theme 10: Civic Ideals and Practices

The NCSS emphasizes that these themes are interrelated and that a topic of study may draw from multiple themes. For example, the study of the U.S. Civil War might use Theme 2, Theme 3, and Theme 10. This focus on integration is evident in the formal definition of social studies adopted by the NCSS in 1992. With the ultimate aim to promote civic competence, this definition shapes the ten themes listed above:

Social studies is the integrated study of the social sciences and humanities to promote civic competence. Within the school program, social studies provides coordinated, systematic study drawing upon such disciplines as anthropology, archaeology, economics, geography, history, law, philosophy, political science, psychology, religion, and sociology, as well as appropriate content from the humanities, mathematics, and natural sciences. The primary purpose of social studies is to help young people develop the ability to make informed and reasoned decisions for the public good as citizens of a culturally diverse, democratic society in an interdependent world (NCSS, 1994, p. vii).

In the revised version, the standards for each theme are presented using the following elements to "sharpen the focus":

• Purposes
• Questions for Exploration
• Knowledge: what learners need to understand
• Processes: what learners will be capable of doing
• Products: how learners demonstrate understanding
  (http://www.socialstudies.org/standards/execsummary)

STATE AND LOCAL STANDARDS

While the implementation of the Common Core State Standards is bringing about greater uniformity at the state levels, a look at state and local standards still reveals an enormous variety in specificity. Some identify the month, week, and day a teacher is supposed to address a particular standard. Some are stated broadly and leave most of the instructional planning (topic, placement in the curriculum, pacing, etc.) to the teacher. To see the extensive variety of standards available, use any of the Internet search tools and search for information on mathematics standards, science standards, social studies standards, or English language arts standards. Among the thousands of results, you will find hundreds of relevant websites about standards. All states and many school districts provide an explicit listing of their standards for your evaluation.

USING STANDARDS TO GUIDE INSTRUCTION

Navigating the world of standards is a challenging task even for veteran teachers. The increasing demands and expectations of using standards in your daily practice will be even more daunting to beginning teachers. Use the following principles as your starting point:

- *Investigate which standards guide the curriculum and instruction in your school district.* Most likely, districts will be following the state standards with modified CCSS standards. However, districts may have another set of standards that are tailored to meet their own needs. Know how to access the standards that you are expected to use and to cite in your lesson or unit plans.
- *Know the degree to which you must meet the standards.* Districts vary in how they meet the standards. Some will expect you to use the standards to guide instruction but not mandate day-to-day instruction. As long as your students are able to perform with proficiency on standardized tests, they will give you room to create your own instructional plans. Some will provide pacing guides and explicitly state the standards you must meet daily, weekly, or monthly.
- *Get to know the standard.* Some standards are easy to understand. They are written clearly and concisely, presenting the benchmark in ways that leave little room for interpretation. Some, you will notice, are written ambiguously, not revealing their precise meaning. Some are written with technical and esoteric language that requires deeper investigation on the part of the content teacher. When in doubt, seek clarification from veteran teachers or curriculum specialists in your school or district to ensure that your interpretation of the standard and your instructional strategies match the intended goal of the standard.
- *Use other standards as resources.* The national professional organizations offer valuable resources for not only meeting their own standards but also

much more. Be sure to check out what each has to offer as you develop lessons and units in your content area.

• *Rely on assessment to know when you have met the standards.* Some standards are written in a way that it is easy to give a traditional summative assessment to gauge whether your students have met them. Some standards will take many lessons over a period of time to teach and to assess through a series of formative assessment tools. Regardless of what the district's pacing guide dictates, keep students at the center in your standards-based instruction.

THEORY TO PRACTICE

Standards should be used as a guide for setting goals and objectives for learning. They also help a teacher to determine if he is setting the right learning goals. Once you have your own classroom, your school district will serve as a guide to standards you are required to use in your yearly (and even daily) curriculum.

We believe that the standards presented in this chapter—the CCSS and the national professional standards—provide valuable professional knowledge you must have in order to be a good teacher. Begin with the standards that are most relevant to your content area. Know all of the elements in your subject standards—content, process, practice, application, and more—well enough so that they can inform your teaching. Then, for the sake of making integration possible, familiarize yourself with the standards in other content areas. As your students are learning a particular topic in your class, what will they also be learning in their other classes? How might you collaborate with teachers in other content areas so that you can integrate your curriculum? Standards are an essential component in your teaching.

REFERENCES

Calkins, L., Ehrenworth, M., & Lehman, C. (2012). *Pathways to the common core: Accelerating achievement.* Portsmouth, NH: Heinemann.

Dillon, S. (2010, March 10). Panel proposes single standard for all schools. *New York Times.*

Kohn, A. (2000). *The case against standardized testing: Raising the scores, ruining the schools.* Portsmouth, NH: Heinemann.

McLaughlin, M., & Overturf, B. J. (2013). *The common core: Teaching students in grades 6 –12 to meet the reading standards.* Newark, DE: International Reading Association.

National Commission on Excellence in Education. (1983). *A nation at risk: The imperative for educational reform*. Washington, DC: U.S. Government Printing Office.

National Council for the Social Studies. (1994). *Expectations of excellence: Curriculum standards for social studies*. Washington, DC: Author.

National Council for the Social Studies. (2002). *National standards for social studies teachers*. Washington, DC: Author.

National Council of Teachers of English and the International Reading Association. (1996). *Standards for the English language arts*. Urbana, IL & Newark, DE: Author.

National Council of Teachers of Mathematics. (1989). *Curriculum and evaluation standards for school mathematics*. Reston, VA: Author.

National Council of Teachers of Mathematics. (2000). *Principles and standards for school mathematics*. Reston, VA: Author.

National Governors Association Center for Best Practices & Council of Chief State School Officers (2010). *Common core state standards*. Washington, DC: National Governors Association Center for Best Practices & Council of Chief State School Officers.

National Research Council. (2012). *A framework for K–12 science education: Practices, crosscutting concepts, and core ideas*. Washington, DC: National Academy Press.

National Research Council. (2013). *Next generation science standards*. Washington, DC: National Academy Press.

Popham J. W. (2001). *The truth about testing: An educator's call to action*. Alexandria, VA: ASCD.

Race to the Top Grant Program (2010). Retrieved January 20, 2013, from www2. ed.gov/programs.racetothetop/index/html.

Ravitch, D. (1995). *National standards in American education: A citizen's guide*. Washington, DC: Brookings Institution Press.

Reutzel, D. R., & Cooter, R. B. (2013). *The essentials of teaching children to read*. Boston: Pearson.

Sacks, P. (1999). *Standardized minds*. Cambridge, MA: Perseus Books.

4

Informing Instruction

Assessment

All there is to thinking is seeing something noticeable which makes you
see something you weren't noticing which makes you see something that
isn't even visible.

—Norman Maclean, *A River Runs Through It and Other Stories*

Tribute to Dr. Moehn

It seems that few college professors understand differentiated instruction or the
benefits of using a variety of assessments to understand what students have learned.
I was fortunate as an undergraduate biology student to have one of those professors
that did understand. I didn't know this at the time, but he would become my husband's
and my favorite professor. His name was Dr. Lawrence Moehn.

My biology class consisted of 120 freshmen in a lecture-style auditorium. Our
first exam took place about four weeks into the semester. On the day the professor
returned our tests, he put all of our scores on the board and drew lines between the
scores where the grades broke from an A to a B, and so on. Mine wasn't the lowest
score on the board, but it was the third lowest score at 54 percent and below the F
line scrawled on the board. I was devastated. My goal had been to be a teacher since
I was four years old, and I felt the dream being swept away from me. After class, I went
straight to the Dean of Students office and told her what happened. She suggested
I meet with the professor—something I did not want to do.

Dr. Moehn was kind, but not sympathetic. He was sure I had scored so poorly because I had not studied. He shared a few studying tips with me and encouraged me to
work harder for the next exam scheduled in three weeks. And I did. But when the day
of the test arrived, I woke up very sick and could not go to class. I called Dr. Moehn
and told him of my situation, and he reluctantly excused me but told me the make-up
test would be essays, not the standard multiple-choice exam and much more difficult.
He suggested I should come in to take it as soon as I possibly could.

The following morning I called his office and scheduled a time to take the exam. When I finished, Dr. Moehn asked if I had studied, and I assured him that I had. He asked me to have a seat in the hall while he graded my test. Ten minutes later, he emerged with a broad smile on his face and asked me to come into his office. He showed me the B+ written across the top of my test and said, "Now that I know you have studied, I would like you to take the test I gave the other students. Do you have time?"

I completed the fifty multiple-choice questions in about an hour. He again asked me to sit in the hall while he graded my test.

"Debbie, come in here," his voice sounding stern.

When I entered his office I could see a 64 percent, D, emblazoned across the top of my most recent test.

"Sit down," he commanded. "Why did you answer this question this way? You actually answered correctly on the first test, but missed the same question on the multiple-choice test. Explain to me *out loud* what you were thinking when you chose this answer."

I explained myself carefully as I believed I had chosen the correct answer. He sat mystified by my response and said, "I understand why you chose that, but it is not correct. Tell me why you chose this one."

Again, I explained the thoughts behind my choice of an answer, and again, he agreed that he could understand my decision—but it was still wrong! After this same conversation happened the third time, he sat back in his chair and thought for a minute, and then said, "You cannot take a multiple-choice test. You know this material and scored higher on what I considered to be a much harder test than the multiple-choice exam. So, here's what we are going to do. When you come to class to take the next exam, I'm going to hand you an essay exam while the others take the multiple-choice exam. Would that work for you?"

It wasn't a hard decision for me—the B+ compared to the D and F seemed like a reasonable choice. I passed the course, and even though this was not one of my teacher preparation courses, I learned a valuable lesson from him that I carry with me every year I teach.

Teachers who embrace the constructivist, sociocultural, and collaborative perspectives of teaching believe that learning is not linear, but instead is multifaceted. They understand that *what* they assess and *how* they assess demonstrates what they *value*. Good teachers use ongoing assessment and evaluation processes to create and foster learning opportunities that maximize students' understanding of worthy concepts, development of important skills, and transfer of knowledge to real-life tasks. These assessment and evaluation processes inform instruction based on students' learning from a variety of assessment tools used before, during, and after the lesson.

You may have wondered how the quote that introduces this chapter has to do with assessment. A good teacher has an intuitive sense about each and every student in his class. Much of this intuition may be invisible to anyone else who walks into the classroom. The teacher knows who is excelling, who is coasting, who is struggling, and who is not even trying. He can separate the "A" students from the "C" students simply by relying on what he has observed and learned in the context of teaching and in the process of authentically interacting with his students. Assessment *documents* these intuitions of a teacher by breathing data into them, making student learning visible in the eyes of the teacher and the students as well as others. As you read on, continue to think of assessment as the documentation process that makes visible what is at first invisible to you and your students.

THEORETICAL FOUNDATIONS OF ASSESSMENT

Teachers often think about which assessment tools they should use after they settle on what they are going to teach and how they are going to teach it. In Wiggins and McTighe's (2005) curriculum model *Understanding by Design* (also referred to as *Backward Design*), they advocate that once learning goals and objectives are clarified, the very next step in the instructional design process is establishing the criteria for success; in other words, what would count as evidence of understanding? What tools or techniques will the teacher use to gather evidence that the students have met the criteria? This process occurs *before* creating lessons and activities. For many veteran teachers who have been introduced to the *Understanding by Design* model, conceptualizing the assessment plan and coming up with actual assessment tools before writing their lesson plans is what seems "backward." Regardless of *when* the teacher designs an assessment, it is important for the assessment to be intentionally, thoughtfully, and specifically made to align with teaching (the objective/goals) and learning (how you structure the lesson).

Using a compilation of scholarly work on classroom assessment (Cooper & Kiger, 2011; Rhodes & Shanklin, 1993; Clarke, 1992; Valencia & Pearson, 1987), we offer the following guidelines for assessment:

- *Assessment should be meaningful.* Assessment should inform teachers about students' strengths and weaknesses so that decisions can be made about instruction. The aim is for better, more appropriate assessment, not simply more assessment.
- *Assessment should be multimodal.* Combinations of assessment tools (i.e., formal and informal, formative and summative, traditional and non-traditional) should be used to fully indicate whether students have met the learning goals.
- *Assessment should be ongoing.* Assessment should occur frequently so that a complete and accurate picture of progress is documented.
- *Assessment should occur in authentic contexts.* As much as possible, assessment should mirror the instructional activities as well as real-life tasks.

In this chapter, a paradigm of assessment consists of effective teaching and meaningful learning. This paradigm places less emphasis on "formal" assessments, typically defined as those with specific test administration and scoring procedures such as state standardized tests or achievement tests developed with larger, more public audiences in mind. Rather, it focuses more on assessment frameworks, tools, and techniques that can be implemented *in* the classroom, *by* the teacher (and the students), *for* the ultimate goal of student learning. The ideas that we share in this chapter are tools for the teachers to use in daily instruction.

ASSESSMENT AND EVALUATION

Assessment and evaluation are separate but interrelated processes. Often used interchangeably, the definitions of these terms vary widely depending on the context for their use (i.e., education, psychology, business, etc.). In educational settings, *assessment* typically refers to the *collection and recording of data* from student learning. *Evaluation* refers to the *interpretation of the data*, making sense and bringing meaning to the data and often resulting in making a judgment of one kind or another.

Echevarria, Short, and Vogt (2008) view the processes of assessment and evaluation as "progressive: first assessment; then evaluation" (p. 18). However, the assessment and evaluation processes are not nearly as linear, sequential, or predictable. While the distinction between the two exist, they are interdependent as they go hand in hand; interpretation cannot take place without first collecting data, and likewise, data void of meaning to illuminate students' progress or effectiveness of the instruction is pointless.

Good teachers use the moment that they deliver content or teach skills to collect some of the data and to evaluate whether their instruction is effective. Most importantly, good teachers make informed decisions as to what to do *next* using that valuable observed data by asking some of these questions:

- Did the students "get it"?
- If so, what worked?
- If not, what needs to be retaught, and to which students?
- Is more modeling needed?
- More guided practice?
- More independent practice?

As you obtain assessment data that directs you off the plan and off the script, keep in mind that data should drive the instruction. You may have to pull together a small group of students to reteach a concept; you may have to reexplain a concept using a different mode of presentation to the entire class; or you may have to return to the lesson you taught the day before to reemphasize a point. Be sure that the time necessary to redirect and refine your lesson is built into the time allocated for the lesson. Especially for beginning teachers, these spontaneous "thinking on your feet" moments may be a challenge at first, but they are an inherent part of good teaching.

TYPES OF ASSESSMENTS

Now that the two processes—assessment and evaluation—have been unpacked, let us use *assessment* to refer to both data collection *and* interpretation in this book for the sake of brevity and clarity. However, be mindful of the interrelated and interdependent processes that make teaching recursive, complex, and unpredictable.

Teachers have known for years that instruction and assessment are difficult to distinguish at times; the same activity that delivers the content may, in fact, be considered data. Table 4.1 shares a range of options for assessment, many of which will be described in detail later in this chapter.

Certainly, you have encountered many of these tools as instructional strategies to promote your learning. You may notice that many of the tools are

Table 4.1. Formative and summative assessment tools.

Formative	Summative
	Formal tests (e.g., standardized)
Observations/Anecdotal Records	
Questioning	
Interviews	Interviews
Discussions	
Conferences	Conferences
Checklists	
Exit/Entrance Slips	
Quick Writes	
Quick Checks (e.g., using whiteboards or thumbs up or down)	
Quizzes/Tests	Quizzes/Tests
Projects	Projects
Working Portfolios	Showcase Portfolios
Logs/Journals	
	Papers
Graphic Organizers	Graphic Organizers
Practice Presentations	
	Presentations

listed in both formative and summative columns. In the hands of a good teacher, the same tool may be used at different times to inform instruction and to summarize a student's learning.

Formative and Summative Assessments

Broadly, assessments come in two forms: formative and summative. This distinction gained stature when Scriven (1967) suggested that there were two different processes for program evaluation: *formative* evaluation to determine the merit of a program while there was still time to make changes in the program during its use; and *summative* evaluation to determine whether to continue or terminate a program, ostensibly at the end of a term or year. In the context of contemporary classroom assessment, Scriven's distinction can still be of use.

Formative assessments are designed to assist the teacher in knowing what her students understand and what they do not yet grasp. According to Popham (2008), formative assessment is "a planned process in which assessment-elicited evidence of students' status is used by teachers to adjust their on-going instructional procedures or by students to adjust their current learning tactics" (p. 6). This planned process involves a number of different activities. Formative assessments can be *informal*, occurring as a result of a direct interaction between the teacher and the students typically during class time (e.g., observations resulting in anecdotal records, discussions, conferences, checklists, questions, etc.), or *formal*, requiring students to complete specific written or performance tasks (e.g., quizzes, tests, student work samples, projects, presentations, portfolios, etc.). Data collected during formative assessments provide useful information for the teacher to modify or reteach the lesson until learning objectives are met.

Summative assessments, on the other hand, do not provide that opportunity for adjustment in instruction. They are used to measure student growth *after* instruction, and such assessment is generally given at the end of a lesson, unit, or course in order to determine if the goals of the instruction have been met. Many of the formal assessment tools such final papers, exams, projects, and performances demonstrate what students have learned from a lesson, a unit, or a course. For many teachers, summative assessments provide data for grades or benchmarks.

One clever way to remember the difference is that formative *informs* instruction and summative lets you *summarize* what the students learned from the instruction. Other playful analogies have been made that might help you remember: an annual check-up at the doctor's office (*formative*) versus an autopsy (*summative*); and a chef tasting the dish while it's being made (*formative*) versus a customer tasting the dish (*summative*). Whichever sticks in your memory, remember that you need both types of assessment—formative and summative—to create a full profile of a learner.

Traditional Assessments

For many of you, the word *assessment* probably conjures up experiences of taking quizzes and tests—complete with multiple-choice, matching, true/false, and short-answer questions—and writing papers at the end of a chapter, unit, or a book. These are considered traditional assessments and are typically characterized by the use of paper and pencil. Traditional assessments are most often used for summative assessment at the end of a learning cycle for grades. There are, however, appropriate uses of traditional tools (like a quiz) for formative assessment to check for understanding in order to adjust instruction.

Summative assessments created by the teacher, the district, and/or by curriculum publishers based on the learning goals are meant to "test" to see if students have learned the right content and developed the right skills. Tests that would be most helpful to the teacher in gathering meaningful data is criterion referenced (Glaser, 1963). A criterion-referenced test is tied directly to instructional objectives and is most often developed by the teacher or the school district to reflect a particular curriculum. Student performance is evaluated relative to mastery of the objectives for each student rather than compared to the scores of other test takers, referred to as norm referenced.

Creating teacher-made tests using many forms of questions such as multiple choice and matching requires both technical knowledge and a set of skills. There are rules for making a multiple-choice test a fair and valid measurement of student learning. For example, stems (or problems) should be written in partial sentences or questions, and alternatives (or choice of answers) should be grammatically consistent and mutually exclusive. Similar rules exist for matching and true/false. An additional course on assessment will provide you with specific knowledge and skills to ensure that you know how to create tests that are developmentally appropriate, fair, and valid. In the meantime, consider this set of guidelines as you create your own exam questions (table 4.2).

Traditional assessments, especially in the secondary levels, do have a role in learning. This is true even in the constructivist approach to teaching and learning that we advocate. However, it is our challenge to you that these assessments do not simply stop at getting the "right" answer. Demand your students use higher-order thinking skills even as they attempt to arrive at a single answer on a multiple-choice question. Rather than asking for a definition, ask for an application, as shown in these examples (table 4.3 and figure 4.1).

Table 4.2. Guidelines for constructing tests.

Format	Description	Guidelines
True/False	• A declarative statement is given and the student determines if the statement is True or False. • Variations of response can include Yes/No, Fact/Opinion, Agree/Disagree, etc. • Can be offered as correction items by underlining the item to be corrected.	• The declarative statement should only include one central idea. • Avoid use of specific determiners such as *never, usually, always,* etc., as they can be used as clue words. • Avoid negative statements, but if you do, highlight/bold the words such as *except* or *not.* Never use double negatives. • Watch for patterns in correct responses (e.g., T, T, F, F, T, T, F, F). • Balance the length and number of T/F statements. • False statements can be offered as correction items. Underline the central idea to be corrected with a space under or above for the correct response. • Avoid trivial statements.
Multiple Choice	• Stem is the problem or the task being presented. Can be written as an incomplete sentence or a question. • Three-to-five alternatives are provided from which to choose either the correct or the best response as per the directions.	• Different number of alternatives can be offered on the same test. • Stem should present a clear enough problem so that the student could answer without looking at the alternatives. • Put as much wording in the stem so as to make the alternatives as concise as possible. However, the stem should not be too wordy. • Put the stem in positive form whenever possible. • All alternatives should be plausible. • Alternatives should be grammatically consistent with the stem. • Avoid clues (e.g., a stem that ends with "an" with the correct alternative that begins with a vowel). • Avoid using "All of the above" and use "None of the above" with caution. • Look for patterns in the correct responses (e.g., A, B, B, D, A, B, B, D) and vary position of correct answer.

Format	Description	Guidelines
Matching	• Variant of the Multiple Choice format. • Written with "Premises" (which act as stems) on the left column and "Responses" (which act as alternatives) on the right column.	• Offer no more than ten items to be matched. • Premises should be numbered and responses should be lettered. • Provide an uneven number of responses to premises. • Directions should state the basis for matching and whether responses can be used once, more than once, or not at all. • Material should be homogeneous (e.g., authors/books) and responses should be listed in a logical order (i.e., alphabetical, numerical, or chronological).
Completion	• Can take a form of a blank at the end of a statement or a direct question. • The student supplies the correct response in either one word or a short phrase.	• The blank should come toward the end of the sentence, never at the beginning. • The correct response should be an essential word or a concept carefully phrased to avoid multiple answers. • Provide only one blank. • Be specific in your guidelines regarding spelling and handwriting. • Blank should be of uniform length so as not to provide clues.
Essay	• Restricted Essay—The content of the response is limited in scope and focus such as "compare and contrast" or "list." • Extended Essay—The response is more open-ended and provides a greater freedom of response. • A scoring rubric (i.e., analytic or holistic) should be provided.	• Sufficient response to a restricted essay should be presented in a short paragraph (in a few sentences). • The prompt should be clearly worded so that it presents a clear problem or a task. • Do not give choices (e.g., answer 2 out of 3) if assessing for content. All students should answer all the same questions. • Grade all the same items (e.g., Question 1) for all students before moving on to the next item. Try to grade anonymously. • Look for fluff or trivial responses (bluffing).

S. Richwine (2014)
General Rules:
• Directions should be clear and concise, telling the student what to do/how to respond.
• Provide answer blanks left of the item number.
• Never split items across pages. For example, all the premises and responses for a matching item should be on a single page.

Another option would be once an answer is found, ask students to document the process or justify their answer. Reading teachers often ask for textual evidence on teacher-made tests, as in: (1) Identify the symbolism of the rose in the book, or (2) Find three passages in the book to justify your answer. Teachers in other content areas can easily adapt this and ask for

Table 4.3 Asking for application rather than definition.

Knowledge Level	Application Level
What does *belligerent* mean?	Who is most likely to be *belligerent*?
1. kind	1. a bully on the playground
2. hostile	2. a neighbor greeting you
3. vulgar	3. a friend who missed your birthday
4. noisy	4. a teacher praising a student

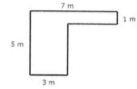

As another example, rather than having students "Find the perimeter," ask them to draw a six-sided irregular polygon with a perimeter of 24 units. What else might you learn about your students' knowledge of geometry using the second task on a test?

Figure 4.1   Mathematics example of asking for application.

elaborations, explanations, justifications, and more to gauge *how* or *how well* the students understand the content.

When used appropriately, traditional assessments will provide meaningful and valid data. With their relative ease of scoring/grading, they can have a role in classroom assessment serving the teacher, the student, and the parent.

Nontraditional Assessment (Performance/Alternative)

The diversity of our student population demands the need for assessments beyond tests, quizzes, and papers. Nontraditional assessment allows students to demonstrate their strengths and growth using a wide range of opportunities. Although this type of assessment is often called alternative assessment, we do not feel that this should be a marginalized option for assessment. Imagine all the possibilities that individual students or collaborative groups of students can use to demonstrate what knowledge they have acquired, what skills they have learned and perhaps even mastered, and what dispositions they have internalized. Much of their transformation may not even be measured or made visible through a paper and pencil test or a final paper.

Nontraditional assessment is also known as performance assessment. Performance assessment covers a broad range of tools as it measures students' learning behaviors or products by their demonstration of knowledge and skills through activities such as writing, oral or visual presentations, dramatizations, videos, simulations, experiments, portfolios, and projects. The characteristics of performance assessment include the following:

- Assessment activity includes performing, creating, producing, or doing.
- Assessment activity taps high-level thinking and problem-solving skills.
- Solution to the assessment activity is student structured.
- Assessment activity emulates real life, invoking application of knowledge.
- Scoring is harder to achieve.

One example of an authentic assessment is GRASPS. GRASPS tasks include Goal, Role, Audience, Situation, Product, and Standards (Wiggins & McTighe, 2005, pp. 157–58). Wren (2009) identifies three steps to developing performance assessments: defining the purpose, choosing the activity, and developing the scoring criteria. Authentic Assessment, a special type of performance assessment, has a higher degree of fidelity to real-life situations (Frey, Schmitt, & Allen, 2012; Reeves & Okey, 1996). Authentic assessments mirror or simulate real-life tasks such as writing a letter to the editor, proposing a solution to a city council, planning an event with a spread-sheet to present a budget, and so on. Every authentic assessment is perform-ance assessment, but not vice versa (Meyer, 1992). Consider this GRASPS example:

> Literary Hall of Fame (English, grades 10–12). The Council of Arts and Letters has announced the establishment of a Hall of Fame to honor the works of not-able U.S. authors and artists. Since your class is finishing a course on U.S. lit-erature, you have been asked to submit a nomination for an author to be admitted to the Hall of Fame. Complete the nomination form for an author whom you believe is worthy of induction. Your essay should include your analysis of the author's contribution to U.S. literature and your rationale for recommending the author for inclusion in the Hall of Fame. (Wiggens & McTigue, 2005, p. 160)

Can you identify each of the GRASPS elements? Goal—to nominate an author; Role—nominator; Audience—The Council of Arts and Letters; Situation—Hall of Fame to honor U.S. authors and artists; and Product—nom-ination letter. Assessment grounded in "authentic work" has two important outcomes: "Learning how adults in the larger world beyond the school *really* [emphasis original] use or don't use the knowledge and skills that are taught in school and how discrete lessons are meaningful, that is how they lead to higher-quality performance or mastery of more important tasks" (Wiggins & McTighe, 2005, p. 155).The teacher could have assigned a more traditional paper with the prompt: "List the contributions made by F. Scott Fitzgerald in American literature." Instead, GRASPS allows for choice (which adults often experience in real-life contexts), students' authentic response (which brings integrity to the task), and a genuine audience (which inspires a quality product). Can you think of a GRASPS task in your content area?

Table 4.4 RAFT.

Role	Audience	Format	Topic
Lawyer	U.S. Supreme Court	Appeal Speech	Dred Scott Decision
Abraham Lincoln	Dear Abby	Advice Column	Frustration with his generals
Frontier Woman	Self	Diary	Hardships of the West
Chemist	Chemical company	Instructions	Combinations to avoid
Square Root	Whole Number	Love letter	Explain relationship
Repeating Decimal	Set of Rational Numbers	Petition	Prove you belong to this set
Interviewer	Those curious about Donner Party survivors	Talk show	James Reed's accounting of his Donner Party experience
Joseph Stalin	George Orwell	Book Review	Reactions to *Animal Farm*
Comma	9th grade students	Complaint	How it is misused
Nucleus	Cell membrane	Letter of Appreciation	The cell membrane's contribution to the nucleus and other organelles
Zero	Whole numbers	Campaign speech	Importance of the number 0
Prime number	Rational numbers	Instructions	Rules for divisibility
Exponent	Jury	Instructions to the jury	Laws of exponents
Acute triangle	Obtuse triangle	Letter	Explain differences of triangles
Nocturnal creature	Diurnal creature	Invitation	You don't know what you're missing!
Charles Darwin	Himself	Journal entries	Biodiversity of the Galapagos

Compiled and adapted from Buehl (2014); Fisher & Frey (2015); and Daniels, Zemelman, & Steineke (2007).

RAFT (Role, Audience, Format, Topic) is a performance-based assessment, not necessarily authentic, used in content area classrooms. An abbreviated version of GRASPS, RAFT captures the spirit of authentic assessment using playful twists on real-life tasks. See table 4.4 for examples that can be used to assess content area learning.

ASSESSMENT TOOLS

Your ability to assess your students' learning is of utmost importance. As you acquaint yourself with the ideas presented in this chapter, think about *how* you should select the appropriate assessment. In order to help you begin to develop your repertoire of effective assessment tools, it is important to remember, like a carpenter's tool belt, it is all about having the "right tool" for the "right job." In the following pages of this chapter, you will find some of our favorite assessment tools. It is important to select the right assessment not only for your lesson but also with your students in mind. To help you find the appropriate assessment, ask yourself these questions:

- What is the purpose of the assessment?
- What would I like to know?
- About which students?
- How much time do I have to collect data?
- What is my instructional approach?
- Can I assess at the time of my instruction?
- Am I looking to assess students' process or their products?
- Do I need a grade for the unit or the marking period?

With so many assessment tools and techniques available to teachers and students in the secondary levels, it is impossible to neatly categorize and catalog them. Many of the tools can be used flexibly serving many purposes; many may not even look like assessment tools. To guide you, the teacher, to select the right tool for the right job, a multitude of tools organized by *who* is most likely to *use* them will be presented. The assessments used or created by the students are referred to as Instructional Assessment Tools. Those created and used by the teacher are referred to as Data Collection Tools.

Instructional Assessment Tools

Using tools presented in this section will align or coincide instruction with assessment. Experiences or activities engaging students during a lesson can be assessments themselves. Using these tools, students will demonstrate knowledge and skills, create samples of work, and offer the most tangible and concrete data to illustrate whether they have met the learning goals. Ideas for such tools, often nontraditional, performance-based, and authentic, can be limitless. You will be able to access a multitude of assessment tools using reputable online resources. However, here are a few examples of instructional assessment tools.

Projects/Exhibitions

Projects or exhibitions are useful because they provide students with opportunities to extend basic knowledge and skills to higher levels of thinking. Because projects usually entail an extended period of time to complete, they reflect the students' ability to manipulate complex information and thinking strategies. Consider the range of products in this category. Beyond the prototypical "projects" that come in science projects and trifolds, think of songs, debates, graphs, diagrams, models, books, pamphlets, websites, wikis, brochures, art projects, and more as "exhibits" of what the student knows and knows how to do.

Multimedia Presentations

From PowerPoint to Prezi to iMovie to GarageBand, there are so many different types of software and programs available to students to produce their own multimedia presentation. With so much of their social and entertainment lives consumed in media, we welcome a chance for students to be producers rather than consumers. In addition to demonstrating their understanding and knowledge, multimedia presentations allow students to put their twenty-first-century technology skills to use (perhaps with more aptitude than the teacher). Multimedia presentations will also provide students with opportunities to consider nonacademic values such as ethics, etiquette, and social protocols of media consumption and production.

Multigenre Projects

Multigenre projects bring a playful twist to student projects. As the name suggests, students are offered a wide variety of options for demonstrating their learning. Possibilities for what counts as a product is only limited by the creativity of the teacher. Figure 4.2 lists some of the possibilities.

Portfolios

Portfolios are collections of student work either on paper or digitally stored. A portfolio can be used to show progress over time (working portfolio) or to exhibit the best work samples (final or showcase portfolio), and function as either formative or summative assessment. Students should choose the artifacts included in the portfolio. A self-assessment can be included by asking students to provide a rationale for each of the artifacts included in their portfolios.

Drama

Drama is a powerful means to illustrate what you know. Through plays, skits, role-plays, readers theater, and other creative ways to dramatize a concept, drama also allows for teachers to witness less tangible outcomes of learning such as emotion, interpretation, and energy. Drama is not just for promoting reading fluency and comprehension; it can also facilitate learning in the

Adventure Magazine Story	Facebook Post	Puns
Advertisement	Future News Story	Puppet Show
Advice Column	Graphic Organizer	Puzzles
Announcement	Greeting Card	Quotes
Article	Horoscope	Radio Broadcast
Artistic Response	How To Guide	Recipe
Autobiography	Human Interest Story	Restaurant Menu
Awards Ceremony	Informational Video	Resume
Baseball Cards	Interview Questions	Satire
Billboards	Introduction	Scavenger Hunt
Birth Announcement	Jingle	Schedule
Board Game	Job Application	Science Article
Book Jacket	Laboratory Report	Shopping List
Book Review	Letter to the Editor	Short Scene
Bucket List	Local News Report	Short Story
Bumper Sticker	Magazine Cover	Sign
Business Letter	Magazine Ad	Slogan
Calendar	Manifesto	Snapchat
Campaign Speech	Membership Card	Song Lyrics
Cereal box	Memory Book	Special Event Invitation
Certificate	Memo	Speech
Character Analysis	Menu	Sport Analysis
Chart	Movie Review	Tableau
Classified Ad	Musical Number	Tabloid Article
Codes	News Report	Talk Show Interview
Comedy Routine	News Announcement	Telegram
	(bulletin)	
Comic Strip	Newspaper Article	Texts
Commercial	Newspaper Editorial	Thank You Note
Contestant Application	Nutritional Label	Tickets
Contract	Obituary	Time Line
Critique	Pamphlet	Tips
Decision Trail	Parody	Top Ten List
Dedication	Personal Letter	To Do List
Dialogue	Persuasive Speech	Tribute
Diary	Picture Book	Trivia
Directions	Poetry	TV Ad
Dream	Poster for Movie/Book	Wanted Poster
Editorial	Prediction	Wanted Ads
Epitaph	Play	Wiki Page
Eulogy	Pop-up Book	Wordless Picture Book

Some examples from this list are from: Frank, M. (1995).

Figure 4.2   Multigenre projects. Marjorie Frank. (1995). *If you are going to teach kids how to write . . . You gotta have this book.* Nashville, TN: Incentive Publication.

content areas. For example, Curriculum-Based Readers Theater (CBRT), in which script topics can derive from curriculum content in the classroom, can teach concepts. Scripts written, rehearsed, and performed by groups of students can increase concept understanding, content vocabulary, and inter-action among peers (Sanacore & Palumbo, 2010). Not all students may be eager to "play" in drama; be ready to offer those students other options to demonstrate their learning.

Experiments

Experiments are a common method to demonstrate a science concept to students, but why not have students demonstrate their knowledge by designing their own? This may reveal more about what they know than com-pleting an experiment designed by the teacher. Beyond the concept, designing experiments will also force students to use higher-level thinking as they use logic, trial and error, hypothesis testing, and problem-solving skills.

Writing Samples

Students' work samples, including writing samples, can be used to assess stu-dent progress. Informal writing such as quick writes or free writes can be used as well as more formal writing including newspapers, newsletters, letters, or even scripts for a play.

Learning Logs/Journals

A student can keep a log or a journal to document his own learning process. Teachers can review on a daily, weekly, or quarterly basis to determine how students are understanding the processes they are using. Teachers can also re-spond to their students' entries in a dialogue journal, shaping their ideas and reinforcing their strengths in anticipation of more formal writing that occurs in other activities (figure 4.3).

Games

Using quality educational games, especially at the middle school level, would be a refreshing occasion for assessment. Specific skills such as mathematical computation and spelling can be observed and documented during games of modified Scrabble and Boggle.

Date: Nov. 2, 2014

Topic: Solving for x

Student: Today we learned how to solve problems like this 2x-5=7.

First, we have to make the -5 go away by adding +5 to both sides and it becomes 2x=12. Basically by doing this, we don't lose the 5, we just move it to the other side of the = sign.

Next divide 2 by both sides of the equation and you get x=6.

I'm still not sure why we added +5 first then divided by 2. Why didn't we just add a -2 to each side of the equation – then it would be x=10. How do I know when to add or subtract and when to multiply or divide?

When solving equations, we use the reverse of the order of operations. Therefore, we always add or subtract before multiplying and dividing. In this problem, we read it 2 times x minus 5 equals 7. We want to get rid of the plus or minus first, so we want to do the opposite of subtracting 5; and add 5 to both sides of the equations. Remember, if you do something to one side you must do it to the other to keep the equation balanced. This will give you 2x = 12. Then since it is 2 times x, you want to do the opposite of multiplication and divide both sides by 2. This will give you x = 6.

Figure 4.3   Learning log.

Brainstorming

Schema theory of learning shows us how important it is to activate and use what students already know about a topic or a concept. Using many "before" learning or reading instructional strategies (such as KWL and its variations and Stickystorms presented in chapter 6), teachers can formally or informally assess students' prior knowledge.

Self-Assessments

Students must be given opportunities to examine their work and be reflective about their strengths and weaknesses. They can use open-ended formats such as logs, journals, quick writes, and exit/entrance slips to document their reflections and insights on the process of their work before, during, and after the lesson. Students can also use rubrics or rating scales to "grade" themselves based on their products. Share rubrics or other grading sheets with students before they complete their work. Have them self-evaluate their work using these assessment tools. You may be surprised at the insights students reveal about themselves as learners through such self-assessments. Ask some of these questions to gather students' insights:

- What do you know now that you did not know before?
- What did you already know?
- What questions do you still have?
- How would you explain this concept to someone being introduced to it for the first time?
- Does your work meet your or my (the teacher's) expectations?
- What needs to be changed?
- What would you do differently next time?
- How does this relate to your "real" life?
- Did you participate in your group work productively?

Data Collection Tools

Tools listed here are specifically designed to *collect* or *measure* data. The measurement tools on their own are not vehicles for learning, whereas tools mentioned in the Instructional Assessment Tools section can be used by teachers as instructional strategies or by the students as learning tools. The tools mentioned in this section are created and completed by the teacher for systematic collection of data from both process and product of student learning. And many of them document behaviors observed before, during, and after instruction.

Even though many tasks completed by the students will have a recognizable product at the end of a lesson or a unit, where process ends and product begins is ambiguous in many other learning contexts. For example, writing is a continuous process even when a "final draft" is submitted. Our point: the process versus product juxtaposition is not as clear as it seems. Many of the tools listed below do not belong to strictly process or product. These tools can be used to collect data from both process and product of student learning. As you read the description of each tool, ask yourself if the tool measures process or product or both.

Checklists

Checklists specify student behaviors or products expected during progression through the curriculum. They are some of the simplest forms of assessment and are used typically when students need to have mastery of a skill. The items on the checklist may be content area objectives. A checklist is considered to be a type of observational technique. Because observers check only the presence or absence of the behavior or product, checklists generally are reliable and

	C			D			E			F			G			A			B		
	#		b	#		b	#		b	#		b	#		b	#		b	#		b
Stephanie	√	√	√	√	√	√	√	√	√	√	√	√	√	√	√	√	√	√	√	√	√
Lauren		√			√									√							
Mark		√						√		√	√	√		√		√	√			√	
Sven	√	√			√									√							
Haley		√						√			√			√					√	√	
Annamarie	√	√												√			√				
Brooke		√			√		√	√		√	√	√		√		√	√		√		
Megan		√						√						√							
Kristen		√			√									√			√				√

Figure 4.4   Music teacher checklist example.

relatively easy to use. Used over time, checklists can document students' rate and degree of accomplishment within the curriculum. Figure 4.4 shows a checklist used by a music teacher to indicate whether each student can name a note. Students can either do it at 100 percent accuracy or they cannot; this form of assessment does not provide partial credit for attempts.

Rating Scales

Rather than recording the "presence" or "absence" of a behavior or skill, the teacher subjectively rates each item according to some dimension of interest during an observation. For example, students might be rated on how proficient they are on different elements of an oral presentation to the class. Each element of the presentation may be rated on a 1 to 5 scale, with 5 representing the highest level of proficiency. The examples shown in figure 4.5 allow students performance on a 1 to 5 scale to rate their and their peers performance.

Questionnaires/Surveys

A questionnaire is a self-report assessment tool with which students can provide information about areas of interest to the teacher. Questionnaire items can be written in a variety of formats and may be forced-choice or open-ended. The open-ended questionnaire with sample student responses is from a summer enrichment math class (table 4.5).

Self-Assessment for Literature Response Group

I completed the assigned reading prior to class.
      1   2   3   4   5

I showed evidence of thoughtful and close reading.
      1   2   3   4   5

I brought the book/article along with questions to support the discussion.
      1   2   3   4   5

I listened to others carefully and responded to their ideas and concerns.
      1   2   3   4   5

I participated respectfully in the discussion today.
      1   2   3   4   5

Peer-Assessment for Literature Response Group

S/he completed the assigned reading prior to class.
      1   2   3   4   5

S/he showed evidence of thoughtful and close reading (completed journal/reflection).
      1   2   3   4   5

S/he brought the book/article along with questions to support the discussion.
      1   2   3   4   5

S/he listened to others and responded thoughtfully.
      1   2   3   4   5

S/he participated appropriately in the discussion today.
      1   2   3   4   5

Figure 4.5   Rating scale examples.

Observation/Anecdotal Records

Teachers learn so much through careful observation. Throughout the school day, a teacher will observe and notice many student behaviors that would be informative. Students' interactions with peers, their responses to your and peers' questions, their enthusiasm or hesitancy for participation in classroom activities, how fluently they have read a piece of text, keeping track of completed homework, not paying attention to instructions, or refusing to use class time to work are just a few examples of anecdotal notes that may come

Table 4.5 Open-ended questionnaire from multiple students.

<Student responses in italics.>

What are your mathematical strengths?	What are your mathematical weaknesses?	What do you hope to get out of this summer course?	Is there anything special I should know about you to help me teach you better?
I'm good at geometry and some algebra.	*I'm not very good with fractions.*	*I hope for this summer course to prepare me for my high school education.*	*I like to do hands-on activities.*
My mathematical strengths are anything that is done in math. I really like math and enjoy doing everything in it.	*My mathematical weakness is geometry and decimals.*	*I hope to get better math skills.*	*Something in math won't come to me as fast as everything else but it differs on what it is.*
My mathematical strengths are showing my work.	*My mathematical weaknesses are not using a calculator on homework.*	*I hope to be advanced or ready for algebra 1.*	*I don't talk much in class.*
Times table graphing and coordinate plans.	*Fractions.*	*Be better at fractions.*	*Need stuff that will be hard to be explained.*
I'm good at the Pythagorean Theorem.	*Word problems. And I'm not really good at math at all. It's really hard to understand and it's hard for me to know how to start a problem.*	*I hope to better understand how to start and finish a problem. And to better understand what I don't know.*	*I work better in small groups, but mostly working with one on one.*
Mainly probability and fractions, decimals, and percentages.	*Sometimes, word problems.*	*Be able to understand math, in general, better.*	*I understand visuals better than explaining.*

in handy when assessing students or holding parent-teacher conferences. These behaviors reveal more about what students know than they can demonstrate on a paper and pencil test.

To take an observation and turn it into data is a tricky task. No teacher can keep consistent records in her head for 175 students. A typical secondary teacher averages twenty-five students each period over seven periods of instruction. In order to monitor students more closely, many teachers develop interesting (and efficient) ways to take notes on student progress while moving around the room. One of our favorites is the use of a clipboard with each student's name drawn in the squares perfectly measured to fit the small sticky note size. As the teacher writes a note on the sticky note, she can paste it to the student on the grid.

Once the students are gone, she can move the notes to a three-ring notebook where she has created a page for each student. For those more technologically savvy, consider using apps such as Evernote and Confer to collect and organize anecdotal records on your tablet or mobile phone. Some teachers use papers with blank spaces where they record student behaviors like the one in table 4.6. No matter the preferred method, the teacher must have a system of recording observations to make this particular assessment tool work. Begin with small steps. Do not expect to observe and record something for every student, everyday; you will only be frustrated with your inability since this is an impossible task.

Questioning

Effective questioning allows teachers to check for understanding, obtain information, and provide indirect cues. Questioning is one of the most effortless methods to monitor student progress and detect problems with student understanding. Good questions, prepared before the lesson, will help a teacher determine whether students use varied approaches to a problem and how well students can explain their own thinking. This process complements observation. Specifically, probing questions are a teaching/assessment strategy that provides insight into the mental processes students use by engaging them in conversation about the subject. The goal of the questions is to deepen students' understanding of the content. Consider this mode of assessment with the anecdotal record form to document student responses. See chapter 10 for more questioning strategies.

Conferences

Students will appreciate the one-on-one time that conferences provide for direct feedback. Conferences can be used to accomplish a particular task such as revising or editing a student's writing, or they can be broad in scope to assess the progress of a student's work. The problem with conferences is the amount of the teacher's time it takes to conduct a one-on-one conference for twenty-plus students per class. New technology does allow a teacher to give verbal feedback with programs like Jing or Blackboard (Bb).

Student-led conferences are also a great tool for parent-teacher conferences. It is important to include a student in the discussion of her progress. Asking students to review their work for their parents in front of the teacher helps

Table 4.6 Anecdotal record example.

Group: A	Date: 2/14/2014
Book/Page: *An American Plague*	Target Skill/Strategy: *Previewing Informational Text*

NAME	OBSERVATIONS/COMMETS
Ayla	Sufficient prior knowledge from reading *Fever, 1793*. Knew about the historical contexts in which the story takes place.
Bella	Immediately began to pay attention to pictures and captions as well as other graphics to make predictions about the text.
Milo	N/A
Mira	Lack of vocabulary knowledge (e.g., plague, epidemic) may pose challenges in comprehension.
Moby	N/A
Otis	Mentioned briefly that he does not like non-fiction.

greatly with self-monitoring and providing them with a better understanding of their progress and accomplishments.

Figure 4.6 shows an example of a form created by Atwell (1987) completed by a middle school teacher during a writing workshop that the teacher subsequently used as a guide for a conference with the student.

Teacher's Conference Record For ___Andrew___

Title of Piece & Date (comments)	Skills Used Correctly	Skills Taught (no more than 2)
"The Edge" 11/4	- Exciting plot. - Strong main Character - Some believable info. about weapons etc. which gives the piece more credibility. - Strong self-editing (Content and mechanics)	* Start a new ¶ each time a different person speaks * Please continue to look out for run-on sentences (You caught a number of them)
"The Edge" D2 11/15	- Excellent revision to short story format. Made sound decisions to simplify the story line: make it more manageable - self-editing - Punctuation for dialogue	* Comma after a "when" clause (When he came rushing in) * Use ¶s for dramatic effect - Force the reader to "pause"

Figure 4.6　Completed writing workshop conference form.

Rubrics

A rubric is a scoring tool to indicate the quality of students' performance or product. Creating a rubric begins with the end in mind using the
question: "Considering the learning goals, what does a good performance/
product look like?" The answer to this question should generate a list of criteria *and* a degree of quality for each criterion (*analytical rubric* shown in
table 4.7) or for the product as a whole (*holistic rubric* shown in table 4.8).

In other words, constructing a rubric requires a scale that reflects the quality levels of performance, gradations, specific description, and criteria for each dimension. Each level of quality may be represented numerically or with qualitative descriptors. A rubric is most often created by the teacher; however, one can be generated with students' input. What criteria would they consider to be part of a good performance/product? Although a rubric is most often used by the teacher to score students' work, we would argue that it is most effective as an assessment tool when students receive a rubric before they begin their work so that they can consult it as they work and to self-evaluate after they have completed work.

A quality rubric addresses all relevant content and performance objectives. A rubric should be easy to understand and to use. When done well, a quality rubric should be both *valid* (measuring what it is intended to measure) and *reliable* (yielding consistent results even from different scorers).

Rubrics are a popular and time-saving way to assess your students' assignments. However, there are some limitations to using the standard rubrics:

- Scores from the rubric may not align easily with a grade for the assignment.
- Feedback is limited to the criteria created on the rubric.
- Students tend to look at their "grade" and not the feedback provided by the criteria.
- Students' work sometimes does not align with the predetermined levels of criteria.
- Students know what is expected and their grades tend to be higher.

Table 4.7 Analytical rubric template

	Level 1	Level 2	Level 3	Level 4	Score
Criteria #1	Performance Descriptors for Criteria #1	Performance Descriptors for Criteria #1	Performance Descriptors for Criteria #1	Performance Descriptors for Criteria #1	Performance Descriptors for Criteria #1
Criteria #2	Performance Descriptors for Criteria #2	Performance Descriptors for Criteria #2	Performance Descriptors for Criteria #2	Performance Descriptors for Criteria #2	Performance Descriptors for Criteria #2
Criteria #3					
Criteria #4					

Note: The numerical descriptors (i.e., 1, 2, 3, & 4) can be replaced with qualitative descriptors (e.g., Needs Improvement, Developing, Sufficient, & Above Average or Needs Improvement, Meets Expectations & Exceeds Expectations)

Table 4.8 Holistic rubric template

5	Student met all criteria and demonstrated deep understanding of all items.
4	Student met most criteria and demonstrated understanding of most items.
3	Students met the minimum criteria and demonstrated adequate understanding of many items and low understanding of some items.
2	Student did not meet the minimum criteria and was not able to demonstrate understanding of most items.
1	Student was not able to complete the assignment at a level showing understanding.

Table 4.9 Single point rubric, student self-evaluation.

How will I revise to better meet criteria	Performance criteria	How I know I met the criteria	How I went beyond the criteria
	Creative introduction grabbed the audience's attention		
	Developed paper with a good flow		
	Directions for the assignment were followed		
	Writing followed conventions: grammar, spelling, etc.		

Adapted from Fluckiger (2010, p.78)

To make rubrics most relevant to specific assignments, teachers can make small or large adjustments to rubric templates readily available online. A rubric the authors recently discovered is getting a lot of attention in the field: the *single-point rubric*. The single-point rubric was originally created for students to self-assess their own work by asking the students to identify (1) How will I revise to better meet the criteria? (2) How will I know I met the criteria? and (3) How I went beyond the criteria (Fluckiger, 2010, p. 24). (See table 4.9.)

The student, with the teacher's guidance or feedback, identifies the performance criteria for the assignment. For each criterion, the student decides if he meets the criterion or goes beyond the criterion.

In the middle and secondary classrooms where grades are part of a teacher's assessment reality, Gonzalez (2014) modified the single-point rubric as a grading rubric (table 4.10).

Table 4.10 Single point rubric, teacher assessment of student work.

Concerns Areas that need work	Single-Point Rubric Criteria Standards for this performance	Advanced Evidence of exceeding standards
	Teacher lists the specific criteria down the middle of the page. If the student meets the criteria, you are done. If they exceed the standards you jot down a few notes clarifying what they did in the Advanced column. If the students did NOT meet your expectations, you jot down a few notes in the left column under Concerns explaining what they could do to improve.	
	Creative Introduction	
	Paper organization	
	Directions followed	
	Writing conventions	

Adapted from Gonzalez (2015⁴)

Under criteria, the teacher lists the specifications of the assignment at the expected level (B grade level). As you grade the student work, most will need a few extra comments from your stated criteria. When a student's work is not where it should be (grades of C, D, or F), you write a comment that shows what they needed to do to achieve the standard in the left column. When a student exceeds your expectations (A grade), you let them know what evidence you have for their higher grade in the right-hand column (table 4.10).

You have been presented with a multitude of ways to categorize assessment tools. One way to select the right tool is to think about how the categories relate to one another. Using a quadrant model found in figure 4.7, you can begin to visualize how to select your assessment tool. More specifically, where do they intersect? What tools are available in those intersections? For example, if you need a formative tool that is also traditional, a quiz or a short paper might be appropriate. If you need a summative tool that is also performance based, you may give a multimedia presentation assignment. What other tools can you add to each of the quadrants?

SHARING ASSESSMENT DATA

Rhodes and Shanklin (1993) identify three broad purposes of assessment based on the 1991 resolutions on assessment issues by the International Literacy Association:

1. for the guidance and improvement of learning;
2. for the guidance and improvement of instruction; and
3. monitoring the outcomes of instruction.

Now that the first two purposes of assessment have been discussed by providing a set of assessment tools for daily classroom instruction, this is an ideal moment to talk about the third purpose, monitoring the outcomes of instruction. Much discussion about the use of nontraditional and self-assessment tools as a way to offer meaningful opportunities for students to participate in the assessment process has been presented in this chapter. Through their participation, students will know what they are learning, how they are developing as learners, what their strengths and weaknesses are, and what they need to do to become better learners. We consider assessment for improvement of learning to be its most important purpose.

For most secondary teachers, much of the assessment data collected and analyzed will make its way into report cards. This is one of your responsibilities as a teacher, and you must have a thoughtful, clear, and transparent process so that students and their parents understand how grades are assigned in your class.

Many school districts use online tools for teachers to post individual assignment grades and course grades, which makes frequent and ongoing communication easier. Believe us; many of the parents will access their children's grades daily so that they, too, can participate in their children's learning process. Consider them as your most important partner in your teaching. However, you may meet parents that do not know how to communicate well, have unrealistic expectations of their children, or are intimidated by your position as a teacher, especially if they were struggling learners themselves. Most of them, if you share how they can help, will do whatever it takes to be helpful. When you are given an opportunity to participate in a parent-teacher conference, use the following guidelines to help communicate your intention to consider them your partners:

- *Be honest.* Share both the strengths and areas of improvement. Start off your conference with a positive comment to set the tone. Just as we use a student's strengths to work on the areas that need improvement, the parents will need both to more effectively help in their children's learning.

- *Be concrete.* Parents may see their children's work samples from school. However, many of the measurement tools such as conference notes, rating scales, self-assessment forms, and rubrics are rarely seen by the parents. Share data that you have collected to demonstrate your evaluation of the student's performance.
- *Seek input.* Parents probably know their children better than you know them as students. Ask about their children's interests and preferences. What ideas do they have that might help in the learning process in your classroom. Ask for questions about their perceptions of their children's academic and social life in your classroom. What they share with you at your invitation can also be used as data for your ongoing assessment.
- *Be open.* Be sure that they know the best way to contact you. Let them know how to access the online grade-sharing tool if it is available in your school district. If you have a web or Facebook page that they can access to learn more about your classroom, be sure that they know how to find your page.

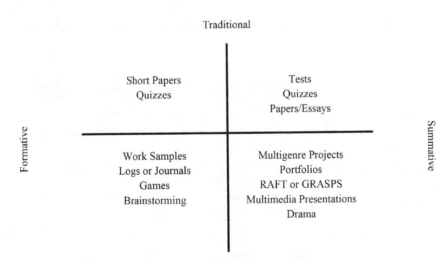

Figure 4.7 Quadrant of assessment tools.

THEORY TO PRACTICE

Assessment is not an afterthought; it occurs simultaneously (or even before) as we consider how we can deliver worthy content and important skills. In this chapter, the goal was to bring clarity to the complexities that are inherent in classroom assessment. With so many terms, categories, types, and other terms thrown all around, even the professionals in the field lose coherence as they discuss assessment. We have attempted to provide both broader frameworks so that you can begin to make sense of its scope and specific tools so that you can make informed choices for effective instruction.

The assessment tools presented in this chapter are not exhaustive; they are a sampling. Hopefully, the tools shared in this chapter make their way into your repertoire, your tool belt, to make assessment meaningful, ongoing, multidimensional, and authentic.

The word *assess* comes from the French word *assidere*, which means "to sit beside." This derivation offers a beautiful metaphor for assessment. What could happen when we mindfully and intentionally "sit beside" the student in an attempt to learn about who she is and what she is capable of knowing and doing? What would that teach us about ourselves as teachers in what we can do to foster a joyful and productive learning environment? Assessment is an essential component of good teaching for this *self-revealing* reason.

REFERENCES

Atwell, N. (1987). In the middle: Writing, reading, and learning with adolescents. Portsmouth, NH: Heinemann.

Buehl, D. (2014). *Classroom strategies for interactive learning* (Fourth ed.). Newark, DE: International Reading Association.

Clarke, D. J. (1992). Activating assessment alternatives in mathematics. *Arithmetic Teacher, 40,* 24–29.

Columba, L. (2001). Daily classroom assessment. *Education, 122,* 372–74.

Cooper, J. D., & Kiger, N. D. (2011). Literacy assessment: Helping teachers plan instruction (Fourth ed.). Belmont, CA: Wadsworth.

Daniels, H., Zemelman, S., & Steineke, N. (2007). *Content-area writing: Every teacher's guide.* Portsmouth, NH: Heinemann.

Echevarria, J., Short, D. J., & Vogt, M. (2008). *Making content comprehensible for English learners: The SIOP model.* Boston: Allyn & Bacon.

Fisher, D., & Frey, N. (2015). *Improving adolescent literacy: Content area strategies at work* (Fourth ed.). Upper Saddle River, NJ: Pearson.

Fluckiger, J. (2010). Single point rubric: A tool for responsible student self-assessment. *Teacher Education Faculty Publications* 5. Retrieved September 9, 2017, from http://digitalcommons.unomaha.edu/tedfacpub/5.

Frank, Marjorie. (1995). If you're trying to teach kids how to write . . . You've gotta have this book. Nashville, TN: Incentive Publications.

Frey, B. B., Schmitt, V. L. & Allen, J. P. (2012). Defining authentic classroom assessment. *Practical Assessment, Research & Evaluation, 17*(2).

Glaser, R. (1963). Instructional technology and the measurement of learning outcomes. *American Psychologist, 8*(8), 519–22.

Gonzalez, J. (2014). Know your terms: Holistic, analytic, and single-point rubrics. Retrieved February 27, 2018. http://www.cultofpedagogy.com/holistic-analytic-single-pointrubrics/

Meyer, C. A. (1992). What's the difference between "authentic" and "performance" assessment? *Educational Leadership, 49*(8), 39–40.

Popham, W. J. (2008). *Transformative assessment.* Alexandria, VA: ASCD.

Reeves, T. C., & Okey, J. R. (1996). Alternative assessment for constructivist learning environments. In B. G. Wilson (Ed.), *Constructivist learning environments: Case studies in instructional design* (pp. 191–202). Englewood Cliffs, NJ: Educational Technology Publications.

Richwine, S. (2014). Guidelines for constructing classroom tests [Class handout]. Allentown, PA: Muhlenberg College.

Rhodes, L. K., & Shanklin, N. L. (1993). *Windows into literacy: Assessing learners K–8.* Portsmouth, NH: Heinemann.

Sanacore, J., & Palumbo, A. (2010). Middle school students need more opportunities to read across the curriculum. *Clearing House: A Journal of Educational Strategies, Issues and Ideas, 83*(5), 180–85.

Scriven, M. S. (1967). The methodology of evaluation. In R. W. Tyler, R. M. Gagne, & Scriven, M. S. (Eds.), Perspectives of curriculum evaluation (AERA Monograph Series in Curriculum Evaluation No. 1, pp. 39–82). Chicago: Rand McNally.

Valencia, S., & Pearson, P. D. (1987). Reading assessment: Time for change. *The Reading Teacher, 40*(8), 726–33.

Wiggins, G., & McTighe, J. (2005). *Understanding by design* (Second ed.). Alexandria, VA: ASCD.

Wren, D. G. (2009). Performance assessment: A key component of a balanced assessment system. *Research Brief: Report from the Department of Research, Evaluation, and Assessment, 2.* Retrieved July 20, 2013, from http://www.vbschools.com/accountability/research_briefs/ResearchBriefPerfAssmtFinal.pdf.

5

Developing a Love of Words
Vocabulary

Knowledge of things and knowledge of the words for them grow together. If you do not know the words, you can hardly know the thing.

—Henry Hazlitt

Maniac Magee

Ms. Livingston's love for literature was evident when I observed her teaching her fifth-grade students. I was fortunate to witness her explanation to her students about the importance of using "just the right word." She held up her journal she had been keeping for ten years and told the students it was a collection of words and phrases that she had found interesting or inspiring. She opened her journal and thumbed through a few pages. Her face lit up as she shared a word from *Harry Potter* that had reminded her of her mother.

She went on to explain that authors have a talent for writing so that their readers could visualize what the author described. All of a sudden, she darted across the room and grabbed a copy of *Maniac Magee* that was in her classroom library.

"Jerry Spinelli is one of those talented authors," she explained as she thumbed through his book. "I remember a passage in this book that really made me stop and think about the way the author used the words he chose." She continued to search the book for the passage as she talked. "If you haven't read *Maniac Magee*, you ought to, it is a very good story. Maniac helps unite the Black part of town, the East End, with the White part of town, the West End . . . here it is, listen."

Maniac loved the colors of the East End, the people colors. For the life of him, he couldn't figure why these East Enders called themselves black. He kept looking and looking, and the colors he found were gingersnap and light fudge and dark fudge and acorn and butter rum and cinnamon and burnt orange. But never licorice, which to him was real black. (Spinelli, 1990, p. 52)

She went on, "I know there's more . . . a few pages later . . . here it is . . ."

> Maniac kept trying, but he still couldn't see it, this color business. He didn't figure he was white any more than the East Enders were black. He looked himself over pretty hard and came up with at least seven different shades and colors right on his own skin, not one of them being what he would call white (except for his eyeballs, which weren't any whiter than the eyeballs of the kids in the East End). Which was all a big relief to Maniac, finding out he wasn't really white, because the way he figured, white was about the most boring color of all. (Spinelli, 1990, p. 58)
> "Wow! Isn't his word choice interesting?"
> There was no expectation for any student to answer. Instead, they all sat quietly contemplating something as simple as the shades of black and white.

Outside of a few hundred high-frequency words in the English language (e.g., *the*, *and*, and *to*), words stand for concepts. They are truly the building blocks by which we describe our world, gain knowledge, share knowledge, express feelings, and color nuances of meaning. Teachers introduce new words, clarify and discuss words, and share new meanings of words on a daily basis. To teach words to enhance comprehension and content learning, especially to lock them in long-term memory to ensure retrieval and use of those words in other contexts, is no easy task. There are many questions a teacher should ask as they prepare to deliberately teach important words in her classroom. Here are just a few:

- What words are essential to teach?
- When, in the lesson or unit sequence, should they be taught?
- How should they be introduced as new words or familiar words with new meanings?
- What do students already know about the words?
- What should students do with the words to connect them to what they already know?

This chapter will discuss the theoretical foundations of vocabulary instruction, including information on the supremely important task of using students' prior knowledge to build conceptual understanding.

THEORETICAL FOUNDATIONS OF VOCABULARY

The vocabulary, or the lexicon of a language, includes all the words of the language. The ever-increasing vocabulary of the English language has well over one million words, and new words become a part of our vocabulary almost every day. Of the three major areas of the study of a language—phonology, syntax, and semantics—the study of *semantics*, words and their meanings, is the most dynamic. Learning the sounds of a language, the *phonology*, begins shortly after birth and is usually completed by age eight or nine. Learning the *syntax*, the organization and grammar of a language, is developed by age eleven or twelve. Most speakers of a language can understand and produce most common syntactic patterns by the time they begin middle school. It is semantic development, the growth of one's vocabulary, that continues, both incidentally and through explicit learning, throughout all the years of an individual's lifetime. The possibility of a teacher introducing new words or expanding understanding of familiar words, in this sense, is certain. The impact of introducing conceptually meaty words, as content area teachers do, makes this chapter an especially important one in this book.

Complexities of the American English Vocabulary

The English language is complex and dynamic. No one knows exactly how many words there are in English; most linguists believe the size of the English language lexicon to be over one million, but some linguists claim it is approaching two million words (Johnson, 2001). Recently published major English dictionaries may contain as many as ten thousand new words, words not contained in the previous edition (Stevens, 2011). English, known to have more words than other comparable languages, is so semantically rich that about 80 percent of our language's ten thousand most common words have at least two meanings, and some as many as thirty (Johnson & Moe, 1983). For example, think of the many definitions or usages of the word *run*. From "walking fast" to "operating an organization" to "opting for an elected office," there are many meanings to this seemingly simple word. The implication of the complexity of the English language is enormous for content area learning, but more on that later.

Not all English speakers know the same number of words. The nature of vocabulary acquisition varies because of (1) the language usage of a student's parents and those around the child; (2) the extent of language stimulation from oral language interactions and reading experiences; and (3) a host of cultural experiences that include travel, live performances, movie/television viewing, and other intellectually challenging and interesting activities. Indeed, many linguists, sociologists, and psychologists believe that an individual's background is the greatest determinant of the size of one's vocabulary (Deutscher, 2011). A sixth-grade student in Dubuque, Iowa, will know dozens of words associated with the Mississippi River (e.g., *barge, channel, locks*, etc.) and dozens of words associated with meat processing and production (e.g., *kosher, slaughter, hocks*, etc.) because of the meatpacking industry in the area. A student in Boise, Idaho, will have a different understanding of the meanings of these words, and in the case of *kosher* may have no meaning at all for the word unless they have some familiarity with Orthodox Jewish dietary practices.

Vocabulary learning also varies depending on the extent of specific instruction of specialized content area terms. With the teaching of a seventh-grade science lesson on the digestive system, there are key words associated with essential aspects of nutrition and human anatomy. In such a use of the key vocabulary (e.g., *vitamin, saliva, intestine,* and *digest*), the meanings of the words must be precise, and they must be taught explicitly. *Saliva* is not just the liquid produced in the mouth, it is an early and essential part of the digestive process, and its meaning must be made clear through discussion, experiments, reading, and writing. Such is the nature of good content area vocabulary instruction. The most important, and perhaps the most challenging, aspect of content area teaching may be that common words have precise and often disciplinary specific definitions. *Energy* and *force* mean something very specific in physics. *Rotate* and *flip* in geometry each refers to an exact way to move a shape.

Cognition and Academic Achievement

Almost one hundred years ago, Terman in *The Measurement of Intelligence* (1916) made the connection between vocabulary and intelligence when he found that no other variable correlated more highly with intelligence than vocabulary knowledge. Terman and others concluded that our vocabulary is often an index of our lives. Further, Vygotsky, in his seminal book *Thought and Language* (1962, 1986), claimed that thought *results from* inner speech, hence drawing a clear connection between cognitive development and language. Vygotsky believed that what starts out as two separate systems at birth—thought and language—merge at around age three as verbal thought and that "thought does not express itself in words, but rather realizes itself in them" (1986, p. 251). This theory challenges the common notion that thought comes before language, and if we believe that language promotes thought and results in cognitive development, the language used in school, most often presented as vocabulary in content area learning, is crucial.

As early as 1925, Whipple emphasized the importance of enlarging the reading vocabulary. In 1942, Davis asserted that there were two essential skills necessary in reading: word knowledge and reasoning. In study after study, over a period of eighty years, the evidence shows that to improve reading instruction and concept learning, vocabulary instruction is the *single* essential element (Terman, 1916; Thorndike & Gallup, 1941; Gipe & Arnold, 1979; Kameenui, Carnine, & Freschi, 1982; Stahl & Fairbanks, 1986; Hairrell, Rupley, & Simmons, 2011; Johnson & Johnson, 2011; Baumann & Kame'enui, 2012; Graves et al., 2013).

When you learn new words you learn new concepts; when you learn new concepts you learn new words. Schools must be language-rich environments that promote the cycle of expanding knowledge, fostering language development, and facilitating thinking. In content areas, content-specific vocabulary should flourish in reading, writing, speaking, listening, and viewing contexts. In the field of educational research, few findings are as clear as the relationship between the teaching of vocabulary and the improvement of academic achievement. Those who have studied school achievement and language development have concluded that (1) academic achievement and vocabulary development go hand in hand; (2) language development, and in particular, vocabulary expansion, is essential to concept development; and (3) vocabulary development is ongoing (Miller, 1996).

Vocabulary and Comprehension

According to schema theory discussed in chapter 1, connecting a student's prior knowledge is essential to learning new concepts. Specifically, a student's ability to comprehend a text *requires* connecting these new concepts to their past experiences.

Teaching essential vocabulary before and during a lesson is fundamentally important for students to comprehend a text and understand concepts. The more words students know, representing more things they know, the more effectively they will be able to create meaning from the reading process. The better readers, in return, read more. And reading is one of the fundamental ways in which we increase our vocabulary; the more we read, the more words we learn. This cycle, as you can imagine, is a powerful one that will impact students' cognitive development and academic success.

EFFECTIVE VOCABULARY INSTRUCTION

As students move to higher grade levels, the difficulty of their instructional materials increases to the extent that the materials become *concept laden* or concept heavy. Studies of middle school social studies textbooks, for example, show that as many as twenty new concepts are introduced in a single page (Irwin & Davis, 1980). This is not only true of the expository textbooks used in science and social studies, but it can also be true of narrative books used in English and the language arts.

In addition, the precise nature of content area vocabulary becomes increasingly important in higher grade levels. Content area textbooks may be filled with discipline-specific vocabulary that students may not have ever encountered before, like *isosceles*, *cosine*, and *hypotenuse*. Other words such as *tangent, congruent,* and *angle* are those commonly seen in daily usage, but they carry concise, technical definitions in mathematics learning. Now imagine teaching all of them in a single lesson or a unit. It may not be an exaggeration that much of content teaching is vocabulary instruction, fundamentally shifting ways in which content area teachers define their role as teachers.

Over a decade ago, the National Reading Panel (NRP, 2000) Report provided nine recommendations for vocabulary development:

1. Provide both direct and indirect instruction.
2. Provide repetition and multiple exposures to words.
3. Present the words in a variety of contexts.
4. Use restructured tasks and differentiated instruction when necessary.
5. Maximize active engagement in learning.
6. Use computer technology, both online and offline.
7. Provide environments that encourage incidental learning.
8. Provide assessment that is based on instruction.
9. Use multiple methods of vocabulary instruction for optimal learning (pp. 4–27).

Not one of the nine recommendations for good vocabulary instruction is "look it up in the dictionary, copy the definition and use the new word in a sentence." Perhaps you recall this dictionary approach used in many of the classes in middle and high schools. Research has found this mode of vocabulary instruction to be one of the least effective ways to teach new vocabulary for a number of different reasons (Nagy, 1988). So what else is a teacher to do in presenting new words and concepts? Many of the strategies provided in this chapter will help students to make connections with words, manipulate the words, and develop a deeper understanding of the word.

"Knowing" a Word

Before we present strategies for vocabulary instruction in the content areas, it is important to briefly mention what it means to know a word. We believe that there are stages of "knowing" a word. We will demonstrate some likely stages of understanding with the word *aileron* in the sentences below:

1. I have no meaning for the word *aileron*.
2. I think an *aileron* has something to do with airplanes.
3. I believe an *aileron* is part of an airplane.
4. I am quite sure there is an *aileron* on each wing of an airplane.

5. I am certain that each wing of an airplane has an *aileron*, which helps raise or lower the wing and thus enables the pilot to put the airplane into a bank so that it will turn.

Note that with each use of *aileron* in the sentences above the use of the word becomes more precise. This is an approximation of the way we learn new words. The full understanding of aileron could have come as a result of a teacher's guidance or because of reading or both.

Implication of students' varied levels of knowledge is an important one for content teachers to consider. If students' knowledge of essential content words are at various levels, it may seem reasonable to assume that the way in which you teach the words should also vary. Let's consider this in action. In a chapter of a sixth-grade science textbook is a unit on "Understanding Living Things." This unit begins with a chapter on cell reproduction and heredity. The first lesson in this chapter contains information on cells and provides a comparison of plant and animal cells. This eight-page lesson provides excellent graphics with depictions of plant and animal cells, a clear theory about cells, and definitions of the key vocabulary concerning cell components. Here are the new, key words used in this lesson (table 5.1).

This introduction to cell biology is done from the perspective of the textbook author. However, that author does not know your students and which words (even beyond this list) they may still not understand after the introduction. You can easily assess their level of understanding by using one of the instructional strategies, Word Knowledge Rating Sheet (figure 5.1). A list of important words from a text is shared with the students. Each student self-selects his level of understanding by indicating it on the chart. This provides the teacher with valuable data to inform which of the words need to be taught.

After you have collected this assessment data, if necessary, you may find you will need to teach or reteach using some of the following techniques:

- Label the terms on a picture of plant and animal cells.
- Make a comparison by listing the parts the plant and animal cells have in common.
- List and compare those cell parts that are different.
- Use semantic mapping as appropriate to clarify similarities and differences.

Table 5.1 Key vocabulary.

Nucleus	nucleolus	chloroplasts
Chromosome	stentor	photosynthesis
vacuole	cytoplasm	mitochondria

Word Knowledge Rating Sheet
How well do you know these words?

	I have never seen this word.	I have heard it, but I do not know what it means.	I recognize it, and I think it means…	I know it, and it means… I also know how to use it in a sentence.
chloroplasts		X		
chromosome				Carries genes
cytoplasm			Material found in a living cell	
mitochondria	X			

Figure 5.1   Word knowledge rating sheet.

• Elaborate further on the essential words students at this grade level should know, like *nucleus*, *chromosome*, and *DNA*.

Elements of Vocabulary Instruction

In Nagy's (1988) book, *Teaching Vocabulary to Improve Reading Comprehension*, he shares three required properties of vocabulary instruction: integration, repetition, and meaningful use (p. 10). Let us examine how these three properties work together.

Integration requires that the new word be connected to existing knowledge. This requires connecting the unknown with the known. For example, new words *cell* and *molecules* may be introduced in a middle school science class based on students' knowledge about living organisms. An extension of this list may include *cytoplasm*, *ribosome*, and *lysosome* as parts of an animal cell are introduced in a high school biology class. The high school teacher introduces these new words in connection to those previously known. How are the new words related to the familiar words? What is the relationship?

There are many instructional tools to make semantic relationships among words explicit. A semantic map, word map, or concept of a definition are just a few that provide space to help students identify relationships and distinguish

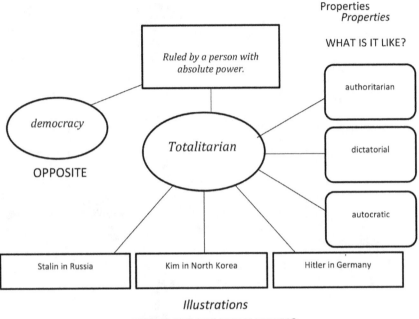

Category
WHAT IS IT?

Properties
Properties

WHAT IS IT LIKE?

Ruled by a person with absolute power.

authoritarian

democracy

Totalitarian

dictatorial

OPPOSITE

autocratic

Stalin in Russia   Kim in North Korea   Hitler in Germany

Illustrations
WHAT ARE SOME EXAMPLES?

Concept of a Definition by Schwartz and Raphael (1985)

Figure 5.2   Concept of a definition.

the nuances of concepts or words that are more abstract. Conceptual words are better understood when students have examined not only the word's definitions but also its characteristics, synonyms, antonyms, examples, and nonexamples. Schwartz and Raphael (1985) created a map called *concept of a definition* that provides a framework for thinking about the nuances of a concept (figure 5.2).

There are also strategies designed to help bring out the semantic distinctions in words that are complex, such as concepts or words with multiple meanings. Select graphic organizers, such as a Venn diagram, flowchart, sequence chart, and classification web, work beautifully in representing semantic relationships between words. Semantic feature analysis (figure 5.3) uses a grid or matrix that allows students to determine which attributes pertain to a list of words. The semantic feature analysis will be described in more detail in chapter 6.

TRAITS

GENRES	Realistic	Not likely to happen	True	Made-up
Modern Fantasy	-	+	-	+
Contemporary Realistic Fiction	+	-	-	+
Biography	+	-	+	-
Informational	+	-	+	-
Historical Fiction	+	+/-	+/-	+
Traditional	-	+	-	+

+ = has the characteristic

- = does not have the characteristic

Figure 5.3 Semantic feature analysis using genres of literature.

Repetition means that students need a number of meaningful encounters with the new word in multiple contexts. Unfortunately, reading a text once, and only once, is a common reading practice in schools. For readers, regardless of age and reading ability, multiple reading of a text is beneficial. Especially if the text is concept heavy, it might require a student to read the same text many times to fully understand a concept. Perhaps the first reading provides an overview with several new words introduced. The second reading may extend the words and meanings to other related words. The third reading may bring to light nuances of meaning regarding a concept. Make each reading purposeful; give students something concrete to do (e.g., highlight the new word and context in which its definition resides) to provide explicit guidance in learning words.

Repetition also refers to encountering words learned in one text discovered in another text. It is useful to provide opportunities to read about a concept in a wide range of texts, both for more information and for enjoyment. Broaden the genre and type of reading materials by offering magazines, web pages, fiction, and even poetry that present the same concept in different language, structure, and tone. The various ways in which these texts use the same set of words will surprise you.

Finally, allow "chance encounters" with words to happen through students' recreational reading. Words learned in a content area reading will pop up in unexpected places as students read for enjoyment. Allow students to be able to choose their own texts to read and, at times, to read for no particular tasks to be completed after the reading. Remember that readers learn new words incidentally as well as through direct instruction, and incidental learning of words will only occur if students read often.

Meaningful use requires readers to go beyond just defining the word, and to be able recognize it and use it accurately in several contexts. Expect students to use the words they have just learned in rich discussions, in both oral and written language. A content area class should be filled with meaningful and substantive discourse using the language of the discipline, specific to the content. The only way for students to accurately and fluently use these words is by using them. Awkwardness will abound and mistakes will be made in their first attempts. Model for students how to use them; show them explicitly. Then give them guidance as they practice in many purposeful activities. Repeat until you see, hear, and read students' new vocabulary, perhaps internalized by then, show up in their usage.

Using Context Clues

In all types of reading, contextual analysis is the easiest, the most natural, and potentially most powerful strategy in learning new words. Undoubtedly, you have been directed to "use context clues" to unpack an unfamiliar word more than once as a student. Particularly in the content areas, students will read texts in which the author has presented the precise definition for a word within a sentence or a paragraph. A context that provides meaning is called *directive contexts* (Beck, McKeown, & Kucan, 2002), leading the reader to a specific and correct meaning for a word:

- Formal definition: A *plow* is a farm implement used to cut and turn the soil in preparation for planting.
- Description: A *butterfly*, which is often brightly colored, is a flying insect with four wings.
- Example: Banjos, cellos, harps, violins, and zithers are *stringed* instruments.
- Synonym: *Peanuts* are also known as groundnuts and ground peas.
- Comparison: *Porpoises* are mammals that look somewhat like dolphins.
- Contrast: The *speed of an airplane* is not determined by its size.
- Origin: *Stanine* is made from the words *standard* and *nine*.
- Appositive: *Otis, my energetic dog*, needs at least an hour of exercise each day.

Words that are central to the meaning of a nonfiction text are often, but not always, presented in directive contexts, fully revealing their meaning. As well, text features such as boldface or italics are often used to highlight the target words.

Unpacking the meaning of a word using contextual analysis needs to be explicitly taught to some students, as it will likely not be in their repertoire of reading skills. Help students identify the context in which the meaning can be found as they read.

Additional Instructional Strategies

Many teacher resource books will offer excellent suggestions for teachers on how to introduce new words and concepts, but often teachers are faced with devising activities on their own. We will share several effective strategies. Many use examples from trade books, a wonderful source of incidental and planned vocabulary instruction.

Direct Teaching

In many cases, simple and direct teaching that explicitly defines the words is the best method. The immediate usefulness of the new word knowledge is one of the motivations to learn words according to research by Ruddell and Shearer (2002). There will be times when it is necessary for secondary teachers to introduce a concept that is completely new—one that is difficult to attach to some prior knowledge. When direct teaching is most appropriate, be direct and be concise. Present the most relevant and meaningful definition or explanation. But put that precise definition in as many contexts as possible. Offer examples, put in other words, list synonyms, or tell a story about it. Draw diagrams with labels or illustrate a magnified part. Show pictures, play songs, or bring in an artifact. Have students say it, see it, feel it, and hear it. In direct teaching, it is the teacher's job to do whatever is necessary to make the words and their definitions attach to memory not only for understanding at that particular moment but also for retrieval and use in the future.

Contextual Redefinition

Contextual redefinition strategy begins by asking students to make a guess as to the definition of the word. After they have written their guess, provide the students with a clue and allow them to modify their original definition. After some discussion from the students, provide them with an accurate definition and ask them to help identify a synonym and an antonym. You may have to

Table 5.2 Key vocabulary.

segregation	Jim Crow laws	racist	Ku Klux Klan
lynching	descendants	aviation	Choctaw blood
barnstormer	ground school	aerobatics	separate-but-equal schools

Word	segregation
What do you think the word means?	
Here is the word in context.	*Because of segregation, my friend and I went to different elementary schools.*
Does that change your definition?	
What is the new meaning?	
What is the actual definition?	*Setting apart or separation of people or things from others or from main body or group*
Think of a synonym.	
Think of a antonym.	

Figure 5.4   Contextual redefinition.

give mini lessons to explore a few of these concepts in greater detail. Artifacts such as photographs may help to build students' prior knowledge.

For example, in *Talkin' About Bessie* (Grimes, 2002), we find an excellent account of one of the first female American aviators. This account of Bessie Coleman's life includes aspects of history (aviation and segregation), geography (United States and Europe), science (flying and weather), as well as the first-person accounts of a remarkable African American woman who became the first woman barnstormer in the United States. Here are some concepts that readers must understand in order to gain an understanding of her life.

Let's take *segregation* as one of the essential words to teach in this vocabulary lesson. An example of the strategy may look like table 5.2 and figure 5.4.

Personal Clues

Personal clues strategy uses the most efficient method of locking new knowledge into memory: personally and deliberately creating a way to remember. Provide students with 3 x 5 notecards. The teacher provides the students with the target word and a definition to be recorded on one side of the card. On the reverse side, students add whatever they think will make the word and

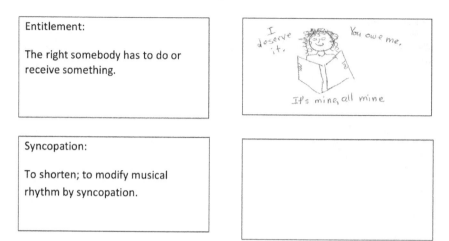

Figure 5.5   Personal clues.

the definition linger in memory (figure 5.5). They may think of a mnemonic device. They may draw a picture or a diagram. They may write what the word means. They may list a set of related words, examples, attributes, or characteristics. Have students share their personal ways to connect with the word. Generate a collective list from the sharing session for ways to "make words stick." Students may return to this list to remember other words you introduce in the future.

Hierarchical Array/Linear Array

Both arrays are used to show differing gradations of terms. Hierarchical array (figure 5.6) is used to show hierarchy such as you might find in biology when classifying species from higher-level orders to lower ones.

Linear arrays are a continuum from a low level to high level, such as temperatures of water. What words would fit between *tepid* and *scalding*? Can you think of a word that might come before *tepid* (figure 5.7)?

Individual students can complete this strategy. However, imagine the richness in students' discussion as they identify words and determine (often subtle and nuanced) meanings when asked to do this in a small group. With either hierarchical or linear array, think of a way to modify for additional steps for students to complete. For example, figure 5.8 asks students to generate a list of words before putting them in order.

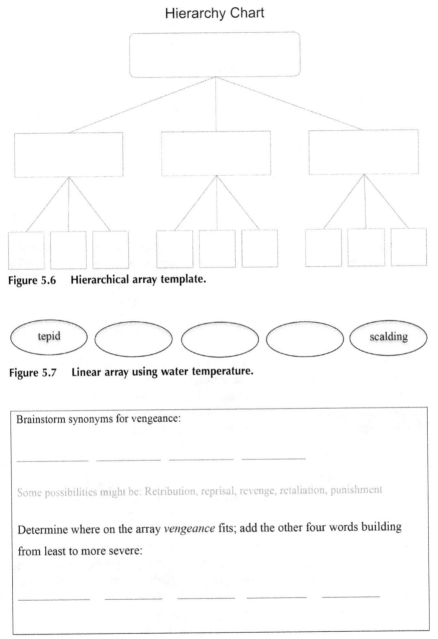

Figure 5.6   Hierarchical array template.

Figure 5.7   Linear array using water temperature.

Brainstorm synonyms for vengeance:

_____   _____   _____   _____

Some possibilities might be: Retribution, reprisal, revenge, retaliation, punishment

Determine where on the array *vengeance* fits; add the other four words building from least to more severe:

_____   _____   _____   _____   _____

Figure 5.8   Linear array using *vengeance*.

SELECTING WORDS TO TEACH

When you attempt to select words to teach from a book as we have demonstrated here, you may be overwhelmed by the number of words that you *think* you must teach. Surely you *must* teach all the words that students may not know, right? Not so. With narrative texts, keep in mind three important factors as you decide which words to teach: (1) Are the words central to the story, and without knowing them, a reader is likely to fail to comprehend the text?; (2) Are the words likely less known or unknown to a reader, in other words "hard" words?; and (3) Are the words presented in ways that the meaning cannot be illuminated through context? Do not feel you have to teach all the "hard" words; teach only those that will impact readers' understanding of the story in the text. And among those words, preteach words that will be difficult for students to figure out the meaning through context clues alone.

With expository texts, keep in mind: (1) the words are conceptually important to the lesson; and (2) the words are semantically related, meaning words that are associated through meaning. In most expository texts, like a textbook, the most important words will be bolded and defined in the glossary at the end of the book. You may not need to preteach as many words as you will with narrative texts, but be prepared to spend time explicitly teaching words and relationships among the words during and after the lesson.

We acquire vocabulary through both incidental and planned learning. The teacher's job is to plan effective instruction for vocabulary learning. Knowing which words to teach and when to teach them will take time to develop. Since learning new words that will be needed in future readings or lessons is especially important, your emphasis should be on teaching a few words well.

ASSISTING ENGLISH LANGUAGE LEARNERS AND STRUGGLING LEARNERS

Academic language is the formal language used in books and in formal settings like classrooms. The language of teaching and learning, business and commerce, and writing and publishing is generally grammatically complete and semantically precise. Academic language is the language we find in all expository textbooks and in many narrative books used in English classes. Students who are native speakers of other languages, however, may need special consideration. These individuals are already challenged as they build a listening vocabulary and attempt oral production of common English words. Additionally, in school, they are expected to deal with the new concepts and new vocabulary in an unfamiliar language. You can see why English language learners need extra support as they learn content area information.

Foremost among the considerations teachers must make is to understand the language differences their English learners are trying to reconcile. Are the language problems ones of phonology, semantics, or syntax? Many languages—Spanish, for example—do not have as many phonemes as English, and some language learners for whom English is the second language will never be proficient in making all the sounds of English. The difficulties with syntax may be minor, as with Spanish, where the modifier follows the noun (as in *casa grande*), or major as in German where the organization of the grammar can be dramatically different than in English.

English learners in your classroom can benefit from the following guidelines:

- Students generally understand more than they are able to express.
- Some apparent language problems are cultural differences.
- All students should participate in speaking and listening activities.
- Routines are beneficial for student learning.
- Assigning an English learner to a peer helper can be beneficial to both students.
- Meet individually with English learners as often as possible.

One crucial fact to remember in working with English language learners in your classroom in the context of vocabulary instruction is that they may have difficulty learning a word if they do not have anything to relate that concept to in their native language. For example, a student without an understanding of *autonomy* will have a difficult time learning it in English. English Language Learners (ELL) students must be taught the word and the concept simultaneously. Generate a list of concepts that you plan to teach and provide it to the students' parents and their ESL support teachers. Ask parents to engage their student in dialogues in their native language about the concepts. You might also find a text written in their native language to assist them in understanding new concepts.

Research findings on the value of vocabulary instruction has found that "students with reading difficulties who were exposed to vocabulary instruction benefitted three times as much as those who were not" (Hairrell, Rupley, & Simmons, 2011, p. 254). This includes students at all grade levels of instruction. The guidelines for helping non-native speakers of English are also recommended for struggling readers who are native English speakers.

THEORY TO PRACTICE

A teacher that models enthusiasm for words and makes a point to share interesting words with her class will inspire students to build their own vocabularies. The strategies shared in this chapter will help you to increase your students' understanding and long-term memory of essential words and concepts. Effective teachers will provide their students with multiple opportunities to hear and see words used correctly.

Since cognition and academic achievement are tied to vocabulary growth, it is essential for teachers to teach vocabulary explicitly. Begin your journal of words and quotes to share with your students. It is not too late to develop your own love for words.

REFERENCES

Baumann, J. F., & Kame'enui, E. J. (Eds.). (2012). *Vocabulary instruction: Research to practice*. New York: Guilford Press.

Beck, I. L., McKeown, M. G., & Kucan, L. (2002). *Bringing words to life: Robust vocabulary instruction*. New York: Guilford Press.

Davis, F. B. (1942). Two new measures of reading ability. *Journal of Educational Psychology, 33*, 365–72.

Deutscher, G. (2011). *Through the language glass: Why the world looks different in other languages*. New York: Picador.

Gipe, J. P., & Arnold, R. D. (1979). Teaching vocabulary through familiar associations and contexts. *Journal of Reading Behavior, 11*(3), 281–85.

Graves, M. F., Baumann, J. F., Blachowicz, C. L. Z., Manyak, P., Bates, A., Cieply, C., Davis, J. R., & Von Gunten, H. (2013). Words, words everywhere, but which ones do we teach? *The Reading Teacher, (67)*5, 333–46.

Grimes, N. (2002). *Talkin' About Bessie* (E. B. Lewis, Illus.). New York: Orchard Books.

Hairrell, A., Rupley, W., & Simmons, D. (2011). The state of vocabulary research. *Literacy Instruction and Research, (50)*4, 253–69.

Irwin, J. W., & Davis, C. A. (1980). Assessing readability: The checklist approach. *Journal of Reading, 24*(2), 124–30.

Johnson, D. D. (2001). *Vocabulary in the elementary and middle school*. Boston: Allyn & Bacon.

Johnson, D. D., & Johnson, B. (2011). *Words: The foundation of literacy*. Boulder, CO: Westview Press.

Johnson, D. D., & Moe, A. J. (1983). *The Ginn word book for teachers*. Boston: Ginn and Co.

Kameenui, E., Carnine, D., & Freschi, R. (1982). Effects of text construction and instructional procedures for teaching word meanings on comprehension and recall. *Reading Research Quarterly, 17*(3), 367–88.

Miller, G. A. (1996). *The science of words*. New York: Scientific American Library.

Nagy, W. E. (1988). *Teaching vocabulary to improve reading comprehension.* Urbana, IL: NCTE.

National Reading Panel. (2000). *Teaching children to read: An evidenced-based assessment of the scientific research literature on reading and its implications for reading instruction.* Washington, DC: National Institute of Child Health and Human Development.

Ruddell, M., & Shearer, B. (2002). "Extraordinary," "tremendous," "exhilarating," "magnificent": Middle school at-risk students become avid word learners with the vocabulary self-sollection strategy (VSS). *Journal of Adolescent & Adult Literacy, 45*(5), 352–63.

Schwartz, R. M., & Raphael, T. E. (1985). Concept of a definition: A key to improving students' vocabulary. *The Reading Teacher, 39*(2), 198–205.

Spinelli, J. (1990). *Maniac Magee.* Boston: Little, Brown and Company.

Stahl, S. A., & Fairbanks, M. M. (1986). The effects of vocabulary instruction: A model-based meta-analysis. *Review of Educational Research, 56*(1), 72–110.

Stevens, H. (November 6, 2011). Dictionary adds 10,000 words, redefines marriage. *Orlando Sentinel,* A12. (Heidi Stevens, Tribune Newspapers).

Terman, L. M. (1916). *The measurement of intelligence.* Cambridge: Riverside Press.

Thorndike, R. L., & Gallup, G. H. (1941). Verbal intelligence of the American adult. *Journal of Genetic Psychology,* 75–85.

Vygotsky, L. S. (1962, 1986). *Thought and language.* Cambridge. MA: MIT Press.

Whipple, G. (1925). *The twenty-fourth yearbook of the national society for the study of education: Report of the national committee on reading.* Bloomington, IL: Public School Publishing.

6

Creating Meaning

Comprehension

The point of reading is understanding, and comprehension is to understanding as getting wet is to swimming. You must do the one before you can hope to do the other, but you don't do the other simply because you do the one.

—Richard Mitchell

Fallen Angels

My "Guys Book Club" consisted of four guys all in their junior year of high school. We had been meeting for about three months when one of the guy's mother called me.

"I had to call you to tell you about a conversation I overheard yesterday. All four guys were talking about your book club when their friend Aaron asked if he could join. They told him no. I remembered from our first conversation that you said you would be happy to work with five to seven students, so I knew when they said you wouldn't take any others they were not being honest with Aaron. I moved closer to eavesdrop on this conversation. A few excuses later, I entered the room and told the guys that I was sure Aaron could join their book club. When he left, I asked them why they were reluctant to let him join, and here is the part you will love, they didn't want to share you with another guy. They liked the dynamics of the group and didn't want to mess it up."

I was flattered by their comment but called Aaron to let him know we were reading *Fallen Angels* by Walter Dean Meyers next week. The guys had decided to read the first one hundred pages, and he was welcome to join us.

We gathered in our usual meeting place and welcomed Aaron to the group. I reminded them that I was going to participate less this week, hoping they could keep the conversation going without me being responsible to ask the questions to jump-start the discussions. Ninety seconds of silence later, Matt threw out the first question.

"How long did it take you to realize that the main character was an African American soldier?"

All four of the guys carried this conversation for about three to four minutes, but Aaron did not add anything or make any comments. Ben threw out a second question, and again the original four all shared their thoughts but Aaron was silent. Finally, Aaron spoke up.

"What book did you read?"

"*Fallen Angels*," I replied. "The book I told you about last week."

Aaron reached down into his backpack and pulled out a book titled *Fallen Angel* by Catherine Hart, *not* Walter Dean Meyers! This book's cover had a busty woman with long, flowing, curly ashen-blonde hair draped down her back as her hot hunk of a shirtless man had both arms wrapped tightly around her scant white blouse.

Not exactly a story about a Black soldier's experiences in Vietnam.

To read is to understand. Comprehension, or constructing meaning while reading, is fundamental to that process. For most of us, the process of reading is a fluid and automatic one. Zwiers (2010) uses the analogy of driving a car to illustrate how many of the conscious and deliberate steps in driving a car have become mere habits for experienced drivers: "Reading is similar to driving in that the brain, from processing pages and pages of text, develops a variety of strategies and connections that facilitate efficient comprehension" (p. 3). The reading process, therefore, is a complex one that requires our brain to simultaneously use multiple skills and strategies in order for the reader to access the text and understand its meaning. If the reading process is as complex and complicated as described by Zwiers, teaching reading requires thoughtful and careful attention to cognitive skills and strategies, texts that we ask students to read, and instructional tools that facilitate a successful and efficient reading experience for all students.

THEORETICAL FOUNDATIONS OF COMPREHENSION

We know much about the reading process from the reading research giants such as Thorndyke (1977), Anderson and Pearson (1984), Anderson (1977, 1985, 1994), and Smith (1988), especially about the roles of prior knowledge in the comprehension process. As discussed in chapter 1, schema theory provides us with an explanation of how we organize and integrate information in our minds. According to Smith (1988), schema theory is linked to comprehension in a rather poetic way:

We can do much more with the theory of the world in our heads than make sense of the world and interact with it. We can live in the theory itself, in worlds that exist only in the imagination. Within this theory we can imagine and create, testing provisional solutions to problems and examining the consequences of possible behaviors. We can explore new worlds of our own, and can be led into other worlds by writers and artists. We can use the theory of the world to predict the future. This ability to predict is both pervasive and profound, because it is the basis of our comprehension of the world, including our understanding of spoken and written language. (p. 16)

In other words, readers use what they already know to make sense of new information that they read. Sometimes called the backbone of comprehension, prior knowledge is *essential* for comprehension. Readers may be able to crack the code of our written language, but they cannot make sense of what they read without prior knowledge. Smith (1988) argues: "It is not possible to demonstrate thought in any way if we do not understand what we are expected or trying to think about" (p. 21). Alvermann and Phelps (2001) claim that prior knowledge must be (1) activated; (2) appropriate; and (3) sufficient for it to be of use in comprehension. It is not enough that the reader has relevant prior knowledge that can connect to the text if that particular prior knowledge is not activated. To be of use to the reader, the reader must know enough about that particular knowledge. Lacking any one of these three conditions, then, results in failure to understand while reading.

Keene (2008) lists other thinking strategies that utilize prior knowledge, or schema:

- Readers spontaneously activate relevant, prior knowledge before, during, and after reading text.
- Readers assimilate information from text into their schema and make changes in that schema to accommodate the new information.
- Readers use their schema to relate text to their world knowledge, text knowledge, and personal experience.
- Readers use their schema to enhance their understanding of text and to store text information in long-term memory.
- Readers use their schema for specific authors and their styles to better understand text.
- Readers recognize when they have inadequate background information and know how to create it—to build schema—to get the information they need (p. 267).

TEXT STRUCTURES

To a large extent, the reading process depends on the text being read, and the structure of that text is one of the elements that distinguish one text from another. The two main text structures are narrative and expository. During the primary grades, much emphasis is placed on reading narrative texts, and it is both philosophically and developmentally appropriate for readers to be engaged in reading "stories." Language of narratives, both oral and written, has powerful impact on the lives of human beings. Most of us grew up listening to and telling stories from a young age; the sense of story that we develop is an intimate part of ourselves. Children's responses to narratives are natural, not forced. The power of a story, when combined with a child's natural instinct to make connections, allows for the use of narratives as one of the essential ways to teach and to learn.

We would argue that such power of stories should be extended to the secondary grades as narratives in literature exploring mathematics, science, and social studies concepts are often an unexploited resource. Stories can be, with their power to inspire, motivate, and relate to students as they learn content area topics, a natural tool for developing mathematical power and scientific ways of thinking, as well as learning about different societies and cultures.

In addition to powerful stories most often presented in narratives, it is imperative to introduce students to a wide range of informational texts. Much of the texts that students will encounter in the content areas will be expository in structure and informational in content. Expository texts demand more from readers than narrative texts (Keene, 2008). Reading expository texts, including textbooks, websites, articles, and primary documents, demands the use of prior knowledge and cognitive strategies in different ways than reading narrative texts. Assuming a stance to gain information as the reader enters the reading process, setting a purpose for reading other than simply to elicit enjoyment and attending to text features, for example, are some of the ways that shifts the reader's engagement with the text even before the first paragraph is read. To make matters more complex, expository texts are potentially more inconsiderate and inaccessible to readers with a greater number of potential unknown words and many different text features and layouts. Also, the prior knowledge necessary to unlock the potential meaning intended by the author (which is narrower than in narrative texts) may be insufficient, inaccessible, or even nonexistent in the reader's mind.

In addition, expository texts come in many different types and structures, which gives the text form, shape, and predictable ways to present content. Research on text structure shows that the lack of awareness of the structure before and during reading hinders the comprehension process. Conversely, teaching students to speculate the structure of the text they are about to read based on previewing the text has proven successful in facilitating comprehension. We share a slightly more sophisticated version of expository text structures (Marzano, 2010) that might be useful as you refine the study of text structures with your secondary students:

- *Description*: describes characteristics of a particular person, place, or thing.
- *Generalization*: begins with a general statement like, "There are a wide variety of consequences for breaking federal rules regarding carry-on baggage on commercial airplanes." Examples illustrating the generalization follow.
- *Argument*: begins with a statement that must be proven or supported. Proof or evidence follows the statement. For example, an argument supporting global warming might list pieces of evidence that make the argument valid. Sometimes qualifiers identify exceptions to the proof or evidence provided, and opposing arguments are presented.
- *Definition*: begins by identifying a specific term and then describing the general category to which the term belongs, along with specific characteristics of the term that distinguishes it from other terms within the category. For example, a text structure might articulate the characteristics of the process of commensalism, first explaining that it is a type of symbiosis and then showing how it is different from other types of symbiosis.
- *Comparison*: identifies two elements, such as commensalism and mutualism, and lists how those elements are similar and dissimilar.
- *Problem/solution*: begins by describing a problem, such as "The problem of the divide in wealth between the upper 10 percent of people in the United States and everyone else can be addressed in a number of ways." Possible solutions follow (p. 83).

Of course, a typical secondary student will read countless pages of textbooks and other academic expository texts, but we also advocate the use of content texts that are more authentic. In simplest terms, *authentic texts* are defined as "print, audio, and visual documents created and used by native speakers" (Annenberg Learner: https://www.learner.org/workshops/tfl/glossary.html). Examples include books, websites, articles, artwork, films, folk tales, music, and advertisements. In the field of second language acquisition, the use of authentic texts has been embraced as a tool for language and cultural learning for quite some time (see Bacon & Finnemann, 1990; Berardo, 2006; Chung, 1995; Day & Bamford, 1998). According to Kilickaya (2004), the main advantages of using authentic materials are:

- They have a positive effect on learner motivation.
- They provide authentic cultural information.
- They provide exposure to real language.
- They relate more closely to learners' needs.
- They support a more creative approach to teaching.

LITERACY STRATEGIES SUPPORTING
THE CONTENT AREAS

With the popularity of professional books on comprehension targeted to in-service teachers (e.g., Keene & Zimmermann, 1997; Duffy, 2003; Harvey & Goudvis, 2000, 2007; Gallagher, 2004; Oczkus, 2004; Kissner, 2006, 2008; Zwiers, 2010; Wormeli, 2009; Beers & Probst, 2012), secondary teachers know much about a variety of literacy strategies that make the meaning-making process possible. Some of the strategies associated with comprehension include the activation of necessary prior knowledge, the efficient use of memory to store and recall information, and inference skills that allow the reader to figure out what the author implies but does not say directly. Literacy strategies help the reader to make predictions, determine importance in order to synthesize what should be remembered as they continue to read, and set the purpose for reading using genuine questions. It is also important for the reader to be able to discern the author's intentions, evaluate writing while taking a stance using appropriate judgments, and transform what they knew about something (hence changing their cognitive structures) to create new knowledge.

To summarize, students' comprehension process includes the following:

- *Connecting to prior knowledge*: determine and use what you already know about a topic.
- *Evaluating author's purpose*: determine the purpose of the author through language, style, tone, and content.
- *Identifying important information*: distinguish what information is important and what is not.
- *Summarizing*: ability to capture the gist of a text using main ideas and important details.
- *Synthesizing*: ability to synthesize what you have read from various locations into a meaningful whole.
- *Inferring*: determine what the author means to say but does not explicitly state.
- *Questioning*: be able to generate and answer questions in order to store in your memory what is important.
- *Drawing conclusions*: evaluate and make judgments based on your reading or listening.
- *Monitoring*: be able to know when you are not comprehending or understanding the information and figure out what you can do to understand it.

Keene (2008) describes comprehension strategies as "the tools to change and manipulate thinking" (p. 168). Readers who use these strategies knowingly, deliberately, and strategically are, simply put, better readers. As we become better readers these strategies become automatic, "something we can't help but use," as Zwiers (2010) puts it. The "split-second thoughts that kick in constantly to help a proficient reader actively construct meaning . . . make up the majority of the thinking processes we use during reading even though we seldom notice them" (p. 4). What is more amazing is that we use these skills simultaneously, and again, quickly to keep the flow of meaning: "The habits work together and overlap as they construct meaning. They are highly intertwined. For example, just after reading the end of one paragraph, I might quickly summarize the last three sentences, question a character's motives, infer possible causes for an event, tweak my main idea, wonder about a word, and predict what may happen in the next section—all while I am reading the first few sentences of the next paragraph" (p. 4). In order for strategies to develop into skills or habits, readers first must learn *what* they are, *how* to use them, *when* to use them, and *why* they must use them, making these strategies *metacognitive*. Once taught, these metacognitive strategies must be used in authentic reading contexts many, many times before they become habits.

The metacognitive strategies that have become habits in readers are referred to as *skills*, according to Afflerbach, Pearson, and Paris (2008). A reading skill is most typically defined as "automatic actions that result in decoding and comprehension with speed, efficiency, and fluency and usually occur without awareness of the components or control involved" (Afflerbach et al., 2008, p. 368). Think about what good readers know how to do automatically, without having to consciously go through the step-by-step process. For example, what do you do when you come to a word in your text that you do not understand but know is important? Your response may vary depending on the purpose you pictured. For example, if it is a term you know will show up on an exam, what would you have "automatically" done to make sure you understood the word? If it is a term in a novel you were reading for pleasure, what would you do? In the latter case, you may have just ignored it. Believe it or not, struggling readers do not understand they have that option.

A set of skills that a first-grader needs to acquire is very different than a set of skills for a secondary student. Now imagine a secondary student and what skills she needs to possess in order to read efficiently and fluently. The literacy skills that were listed earlier as necessary for secondary readers may or may not be in the repertoire of abilities for a particular student. For a student, lacking some of the skills, strategies provide a method to help students attain the necessary skills. *Strategies*, defined as "deliberate, goal-directed attempts to control and modify the reader's efforts to decode text, understand words, and construct meanings of text" (Afflerbach et al., 2008, p. 368), help to develop skills. For example, a student may struggle with the ability to "identify important information" in a text. For that student, this requires deliberate and explicit instruction on why and how to identify and collect information in order to eventually, after much guided and independent practice, use it as a skill. For another student, this may have been in his skill set to easily use it in many different reading contexts. While we are presenting an argument here that a skill or a strategy is age dependent and reader specific (hence a fluid notion rather than rigidly defined), for the sake of consistency, we refer to instructional and cognitive strategies as simply *strategies* in this book.

Developing Comprehension

Students in content area courses need to be able to infer, identify important information, synthesize, and monitor their understanding when using either narrative or expository texts. Teachers should have a repertoire of *instructional* strategies at their disposal. Strategies are designed to aid the reader in understanding the text. Good instructional strategies consist of processes that are deliberate and intentional and use a step-by-step approach to guide the reader to construct meaning. Through this process, the reader gains a conceptual understanding of what the strategy is, why readers use it, and when to use it for effective and efficient reading. Instructional strategies typically have names (KWL, Venn diagram, etc.). Literacy scholars create these strategies to help teachers develop specific reading skills at all levels. However, some strategies, such as questioning, cannot be attributed to one scholar. This text includes powerful instructional strategies that you can use as you design your lessons.

The strategies presented in this chapter are used widely in middle-level and secondary classrooms by teachers to support learning in all content areas. The authors of this text have created some of the strategies described in this book. As you read and think about how you might use each strategy, think about how the strategy will facilitate learning through the use of reading and writing in *your* content area.

Activing Prior Knowledge

Since prior knowledge is essential for comprehension, it only makes sense that each lesson, whether you are teaching from a narrative or expository text, should include activities that assess what the students already know, then activate their prior knowledge by expanding and/or refining or building upon their prior knowledge. Many instructional options are available to assess, activate, expand or refine, and build prior knowledge.

Preteaching vocabulary in a content area class is perhaps the most common way to activate and/or build relevant prior knowledge. Refer to chapter 5 for how to select essential words to preteach and how to deliver effective vocabulary instruction. There are many other ways to activate and build prior knowledge. With easy access to the internet these days, using multimedia artifacts such as pictures, videos, podcasts, and primary documents, to name just a few, is perhaps one of the easiest ways to accomplish this task. Here are some concrete examples of what is possible.

Using Photographs. Before studying the Dust Bowl or reading Steinbeck's (1939) *The Grapes of Wrath*, show a hauntingly beautiful series of Dorothea Lange's photographs taken for the U.S. Farm Security Administration (figures 6.1, 6.2, and 6.3). These images and others related to a range of

Figure 6.1   Migrant mother. Dorothea Lange (1936). Mother of seven children, age thirty-two, Nipomo, California. Library of Congress photo and print archives.

Figure 6.2   Farm implements. Dorothea Lange (1935). These farm implemnts destroyed a naturally rich grazing area, Mills, New Mexico. Library of Congress photo and print archives.

Figure 6.3   Dust storm. Dorothea Lange (1935). It was conditions of this sort that forced many farmers to abandon the area, spring 1935, New Mexico. Library of Congress photo and print archives.

content area topics such as Jim Crow and the civil rights movement are available to teachers for use in the classroom from the Library of Congress's Prints & Photographs Online Catalog (PPOC). Visit: http://www.loc.gov/pictures/ to search.

Using Artifacts. The Prints & Photographs Online Catalog (PPOC) can also be used to obtain artifacts to teach content area topics. For example, imagine using a collection of posters produced by the Work Projects Administration (WPA) during the Great Depression. Of the two thousand WPA posters known to exist, the Library of Congress acquired 907 of them in 1940s. According to the Library of Congress, "The posters were designed to publicize exhibits, community activities, theatrical productions, and health and educational programs in seventeen states and the District of Columbia, with the strongest representation from California, Illinois, New York, Ohio, and Pennsylvania" (http://www.loc.gov/pictures/collection/wpapos/). The posters can be used to illustrate the multidimensional and interdisciplinary nature of the topic at hand, engaging students to explore a range of subtopics (figures 6.4, 6.5, and 6.6).

Using Media. PBS's award winning show *American Experience* (http://www.pbs.org/wgbh/americanexperience/) is an excellent resource for a range of topics for content area teachers. Stories of surviving the Dust Bowl to the rising of the militia movement to creating the first subway to the University of Washington's rowing team winning the gold medal in 1936, this PBS series offers engaging multimedia artifacts (e.g., films, videos, articles, time lines, and an image gallery) to accompany social studies and science topics.

A web search on national professional organizations will yield many worthwhile audios, videos, primary sources, and "interactives" that you can use to introduce a challenging topic. A search for the "Civil Rights Movement" in preparation for Christopher Paul Curtis's (1995) powerful novel, *The Watsons Go to Birmingham—1963*, resulted in such artifacts as freedom songs from

Figure 6.4   WPA Poster. "Stamp out the Axis." Library of Congress photo and print archives.

Figure 6.5   WPA Poster. "Welcome to Montana." Library of Congress photo and print archives.

Figure 6.6   WPA Poster. "Safety Is Home Defense." Library of Congress photo and print archives.

Smithsonian's History Explorer and a collection of pictures and descriptions of historic places of the civil rights movement from the National Endowment for the Humanities EDSITEment! (https://edsitement.neh.gov/).

KWL. The KWL (Ogle, 1986) is one of the universal strategies that can be used across all grades and subjects. The strategy begins by asking the question, "What do you Know?" The purpose of this section is to activate prior knowledge and develop interest. Students can either respond orally or in writing, listing all that they know about the topic in a chart such as the one found in table 6.1. Teachers can use this as a brainstorming exercise with an entire class. Next, the teacher asks, "What do you Want to Know?" which generates interest and set them on a direction for their learning. Finally, when the lesson/unit is completed, the teacher asks, "What have you Learned?" Students then list the items they learned about the topic. Many teachers introduce a KWL chart at the beginning of a lessons/unit and allow the students to add to the chart as it progresses. Many students will find that they want to learn more about something when they are investigating one issue and then become curious about another.

KWL Plus. Carr and Ogle (1987) noted that the list created by the student under the "L, what students had learned," could serve as a writing outline for the students. By grouping the "learned" items in categories, these findings would serve as headings or topics for writing a report or essay on the topic.

KWL charts can be modified by teachers to meet the needs of a specific lesson. The example of modified comparative KWL was used by preservice teachers in a college literacy class. Students compared the *Time* magazine account of the church bombings in Alabama on September 15, 1963, with Christopher Paul Curtis's account in his novel *The Watsons Go to Birmingham—1963* (figure 6.7). Under the K column, each student answered the five questions based on the fictional text they had just completed. Once those questions were answered, the professor asked the students what questions they had about the actual event. Students were then given a copy of the article "Civil Rights: The Sunday School Bombing" written in *Time* magazine (September 27, 1963) the week after the event. Students used the L or learned column to answer the same questions but based on the information in the *Time* article. The KWL comparison provided an additional lesson to students on how authors can use an actual event to tell a fictional story. Teachers may also find the Paired Text Comparison Guide (table 6.2) to be another effective way to compare information found in texts. The discrepancies can be either generated by the teacher or found by the students.

KWHLH. The KWL strategy is often expanded by including other components that promote learning. KWHLH adds a question before the L: "How we think we could find it out?" and a question for citing what they found: "How we learned about it." (Table 6.3.)

Table 6.1 KWL chart.

Topic: _____

K	W	L
What do you Know?	What do you Want to know?	What have you Learned?

Anticipation Guide. This strategy activates prior knowledge before reading an informational text by presenting readers with a set of statements about the topic pulled from the text. Each statement is written as either a true or a false statement, and readers have to make a stance on whether a statement is true or false (Smith, 1988). See figure 6.8 below for an example of an anticipation guide regarding Jim Crow. After having read the text, readers return to the

Table 6.2 Paired Text Comparison Guide

Text One:_____

Text Two:_____

Examples from Text One:	Examples from Text Two:	I am curious…
Discrepancy 1:		
Discrepancy 2:		
Discrepancy 3:		
Discrepancy 4:		

anticipation guide this time. This strategy provides teachers a way to gauge students' level of prior knowledge about the topic, and it provides readers a purpose for reading as they read to locate the statements in the text to determine if they were correct in their initial stances.

Stickystorms. Cathy, one of the authors of this text, uses Stickystorms as an interactive way to activate prior knowledge before instruction on a topic or reading about a topic. On a work board, each student puts six to eight sticky

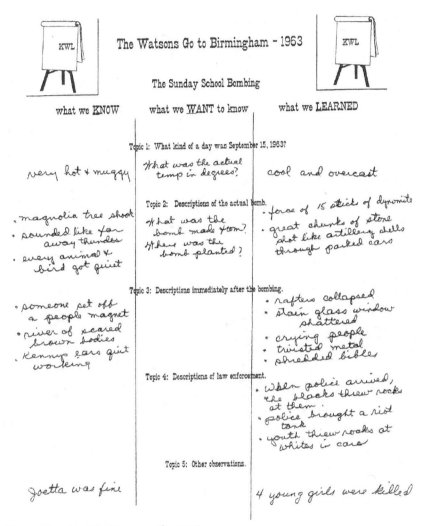

The Watsons Go to Birmingham - 1963

The Sunday School Bombing

KWL   KWL

what we KNOW   what we WANT to know   what we LEARNED

Topic 1: What kind of a day was September 15, 1963?

very hot & muggy   What was the actual temp in degrees?   cool and overcast

Topic 2: Descriptions of the actual bomb.

• magnolia tree shook
• sounded like far away thunder
• every animal & bird got quiet

What was the bomb made from? Where was the bomb planted?

• force of 15 sticks of dynamite
• great chunks of stone shot like artillery shells through parked cars

Topic 3: Descriptions immediately after the bombing.

• someone set off a people magnet
• river of scared brown bodies
• Kenny's ears quit working

• rafters collapsed
• stain glass window shattered
• crying people
• twisted metal
• shredded bibles

Topic 4: Descriptions of law enforcement.

• When police arrived, the blacks threw rocks at them
• police brought a riot tank
• youth threw rocks at whites in cars

Topic 5: Other observations.

Joetta was fine   4 young girls were killed

Figure 6.7   Modified Comparative KWL

notes (figure 6.9). On each sticky note, one fact that the student thinks she knows is written. Then in partner groups, the partners take turns sharing a fact. When the same fact is found on both lists, it is considered as a single fact, so eventually the partners' lists are collapsed into one. Then a partner group pairs up with another partner group to repeat the process. Finally, the teacher asks for facts from students. As each fact is presented to the class, a sticky note is posted on the board to represent a collective set. As each student shares a fact, other students look at their board to see if they have that

Table 6.3 KWHLH

K What is known	
W What we want to know	
H How we think we could find it out	
L What we learned	
H How we learned about it	

fact; if so, it gets removed from their boards. What will remain on the board at the end of the whole group process is the class's collective list of what they know about the topic. Some of the facts may be misconceptions as the teacher has yet to deliver the lesson on the topic, but it provides an excellent time to assess students' prior knowledge. The collective list can be categorized, webbed, lined up according to simplest to most complex facts, timelined, and other methods to generate a further discussion about the topic. Students can do quick writes after the class discussion, perhaps posing questions that they

This anticipation guide is done before students read an expository text about Jim Crow laws.

ANTICIPATION GUIDE

Jim Crow

Before Reading		After Reading
T or F		**T or F**

_____	Jim Crow lasted nearly 100 years.	_____
_____	Christians defended the blacks' rights.	_____
_____	Jim Crow laws are also known as "slave codes."	_____
_____	Jim Crow etiquette is same as Jim Crow laws.	_____
_____	Plessy vs. Ferguson enforced the constitutional rights based on the 13th, 14th, and 15th Amendments.	_____
_____	Violations of Jim Crow laws could result in lynching.	_____
_____	In the mid-1800, more whites were lynched.	_____

Figure 6.8   Anticipation Guide

now have about the topic. The collective class list can stay throughout the lesson or the unit. This whole process can be repeated after the lesson or the unit to compare how much the students have learned.

Generating and Answering Questions

QAR. QAR stands for Question-Answer Relationships (Raphael, 1984). At the core, this strategy facilitates an understanding that there are different types and levels of questions. For every type of question—Right There; Think and Search; Author and Me; and On My Own—the answer is found in a particular location—In the Book or In my Head. Table 6.4 lists the four types of questions and descriptions of where answers are found for each question. Before students attempt to answer a question, they first think about what type of question they are about to answer. Once they identify the type, then they look for the answer based on the type. For example, answers to Think and Search questions are found in multiple places, and the reader has to piece together the bits of answers to synthesize an answer. If a student has decided that she is about to answer a Right There question, she knows that the answer

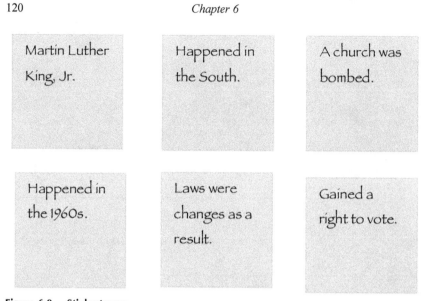

Figure 6.9   Stickystorms

will be located in a single sentence or a paragraph. For the Author and Me question, she knows that the answer should be based on what she has read, but she can interject her own perspective as a reader. Students can also be asked to generate each type of question after reading, rather than answering questions posed by others.

Central Question. This instructional strategy is used to facilitate synthesizing. After reading or a lesson/unit, an important question that uses the knowledge gained through instruction is posed. Students must choose an answer. Then they list reasons to justify their stance along with finding page numbers of textual evidence. For example, the ending of Lois Lowry's (1993) *The Giver* has an ambiguous ending. Readers often finish the book believing that the main character either died or has reached his ultimate destiny. The central question in this example would be: "Does Jonas die at the end of the book?" Readers taking the "YES" stance will have to prove it through their justifications and examples from the book. Examples in table 6.5 and table 6.6 show possible reasons for each stance.

Synthesize and Analyze

Inquiry chart. An inquiry chart (Hoffman, 1992) can be considered as an expanded KWL through the use of a matrix (table 6.7). For a given topic, a set of guiding questions is generated (Want to Know), either by students, the teacher, or both. For each question, students have an opportunity to list

Table 6.4 QAR, Question-Answer Relationships

Question-Answer Relationships

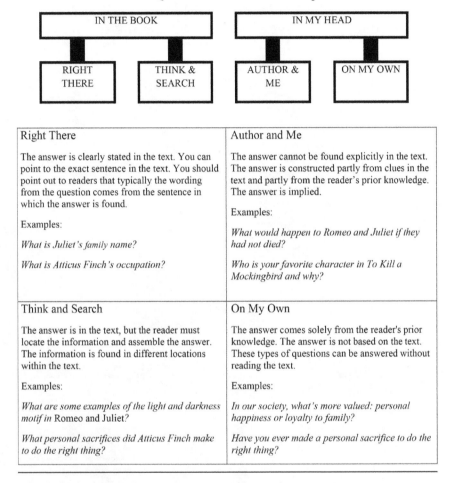

Right There	Author and Me
The answer is clearly stated in the text. You can point to the exact sentence in the text. You should point out to readers that typically the wording from the question comes from the sentence in which the answer is found.	The answer cannot be found explicitly in the text. The answer is constructed partly from clues in the text and partly from the reader's prior knowledge. The answer is implied.
Examples:	Examples:
What is Juliet's family name?	*What would happen to Romeo and Juliet if they had not died?*
What is Atticus Finch's occupation?	*Who is your favorite character in To Kill a Mockingbird and why?*
Think and Search	On My Own
The answer is in the text, but the reader must locate the information and assemble the answer. The information is found in different locations within the text.	The answer comes solely from the reader's prior knowledge. The answer is not based on the text. These types of questions can be answered without reading the text.
Examples:	Examples:
What are some examples of the light and darkness motif in Romeo and Juliet?	*In our society, what's more valued: personal happiness or loyalty to family?*
What personal sacrifices did Atticus Finch make to do the right thing?	*Have you ever made a personal sacrifice to do the right thing?*

answers to that question that they might already know (K). Then, using a range of sources (i.e., informational texts, online sources, trade books, textbooks, etc.), students locate answers to the remaining guiding questions (L). The matrix allows an alignment between the question, the source, and the answer. For example, if a student finds an answer to the guiding question 3 using source 2, there is a specific box reserved for the student to write down the answer. The chart provides space to synthesize a succinct answer to each question from multiple sources as well as space to gather interesting facts and new questions.

Table 6.5 Central question "Yes" response using *The Giver*.

Text: *The Giver*

Central Question ___ Does Jonas die at the end of the book?

YES		NO	
Reason	**Textual Evidence**	**Reason**	**Textual Evidence**
The metaphor of sledding down the hill to "Elsewhere" implies that Jonas is traveling to the afterlife.	"The hill was steep but the snow was powdery and soft, and he knew that this time there would be no ice, no fall, no pain" (179). "…they sped in a straight line through an incision that seemed to lead to the final destination, the place that he had always felt was waiting, the Elsewhere that held their future and their past" (179).		
References of light in the last scene means Jonas sees death.	"…and all at once he could see lights, and he recognized them now…they were the red, blue, and yellow lights that twinkled from trees where families created and kept memories, where they celebrated love" (179).		
Death is the ultimate sacrifice. Jonas dies to save Sameness.	"'If you get away, if you get beyond, if you get to Elsewhere, it will mean that the community has to bear the burden themselves, of the memories you had been holding for them'" (155-156).		
Lowry refers explicitly to the deterioration of Jonas's body and strength.	"It became a struggle to ride the bicycle as Jonas weakened from lack of food…His sprained ankle throbbed as he forced the pedal downward in an effort that was almost beyond him" (174).		

Table 6.6 Central question "No" response using *The Giver*.

Text: *The Giver*

Central Question ___ Does Jonas die at the end of the book?

YES		NO	
Reason	**Textual Evidence**	**Reason**	**Textual Evidence**
		As the story resolves, Lowry indicates that Jonas's courage and love can conquer all obstacles.	"But somewhere ahead, through the blinding storm, he knew there was warmth and light…Inside his freezing body, his heart surged with hope" (179).
		This happens on Christmas day. Gabriel may represent baby Jesus, and this is the day of his birth.	"Suddenly he was aware with certainty and joy that below, ahead, they were waiting for him; and that they were waiting, too, for the baby" (180).
		The human will is a powerful force. Jonas is determined to stay alive for the sake of the child.	"Jonas felt himself losing consciousness and with his whole being willed himself to stay upright atop the sled, clutching Gabriel, keeping him safe" (179). "Warming himself ever so briefly had shaken away the lethargy and resignation and restored his will to survive" (177).
		Jonas hears symbolic music coming from a distant place, implying that he is still alive to witness his success in releasing his memories to the community.	"Behind him, across vast distances of space and time, from places he had left, he thought he heard music too" (180).

Table 6.7 Example of Inquiry Chart about the Dust Bowl using *The Grapes of Wrath* **(Steinbeck, 1939).**

Dust Bowl using *The Grapes of Wrath (Steinbeck, 1939)*

	GUIDING QUESTIONS					
TOPIC Dust Bowl	1. When and where did it occur?	2. Why did it occur?	3. How did the government respond?	4. Is this a common phenomenon?	INTERESTING FACTS AND FIGURES	NEW QUESTIONS
WHAT WE KNOW	Oklahoma 1930s				Got its name after Black Sunday, 4/14/1935	
1. www.english.illinois.edu/maps/depression/dustbowl.htm	Colorado, Kansas, Oklahoma, Texas, and New Mexico		Established Drought Relief Service			
2. History.com	1931-1939	Drought and farming practices			Affected 150,000 square-mile area	
3. HowStuffWorks.com	Coincided with the Great Depression	Migration to the plains region, populating those states				
4. livinghistoryfarm.org		Poor farming practices, leaving too much top soil	Congress passed the Soil Conservation Act in 1935			Are the congressional acts still effective?
SUMMARY						

(Left margin label: SOURCES)

List of Similarities, Web of Differences. As an alternative to the limited space available on a Venn diagram, use the list of similarities, web of differences, which resolves the issue (Fordham, Wellman, & Sandmann, 2002). Students are able to compare and contrast two items by making a list of how the two are similar and then creating a web for each of the concepts depicting how they are unique. An example of this strategy is presented in figure 6.10.

Semantic Feature Analysis. A semantic feature analysis expands the concepts of words using their features (Anders, Bos & Filip, 1984). You saw one example in chapter 5 using genres and types of children's literature. Historical fiction, one of the target words in the example, is examined through the features—genre, realistic, unrealistic, true, made-up, narrative, and expository. According to the example, historical fiction is a genre, it is realistic because it has an element of truth, but it is made-up and written in narrative text structure. To explore one word this way would be considered an effective

List of Similarities; Web of Differences

1. _____
2. _____
3. _____
4. _____
5. _____
6. _____
7. _____
8. _____
9. _____
10. _____
11. _____
12. _____

Figure 6.10   List of Similarities, Web of Differences

way to learn words. The beauty of this strategy, however, is that it provides an opportunity to analyze the features of many words at once, making it possible to build semantic relationships among those words. Reading teachers often use Semantic Feature Analysis for reading comprehension, not just to teach vocabulary. In table 6.8, characters from the classic novel *Lord of the Flies* (Golding, 1959) are analyzed through character traits after reading the first two chapters. In place of target words, character names are listed. In place of features, adjectives to describe characters are listed. In addition to noting positive (+) or negative (-) relationships between the word and the

Table 6.8 Semantic Feature Analysis using Golding's *Lord of the Flies.*

Sematic Feature Analysis of Characters from the *Lord of the Flies*

	charismatic	devious	detached	idealistic	humane	defiant	ambitious	brave	selfish	confident	naïve	sadistic	sensitive	stubborn	egotistical	smart
Ralph																
Jack																	
Simon																	
Piggy																	
Roger																	
Sam and Eric																	

+ = positive relationship
- = negative relationship

feature, readers using the Sematic Feature Analysis are asked to identify page number(s) on which the evidence for the character trait can be found.

Reciprocal Teaching. Reciprocal teaching features four reading skills crucial for comprehension—questioning, clarifying, summarizing, and predicting (Palincsar & Brown, 1984; Palincsar & Brown, 1986). A content teacher may consider substituting prediction with application. Students create meaning from their reading by explicitly using these skills during an active engagement with their teacher or their peers. Often teachers will provide a bookmark listing the four strategies as a reminder or a chart to document their use of skills (table 6.9). The name of this instructional strategy comes from the role that students play in small group reading as the "teacher" guiding the discussion using the four strategies. Typically, each student takes a role in completing one of the four strategies before meeting with the small group. However, adaptations can be made to the strategy in the middle grades for students complete all four strategies during their independent reading.

Table 6.9 Reciprocal Teaching Chart

RECIPROCAL TEACHING

As I read, I am thinking that this text will be about...	These questions are forming in my mind...
I need to clarify these words/concepts...	To summarize what I have read so far...

Because this instructional strategy requires a reader to eventually take on all four roles, it is important for the teacher to provide sufficient instruction in teaching each and every strategy as well as scaffolding through modeling and guided practice before expecting students to be successful.

THEORY TO PRACTICE

By the time students are in the middle grades, they most likely have learned a variety of strategies that support their ability to comprehend different text structures. Teachers are encouraged to use challenging texts, but they should remain cognizant of the challenges these texts bring to their students. The ultimate goal is to provide students the tools they need to be successful. This chapter provides teachers with a variety of strategies they can implement to help their students grasp and understand the intricacies of each of the content areas. We know learning escalates when students have teachers who understand the importance of activating prior knowledge and are skilled at providing the support they need to comprehend the information.

REFERENCES

Afflerbach, P., Pearson, P. D., & Paris, S. G. (2008). Clarifying differences between reading skills and reading strategies. *The Reading Teacher*, *61*(5), 356–73.

Alvermann, D., & Phelps, S. F. (2001). *Content reading and literacy: Succeeding in today's diverse classrooms*. New York: Ally & Bacon.

Anders, P. L., Bos, C. S., & Filip, D. (1984). The effect of semantic feature analysis on the reading comprehension of learning disabled students. In J. A. Niles & L. A. Harris (Eds.), *Changing perspectives on reading/language processing and instruction* (pp. 162–66). Rochester, NY: National Reading Conference.

Anderson, R. C. (1977). *Schema-directed processes in language comprehension (Tech. Rep. 50)*. Urbana: Center for the Study of Reading, University of Illinois.

Anderson, R. C. (1985). *Becoming a nation of readers: The report of the commission on reading*.

Anderson, R. C. (1994). Role of the reader's schema in comprehension, learning, and memory. In R. B. Ruddell, M. R. Ruddell & H. Singer (Eds.), *Theoretical models and processes of reading* (4th ed., pp. 469–537). Newark, DE: International Reading Association.

Anderson, R. C., & Pearson, P. D. (1984). A schema-theoretic view of basic processes in reading comprehension (Technical Report No. 306). Cambridge, MA: Bolt, Beranek, & Newman; Urbana, IL: University of Illinois. *Center for the Study of Reading. (ERIC Document Reproduction Service No. ED 239 236)*.

Annenberg Learner. (2017). Glossary. Retrieved from http://www.learner.org/index. html.

Bacon, S., & Finnemann, M. (1990). A study of the attitudes, motives, and strategies of university foreign language students and their disposition to authentic oral and written input. *Modern Language Journal*, 74, 459–73.

Beers, K., & Probst, R. E. (2012). *Notice & note: Strategies for close reading.* Portsmouth, NH: Heinemann.

Berardo, S. A. (2006). The use of authentic materials in the teaching of reading. *The Reading Matrix*, 6, 60–69.

Burke, J. (2010). *What's the big idea?: Question-driven units to motivate reading, writing, and thinking.* Portsmouth, NH: Heinemann.

Carr, E., & Ogle, D. (1987). K-W-L Plus: A strategy for comprehension and summarization. *Journal of Reading*, 30(7), 626–31.

Chung, H. (1995). *Effects of elaborative modifications on second language reading comprehension and incidental vocabulary learning.* University of Hawai'i Working Papers in ESL, 14, 27–61.

Civil rights: The Sunday school bombing. (April 27, 1963). *Time*, 19.

Curtis, C. P. (1995). *The Watsons Go to Birmingham—1963.* New York: Delacorte Books for Young Readers.

Day, R., & Bamford, J. (1998). *Extensive reading in the second language classroom.* Cambridge: Press Syndicate of the University of Cambridge.

Duffy, G. G. (2003). *Explaining reading: A resource for teaching concepts, skills, and strategies.* New York: Guilford Press.

Farrell, E. J., & Squire, J. R. (Eds.). (1990*). Transactions with literature: A fifty-year perspective.* Urbana, IL: National Council of Teachers of English.

Federal Art Project (between 1936 and 1941). See America: Welcome to Montana. [WPA Poster]. Retrieved September 6, 2017. From http://www.loc.gov/pictures/ item/96503136/.

Fordham, N., Wellman, D. K., & Sandmann, A. L. (2002). Taming the text: Engaging and supporting students in social studies readings. *The Social Studies*, 93(4), 149–58.

Gallagher, K. (2004). *Deeper reading: Comprehending challenging texts, 4–12.* Portland, ME: Stenhouse.

Golding, W. (1959). *Lord of the flies.* New York: Capricorn Books.

Harvey, S., & Goudvis, A. (2000). *Strategies that work: Teaching comprehension to enhance understanding.* Portland, ME: Stenhouse.

Harvey, S., & Goudvis, A. (2007). *Strategies that work: Teaching comprehension for understanding and engagement.* Portland, ME: Stenhouse.

Hoffman, J. V. (1992). Critical reading/thinking across the curriculum: Using I-Charts to support learning. *Language Arts*, 69, 121–27.

Keene, E. O. (2008). *To understand: New horizons in reading comprehension.* Portsmouth, NH: Heinemann.

Keene, E. O., & Zimmermann, S. (1997). *Mosaic of thought: Teaching comprehension in a reader's workshop.* Portsmouth, NH: Heinemann.

Kilickaya, F. (2004). Authentic materials and cultural content in EFL classrooms. *The Internet TESL Journal*, Vol. X, No. 7. Retrieved February 11, 2012, from http://iteslj.org/Techniques/Kilickaya-AutenticMaterial.html.

Kissner, E. (2006). *Summarizing, paraphrasing and retelling: Skills for better reading, writing and test taking*. Portsmouth, NH: Heinemann.

Kissner, E. (2008). *The forest and the trees: Helping readers identify important details in texts and tests*. Portsmouth, NH: Heinemann.

Lange, D. (1935). *These farm implements should never have been used for they destroyed a naturally rich grazing area. Mills, New Mexico* [photograph]. Retrieved August 6, 2017. From http://www.loc.gov/pictures/item/fsa1998018586/PP/.

Lange, D. (1935). *Dust storm. It was conditions of this sort which forced many farmers to abandon the area. Spring 1935. New Mexico* [photograph]. Retrieved August 3, 2017. From http://www.loc.gov/pictures/item/fsa1998018583/PP/.

Lange, D. (1936). *Destitute pea pickers in California. Mother of seven children. Age thirty-two. Nipomo, California* [photograph]. Retrieved August 6, 2017. From http://www.loc.gov/pictures/item/fsa1998021539/PP/.

Library of Congress. (2017). Posters: WPA Posters. Retrieved August 6, 2017. From http://www.loc.gov/pictures/collection/wpapos/.

Lowry, L. (1993). *The giver*. New York: HMH Books for Young Readers.

Marzano, R. J. (2010). Summarizing to comprehend. *Reading to Learn, 67*(6), 83.

National Endowment for the Humanities. (2017). EDSITEment! Retrieved August 12, 2017. From https://edsitement.neh.gov/.

Oczkus, L. (2004). *Super six comprehension strategies: 35 lessons and more for reading success*. Norwood, MA: Christopher-Gordon.

Ogle, D. M. (1986). K-W-L: A teaching model that develops active reading of expository texts. *The Reading Teacher, 39*(6), 564–70.

Palincsar, A. S., & Brown, A. L. (1984). Reciprocal teaching of comprehension-fostering and comprehension-monitoring activities. *Cognition and Instruction, 2*, 117–75.

Palincsar, A. S., & Brown, A. L. (1986). Interactive teaching to promote independent learning from text. *The Reading Teacher, 39*(8), 771–77.

PBS (2017). *American Experience*. Retrieved August 9, 2017. From http://www.pbs.org/wgbh/americanexperience/.

Raphael, T. (1984). Teaching learners about sources of information for answering comprehension questions. *Journal of Reading, 27*(4), 303–11.

Smith, F. (1988). *Understanding reading: A psycholinguistic analysis of reading and learning to read* (4th ed.). Hillside, NJ: Lawrence Erlbaum Associates.

Steinbeck, J. (1986). *The grapes of wrath*. New York: Viking.

Thorndyke, P. W. (1977). Cognitive structures in comprehension and memory of narrative discourse. *Cognitive Psychology*.

Tworkov, J. (between 1936 and 1941). *Home safety is home defense.* [WPA poster]. Retrieved September 6, 2017. From http://www.loc.gov/pictures/collection/wpapos/item/92500641/.

Von Phul, P. (1941). *Stamp out the Axis / P.V.P.* [WPA poster]. Retrieved August 16, 2017. From http://www.loc.gov/pictures/collection/wpapos/item/2010648603/.

Wormeli, R. (2009). *Metaphors & analogies: Power tools for teaching any subject.* Portland, ME: Stenhouse.

Zwiers, J. (2010). *Building reading comprehension habits in Grades 6–12: A toolkit of classroom activities* (2nd ed.). Newark, DE: International Reading Association.

Understanding and Expressing Ideas

Fluency

I promised myself that I would write as well as I can, tell the truth, not to tell everything I know, but to make sure that everything I tell is true, as I understand it, and to use the eloquence which my language affords me.

—Maya Angelou

Guys Book Club Reads Eminem

When I started my "Guys Book Club" with four high school boys, I chose their first book. I wanted them to have some say in the second book, so during our first meeting I did a book talk on three books I thought they would enjoy and let them vote on the one they preferred to read. When it was time to choose the third book, I insisted that they had full authority to choose the book. They were surprised that I meant they could choose to read *anything* they wanted. Then another problem arose; they had no idea how to choose a book—something that had not occurred to me. I told them they could have the week to decide. They could seek recommendations from their parents, teachers, and friends, meet together to discuss their options, and then let me know their decision the following Wednesday. That would give us all time to go to the bookstore or order it online.

I would be lying if I said I greeted their choice with enthusiasm: *Whatever You Say I Am: The Life and Times of Eminem* by Anthony Bozza. I later learned this decision was my first true "test" to see if I was sincere that it really was *their* choice. I faked excitement and told them how much I enjoyed Eminem's music; truth be told, I did like one of his current hits, but not much else.

Quite literally, this was the worst book I had ever read. *But*, I did read it, and the six of us had one of the most interesting book discussions I've ever encountered. The guys brought up points from the book to substantiate their statements, and all of them had identified vocabulary that was new or interesting to them. They sounded like a group of old men at the coffee shop as they shared their disgust with the overuse of the "f" word throughout the book. One of the guys commented that the book would probably have been fourteen pages shorter if Bozza had omitted that one word—and I believe he was accurate.

The discussion bounced around from Eminem's treatment of his mother, to the impact of fame on a person, and whether Eminem was like Horatio Alger, as he claimed. I discovered a "teachable moment" when they all insisted he was the Horatio Alger of our times yet they couldn't tell me anything about Horatio Alger. I shared the history of Horatio Alger's dime novels and described them as revolving around the theme of the American Dream: the idea that anyone with effort could pull themselves up by their bootstraps and be successful. I was able to sit back and watch in amazement as the four guys split into pro and con sides and then discussed counterpoints for more than twenty minutes. At the conclusion of that hour together, they looked at me and asked me to help them choose their next book—they wanted something with more depth.

It was one of my moments of pride!

Fluency is typically defined as the skills needed to read with expression at a steady pace and comprehend what was read. According to *The Literacy Dictionary* (Harris & Hodges, 1995), fluency is "the clear, easy, written or spoken expressions of ideas" (p. 85). Fluency, most often discussed in the context or oral reading fluency in the elementary grades, has relevance in middle and secondary content areas when the emphasis is placed on the *expressions of ideas*. How well do your students express their ideas in content areas as they read and listen (*receiving* information) and as they write and speak (*generating* information)? What would fluency in these language processes—reading, writing, listening, and speaking—look like?

THEORETICAL FOUNDATIONS OF FLUENCY

Instructional strategies in this chapter provided will support students who are struggling with fluency as well as those that are progressing well but need to continue to improve their fluency skills. Content areas, known for the introduction of new vocabulary and the use of sophisticated texts, will most likely challenge many of your students. Provide your students with plenty of opportunities to help them improve their fluency skills as they are learning the course content.

Unfortunately, many educational ideas become modified from their original intent with unintended consequences, and fluency may become one of those mishaps. Writer's Workshop serves as a perfect example. The five stages of Writer's Workshop are: brainstorm, organize, write, edit, and publish. These stages sometimes are morphed into the lesson plans for the week: Monday: brainstorm; Tuesday: organize your ideas; Wednesday: write the story; Thursday: self and peer edit your work; and Friday: publish your story. No writing expert imagined that the stages of writing would be translated this way in classroom practice.

Fluency instruction, too, is beginning to show some unintended consequences when applied in classrooms. Rasinski and Padak (2013) warn us of a few emerging trends that teachers should avoid:

- trying to get their students to read faster today than yesterday
- bar graphs documenting reading speed over time
- making speed of reading a competitive exercise
- ignoring the importance of prosody (intonation, tone, stress, and rhythm) while students read
- forgetting that pleasure and understanding is still the ultimate reading goal (p. 280).

Keeping these important warnings in mind, let us begin to examine how to improve fluency in the content areas.

READING FLUENCY

A fluent reader can read at an appropriate pace, pronounce words accurately while using proper inflection, and most importantly, understand what they have read. Most students are fluent readers by the time they become middle school students, but not all of them. Teachers will encounter a few students who need continued support with their reading fluency skills. Some students who continue to read with a great deal of effort and who are unable to read words in passages without assistance *may* still understand what they have read. However, for the most part, reading fluency has a strong, positive relationship to comprehension (Samuels & Farstrup, 2006); a student would have a hard time comprehending a text that he cannot read with some level of automaticity, the ability to read without paying attention to the rules of phonetics. When students are bogged down by the need to pay a great deal of attention to decoding words, comprehension drops. Other students who may be able to read with what sounds like fluency—automaticity, ease, and expression—may not be able to tell you what they have read. Both automaticity and comprehension are necessary to be considered a fluent reader.

Reading fluency is aided by a reader's automaticity—having a large stock of sight words that they can recognize instantly as they read. The freedom to read without having to frequently stop to decode provides the brain with more opportunities to pay attention to creating meaning while reading. Most middle and high school students will have a substantial stock of sight words large enough to read some text rather quickly. However, secondary reading in the content areas, with content-specific words that they may not have seen or even heard before, often requires students to revert back to using some decoding strategies as they read. As discussed in chapter 5, students' repeated encounters with words in meaningful contexts will turn them into sight words that they can read automatically. Think about all the words that have become sight words as you read educational texts (e.g., *Piaget, pedagogy, construct-ivism, schema theory, Vygotsky*). These are probably words that you now know the meanings of (as part of your vocabulary development) and that are now in your sight word repertoire contributing to the fluency of your reading.

Strategies to Improve Reading Fluency

The key to reading at a proper pace—not too fast and not too slow—while using good inflection is practice, practice, practice. Middle-grades students will balk at the idea of rereading a text, so it is up to you, the teacher, to provide them with authentic purposes to engage them in the rereading.

Readers Theater

Readers theater uses a script like a play, but the students can read from the script; they do not have to memorize their lines. A variety of websites will have readers theater scripts available, but your students have the ability to create their own scripts. They can use their creativity to create scenes from historical situations or even scientific discoveries.

Tableau

Tableau is a not a stand-alone strategy to support any fluency. Rather, this is a companion strategy to use with readers theater. A tableau is a human "picture," just as one might draw a picture to represent what is being read. In a tableau, three to five students pose as a picture to visually represent what is being read.

Read-Alouds

The best mode of reading for understanding is silent reading. Especially with challenging content area texts, students must be asked to read a text multiple times for particular purposes such as generating or answering questions and summarizing or synthesizing main points. However, oral reading, done grade and content appropriately, should also have a place in the middle and secondary levels. During discussion, return to the text and have students read aloud small sections with important information. Listen to students as they read to see if they are reading the content-related words with fluency.

A common practice of reading aloud in classrooms is referred to as "round robin reading." In this section promoting oral reading, there is one practice we do not advocate: round robin reading. You may have seen or done round robin reading many times: the practice of allowing each student to read a paragraph aloud. You may be one of those students who loved to read aloud a text and could not wait until it was your turn (in which case you probably had high fluency skills). Or, you may be like the majority of students who: (1) counted ahead by counting how many students were ahead and determining which paragraph you would be called on to read; (2) rehearsed your paragraph in your head multiple times; (3) all the while *not* paying any attention to what the others were reading. Round robin reading is a proven ineffective way to read in a classroom setting.

Teacher Read-Alouds

Teachers who are fluent readers should serve as effective reading role models for their students. While many elementary schools include teacher read-alouds as part of their daily routine, it is rare to find a secondary teacher reading to her students. Reluctant readers, those students who do not read for pleasure, may be prodded to pick up a book that a teacher shared with her class. The authors of this text encourage teachers of all content areas to read aloud a chapter (or a few pages) of a chapter book every day at the start or end of a class period. Teachers should read with good inflection and the proper rate. Many of our former students tell us they continue to hear our voice in their heads when they read texts to their students that we read to them.

Choral Reading

Involve a small group of students or an entire class in an echo reading, or choral reading. Choral reading can also be done without the teacher modeling the paragraph. Allow the students to try to read together using the proper inflection and rate.

Partner Reading

Partner readers sit and read a common text. After reading the text on their own silently, partners can reread the text taking turns. They can also be offered different turn-taking patterns such as one partner reads while the other makes a comment or asks a question about what has been read.

DEAR (Drop Everything and Read) or SSR (Sustained Silent Reading)

No matter the name, this strategy is designed as uninterrupted individual reading time and is important to students' ability to read with prosody.

Providing time in a school day for students to participate in personal reading such as books, magazines, or even short texts is important for reading growth. Offer a wide range of texts related to the content you are teaching at the moment so that the students can read about the topic in a different format or a genre. Be open to students reading a text they have found that may be, even tangentially, related to the topic. We strongly suggest that you serve as a model by reading your own books, for pleasure, during this time.

WRITING FLUENCY

Teaching students to become fluent writers takes a great deal of time and patience. In fact, because of the amount of time a teacher must commit to assisting students and because some teachers do not consider themselves writers, quality writing instruction may be difficult to find in the secondary school curriculum. And yet the only way for students to learn to write and write to express ideas fluently is for them to write. Fluency in writing also develops when students write frequently. As reading fluency was best developed through repeated reading, so does writing. In addition to the few longer papers that you assign for formal assessment, allow opportunities for short and spontaneous writing (on index cards, sticky notes, or even small scraps of paper) during each class. Have them "try out" new ideas and thoughts. It is through these small writing moments that new thoughts emerge.

Strategies to Improve Writing Fluency

In chapter 8, we discuss the importance of students being able to create new knowledge to show what they have learned. Because our next chapter is dedicated to writing, we will share a few strategies that will promote writing fluency—the ability to get their ideas on paper in a fluid, organized fashion.

Writers' Workshop

The spirit of writers' workshop allows students to explore and practice a variety of types of writing purposes. Writers' workshop is an approach we would like to see every student experience. Students progress through the five stages: brainstorming, organizing, writing, editing, publishing—not necessarily in this five-step order as the writing process can be a complex and messy one. Writers need to be allowed to vary these steps and perhaps more importantly to be able to abandon or quit a writing project that is not coming together. (See chapter 8 for more information on the writing process.)

Quick Writes

There are many variations and just as many names to describe short, timed, informal, and nonevaluative writing. One way quick writes are used is to have the students write continuously without stopping and document as much thought as possible on paper in a given amount of time (e.g., one minute, five minutes). Quick writes are often used to brainstorm, to prepare for a discussion, or to recall important points before or after a lesson. Quick writes are great for assessing students' understanding, but we caution that a quick write should not be used to grade grammar and spelling. The point of a quick write is to get the information down quickly, not carefully. (See chapter 8 for other varieties of quick writes.)

Invented Spelling

This is not a strategy only to be used in the early grades. Adults, who are fluent writers, use invented spelling. Their purpose for using them may slightly vary, of course, as older writers have different purposes and habits in writing. The willingness for you to allow your older students to use this strategy just might allow a struggling or reluctant writer in your class to write. We want students to get in the flow of writing. One of the most frustrating things for students to encounter is to have to stop their train of thought because they do not know how to spell a word or cannot think of the exact word. During writing time, we encourage you to allow your students the freedom of using invented spelling on their draft writing papers. Teachers who understand and value the importance of students getting their ideas down on paper do not want them to get hung up on how to spell a word and lose their momentum. Just as young children are encouraged to "sound it out," our students can be encouraged to use invented spelling during the rough draft stage of writing. Spelling corrections and finding "just the right word" can be altered in the editing stage. Students should be encouraged to mark the word in some way, such as underlining or jotting a "sp" for spelling or "wc" for word choice next to the word, so the student remembers to come back to it later.

Playing with Words

Allowing students to be playful with words helps to build their reading vocabulary while enabling them to write more fluidly. In those final minutes at the end of class, why not encourage some purposeful play? One approach is the use of games such as crossword puzzles, Boggle, or modified Scrabble. Students can create an amusing text using playful language. Have them create a short song or write a poem using words you introduced in your content lesson. Have them write a script for a performance to explain a concept, which then can be filmed on a camera phone.

SPEAKING FLUENCY

A fluent speaker is able to express ideas in a coherent and interesting manner. Those students with confidence to speak up in class are improving their speaking fluency. We all know students who never raise their hand and are hesitant to answer when called on. Although teachers should have respect for the introverts in their classroom, it is important to help all students learn how to express themselves through their oral skills.

Sharing podcasts, TED talks (https://www.ted.com/talks/browse), and famous speeches with students provides opportunities to hear speaking fluency modeled. Every student should hear Martin Luther King's "I Have a Dream" speech. Hearing Dr. King speak those words—"I have a dream . . ."—is a great example of a fluent and moving speech. Teachers need to provide feedback to students on their oral speaking abilities and provide guidance on how to improve these skills.

Strategies to Improve Speaking Fluency

Classrooms ought to be a place for talk; it is not the quiet classrooms in which the teacher seems to have all things in order and under control at all times that genuine learning takes place. A space in which students are talking—talking with peers, talking in small or whole group, talking to rehearse or talk out loud an emerging thought, and talking to present a more refined thought—is where vibrant learning resides. Surely, all this talking will be done purposefully, following the rules and guidelines established by the learning community, using the meaningful language that facilitates further learning, and learning the rules of engagement—when and how—for effective expression and communication.

Readers Theater

This power strategy makes an appearance again. This technique provides students with a script, but they are not expected to memorize their lines. Having the script in front of them provides a level of security. Students will reread a readers theater script multiple times in order to get their parts fine-tuned. However, if they know they are going to perform, their interest in rereading and practicing their delivery has an authentic reason. Think creatively in the content areas. Expository texts and informational texts may make the most creative scripts for readers theater with peculiar characters like protons and electrons.

Debates

Teach the principles of debate and involve students in the process of expressing ideas with clarity and conviction. Debates also help develop critical-thinking skills such as analyzing, synthesizing, organizing, and logic.

Speech Competitions

Introduce students to scripts prepared for speech competitions. Many schools participate in speech competitions where the school winners go on to regional and state competitions.

Impromptu Topics

In this activity, teachers provide students with a topic, and they must speak for sixty to ninety seconds about that topic. Create an engaging experience by using "dinner party" topics, conversation starters, or even fortune cookies. "What's your small pleasure?" or "What's something you can't forget?" will generate spontaneous, informal expression of ideas.

Small Group Work

This work provides students with ample opportunities to share their view and argue their points. Too many students lose opportunities to discuss their insights in whole-class discussions.

Presentations

Sharing with others what they have learned is an important process in classrooms. Students need to be shown what makes up a quality presentation and how to use the skills of eye contact and preparing for giving a talk. No one wants to hear someone read a report. The appropriate and effective use of technologies such as PowerPoint and Prezi to support presentations is a skill students may need to master for real-life reasons. Of course, not every presentation needs to be supported by a slide presentation. Helping students to discern when these tools would be useful and how to support their points through powerful visuals and succinct texts are important skills.

Discussion Circles

Engaging students in discussions benefits their learning. Discussion circles, similar to literature circles, refer to the practice of students discussing what they have read with their peers. While literature circles make sense when reading novels or in English class, many times students will find discussing an expository or nonfiction text equally stimulating. Another term, Socratic circle, is a

> formal discussion, based on a text, in which the leader asks open-ended questions. Within the context of the discussion, students listen closely to the comments of others, thinking critically for themselves, and articulate their own thoughts and their responses to the thoughts of others. They learn to work co-operatively and to question intelligently and civilly. (Israel, 2002, p. 89)

Finding books, articles, newspapers, and other texts that bring controversial issues to the classroom help students to state and support their opinions. Also, working in small groups provides more chances for a student to share his or her opinion and participate in reciprocal dialogue.

Take a Position

Introduce a controversial topic to your students such as a "school dress code." Students must choose which position of the argument they support and commit to that position. Some teachers have students move to one side of the room for the con position and the other side for the pro position. Have students list their personal reasons for choosing this position and then move to the other side when a compelling argument changes their opinion on the topic.

LISTENING FLUENCY

Listening can be compared to reading, as both are receptive processes. Like comprehension, listening is an active process of deciphering and understanding, but from an oral, or speaking, source. Although we understand the importance of listening, there has not been much attention given to this area of literacy development by education scholars. Typically, when we think about communication, we tend to think about the delivery or the speaking process, but the entirety of the complete experience needs a receptor (the listener or the reader). Teaching students how to listen is an important life skill, one that we expect students to be able to do. However, we have not developed as thorough a repertoire of strategies as we have for reading, writing, and speaking. Listening expert Rick Bommelje (2013) lists five major purposes of communication:

- social
- informative

- persuasive
- emotional
- entertaining.

"*Social* communication is the small talk of life: weather, news, sports, movies, and all kinds of everyday topics of conversation" (Bommelje, 2013, p. 153). Students participate in daily social communication situations between friends and family. The give and take (speaking and listening) moves back and forth between speakers and listeners. Knowing when to share a comment and when to keep quiet are learned skills usually learned through interactions with peers, family members, and teachers.

"*Informative* communication deals with facts, details, and ideas" (Bommelje, 2013, p. 153). This is typically the communication used in schools. Teachers, through lectures and discussions, introduce students to new concepts, and students need to be receptive to hearing and understanding the messages being delivered. Teachers can help prepare students for listening to new information in many of the same ways they prepare them for comprehending a text passage. Activating prior knowledge helps set the stage for students to hear and understand new terms and ideas.

"*Persuasive* communication involves one person trying to influence someone else" (Bommelje, 2013, p. 153). This is the language used by politicians and commercials as they try to convince their audience to agree with their point of view or spend money on a particular product. A variety of skills needs to be taught to help students listen to and make judgments about persuasive messages. Understanding the source of the persuasive rhetoric will be helpful, such as when a product manufacturer is trying to convince an audience that if they use a product they will be more beautiful or wealthy.

"The *emotional* purpose is about sharing feelings with others, either venting as a speaker, or listening with empathy to someone who is expressing emotion" (Bommelje, 2013, p. 153). The listener's ability to understand the presence of emotion in the speaker's message is essential for communication. When students' preconceived notions of the world are challenged by topics and situations introduced to them in school, it can be an exciting but often scary time. This type of cognitive dissonance is an important, yet uncomfortable, part of having our own beliefs challenged and at times changed.

"Finally, the *entertaining* purpose is speaking and listening to gain pleasure and appreciation" (Bommelje, 2013, p. 153). Enjoyment should be a part of the learning environment. We are enthusiastic about teachers who add the right amount of humor or entertainment to their lessons in order to help students enjoy the learning process. A teacher with a sense of humor may use an anecdote or joke to keep the students' attention on the subject.

Strategies to Improve Listening Fluency

With an abundance of digital tools readily available to both teachers and students, there are many new and exciting ways to foster learning in secondary classrooms. And many of these are specifically created to develop listening and speaking skills. Mobile apps, web-based platforms, video and audio recording devices, tools to insert sound effects or music, and more are creating endless possibilities for creative ways to turn students into producers of digital content.

Audio Books

Many contemporary adolescent books are now professionally recorded for our listening pleasure. Audio books are available in bookstores and can easily be downloaded from iTunes or other digital sites. The professional readers used to record books are typically great models of proficient, fluent reading. It is important to note that students, even secondary students, benefit from a teacher read-aloud. Listening to fluent readers reading texts, or even portions of texts, to students will help to improve their own reading ability.

Podcasting

This updated version of readers theater can be produced and saved to a class website so it can be shared with students' families and friends. There are a multitude of opportunities to create podcasts of your students' work: sharing reports, providing daily newscasts, recording presentations, and more. The importance of allowing students to see and hear themselves reading has been made easy with new technology. The old days of cassette tapes made this process cumbersome and difficult to store and locate at a later time. Encouraging students to practice reading by listening to themselves on a podcast is also one way to document improvements over time.

Note Taking

There are many free note-taking apps available to students; however, note taking can be done simply using paper and pencil. Learning to take notes is not something that comes automatically to all students. Just as modeling and guided practice is important with most things we learn, note taking is a skill that needs explicit teaching and practice to develop. Think about the many tasks are required in good note taking. Students need to listen attentively and determine important points while continuing to listen and write. When you are using a lesson to teach and practice note-taking skills, offer useful frameworks like column notes, outlines, or graphic organizers as a scaffolding tool. Pause often to check understanding. Have students do pair work to compare notes. Share models when necessary. Reviewing what your students have written down as notes during your class may surprise you. What you think you may have emphasized may not be what your students considered important. Be prepared to be reflective about your own teaching in terms of presentation style, communication skills, pacing, and more.

BookTrack

With this free digital tool, students can create soundtracks to accompany a story to create or enhance the mood of the story. The story might be an excerpt of a longer text, a poem, or a script. It can be a story authored by someone else or written by the student.

THEORY TO PRACTICE

While we expect that most of the students you encounter will have already mastered reading fluency by the time they enter your classroom, some will still need your assistance. Keep in mind that as students progress through middle and secondary levels, the level of fluency also rises. What was exceptional for a sixth-grade student might be adequate for a tenth-grade student. All teachers—yes, even content area teachers—need to participate in helping students develop stronger skills in reading, listening, speaking, and writing.

As content area teachers, while you are carefully planning your curriculum, you should think about ways you can support students as they increase their skills in all four areas (reading, writing, listening, and speaking) toward fluency. What assignments can you assign that would help students gain fluency in these areas? How do you organize instruction that supports your students in these areas? Think about how skills in these areas will support their learning or your content area but also support their ability to join the workforce or succeed in college.

REFERENCES

Bommelje, R. (2013). *Listening pays*. Orlando, FL: Leadership & Listening Institute.

Hall, A. K. (1995). Sentencing: The psycholinguistic guessing game. *The Reading Teacher, 49,* 76–77.

Harris, T. L., & Hodges, R. E. (1995). *The literacy dictionary: The vocabulary of reading and writing*. Newark, DE: International Reading Association.

Israel, E. (2002). Examining multiple perspectives in literature. In J. Holden & J. S. Schmit (Ed.), *Inquiry and the literary text: Constructing discussions in the English classroom*. Urbana, IL: National Council of Teachers of English.

Rasinski, T. V. (2003). *The fluent reader: Oral reading strategies for building word recognition, fluency, and comprehension*. New York: Scholastic.

Rasinski, T. V., & Padak, N. D. (2013). *From phonics to fluency: Effective teaching of decoding and reading fluency in the elementary school*. Boston: Pearson.

Samuels, S. J., & Farstrup, A. E. (2006). *What research has to say about fluency instruction*. Newark, DE: International Reading Association.

Vasinda, S., & McLeod, J. (2011). Extending readers theater: A powerful and purposeful match with podcasting. *The Reading Teacher, 64*, 486–87.

8

(Re)Constructing Knowledge

Writing

> In order to own a piece of knowledge—really own it—one must reconstruct it and make it new.
>
> —Wolfe and Reising (1983)

Begging to Write

Ms. Learnard was alone at her desk when I passed by her room. A year before, she had supervised one of my student teachers, and I had been impressed with her mentoring and teaching skills. With no students in sight, I popped in for a quick visit. After about five minutes of chatting, the second-grade children started returning from PE class. I excused myself, but Ms. Learnard encouraged me to stay,

"This is their writing time. Give me just a minute to get them started and we can visit a bit longer."

As the students entered, one boy asked, "What are we doing next?"

Ms. Learnard answered, "It's time for writing!"

I taught writing for fourteen years and never got the response Ms. Learnard received that day. Her boys and girls started high-fiving each other and applauding—*because* it was writing time. I had to see what she did to get this kind of response from her students.

Students began by retrieving their writing folders from the file box in an orderly manner. Some students moved to another table and selected paper from a variety of sizes and colors, some went straight to their desks to work on their story, while others asked a peer to edit their work. Ms. Learnard and I continued to chat as I observed this well-orchestrated event occurring around me.

A few minutes later, I observed a little girl with tears running down her face just over Ms. Learnard's left shoulder. I alerted Ms. Learnard to this, and she called Amy over to her side.

"What's wrong, Amy?"

Amy took a deep breath and began to sob as she spoke. "I (sob) picked (sob, sob) up seven little sheets of paper (sob) to write a seven-page story (sob, sob) and folded them in half, (sob) and stapled them and (sob) it became a fourteen-page book." Amy took another deep breath and continued, "I had enough information to write a seven-page book but (and now she begins to cry even harder) but I don't have enough to write a fourteen-page book!"

Ms. Learnard put her arm around Amy and asked to see her book. Amy handed her the fourteen-page book, and Ms. Learnard took a pair of scissors and cut off the last seven pages. Miraculously, the tears dried up and Amy's face turned from despair to happiness as the smile spread across her face.

Moments later, the timer rang signaling the end of writing time, and the class with one unanimous groan showed their displeasure. Two boys came running toward us, and one dropped to his knees and folded his hands as if in prayer, asking, "Please, please could we have a ten more minutes to write?"

The students from across the room chimed in, and all were requesting to lengthen writing time. I sat in disbelief! My students moaned when I introduced writing, not when it was ending!

Ms. Learnard agreed to ten more minutes. The students cheered and quickly got back to their work. Ms. Learnard recognized the astonishment on my face and told me that once she implemented the writing process, the attitude about writing changed. While she still conducted brief writing lessons, she allowed her students to choose their own writing topics and showed them how to peer edit their work. Each student was responsible for bringing three pieces of writing to the final published stage each month, and in her words, "their writing was impressive."

Writing is a fundamental learning tool. It allows us to *construct* and *reconstruct* knowledge, helping to lock what we know into memory. Many of us experience the marvel of discovering what we know through the process of writing. It is not until the words are on paper that you realize that you know something you did not even think that you knew. The deliberate and conscious attempts to digest and process what we have heard, read, and experienced provide the learner opportunities to internalize knowledge.

As the movement to teach reading and writing in the content areas began to flourish, many content area teachers worried that finding time for writing in their curriculum would take away from the time they had to teach their content. Some were also concerned that incorporating writing would be cumbersome. Many of these concerns have been alleviated after teachers began to see the benefits of writing. One issue that continues to be a concern is that in many teacher education programs, future teachers may not be required to take a course on teaching writing and may therefore lack the confidence to assist and grade their students' writing. In this chapter, we present the importance of students engaging in writing activities and strategies that help to infuse writing in the content areas.

THEORETICAL FOUNDATIONS OF WRITING

When we read we are receiving and making sense of the information presented to us. When we write we are producing information that must make sense to ourselves and to the reader. Writing is a unique and potent form of learning, a "uniquely multi-representational and bi-spheral languaging process that corresponds to other powerful learning strategies" (Emig, 1971, p. 125). When students get the instructional support to improve their *writing* skills, we are providing them with essential *learning* opportunities. According to the National Institute for Literacy (2007), improving one's writing skills improves one's capacity to learn. Writing can also accomplish the following (adapted from Azzolino, 1990):

- helps students to summarize, organize, relate, and associate ideas
- provides an opportunity for students to define, discuss, or describe an idea or concept
- encourages the personalization, assimilation, and accommodation of the content area being taught
- provides an appropriate vehicle for students to express and focus on negative feelings and frustrations as well as to emote and rejoice in the beauty of learning in content areas.

In other words, writing becomes the means for translating the strange into the familiar and the seemingly foreign or new concept into a comprehensible or understandable idea (Grossman, Smith, & Miller, 1993).

Writing is inherently an integrative process, combining the total intellectual capacities of the writer (Risinger, 1987). In this way, the writing process incorporates active and vibrant learning. When students write, it creates a situation in which students must engage in personal learning, shifting the responsibility from the teacher to the student. It is important to reemphasize that students not only express knowledge by writing; they also *discover* knowledge as they write.

The goal in content area classrooms should be for our students to begin to ask,

- What do I think I know?
- Do I know enough to explain this concept?
- How can I represent what I know in a way that is comprehensible to others?

Think about the process of writing—as students write, they begin to understand what they do not know sufficiently or what needs to be clarified in their own head. Writing *requires* students to synthesize information, one of the higher-order thinking skills addressed by Bloom (Bloom, Engelhart, Hill, Furst, & Krathwohl, 1956). As students gather and think about relevant content, they typically will need to review what they remember and add details by going back to the text. This process of reconstructing knowledge through rereading and reflecting on what they know is one of the great learning tools.

WRITING-RICH CLASSROOMS: DEVELOPING WRITERS

Content area teachers are passionate about their content and want to pass this love on to their students. While they may be primarily interested in helping their students understand their content area, they also understand the importance of helping students improve their literacy skills. Using writing tasks to learn content offers students opportunities to develop as writers in a number of different ways: (1) to improve the conventions of writing such as grammar, spelling, and punctuation in the context of writing; (2) to understand and to use the process of writing that includes planning, composing, revising, editing, and publishing for authentic purposes; (3) to effectively use modes of argumentation appropriate for the content area; and (4) to use technical writing appropriate for the content (Yore, 2003). Students learn to write by writing. They need a variety of opportunities to write to serve many different purposes. And the resources that foster a writing-rich classroom environment include, but are not limited to, the following:

- an abundant supply of many authentic texts
- time for discourse and writing to share thoughts, ideas, and beliefs
- planned instruction to enhance specific skills
- frequent activities to engage students to practice writing for various purposes
- students writing individually, with a partner, in a small group
- opportunity to reflect on their writing
- a variety of student responses, short and long.

An integral part of classroom organization is creating an effective structure where students engage in the process of learning in a social environment in which students are offered the opportunity to work as a classroom community (Benninga et al., 1991). This type of environment is enhanced when a teacher organizes their teaching so that students share tasks and work cooperatively. In a caring environment, students are given a voice in the classroom and share in the responsibility of maintaining a productive learning community in which *all* students are learning. This instructional setting creates a more positive and encouraging classroom atmosphere for *writing-as-a-way-of-learning* community. Assisting students in achieving this clarity should be our goal as teachers in content area classrooms.

The Writing Process

Writing is a process with interrelated and overlapping stages—prewriting/planning, drafting, revising, editing, and publishing. Writers move through the writing process in their own unique ways that are often messy, unpredictable, cyclical, and recursive. As you write your draft, you may realize that you did not know enough about the topic, looping you back to prewriting. You research more, plan more, then continue writing, only to realize that this may not be what you wanted to write about in the first place. So you abandon that draft. You select a new topic, prewrite, then write again, this time to complete the first draft, and so on. It is not a linear process.

This way of teaching writing (as a process) contrasts with the product-focused writing experiences that some of you may have experienced as a student. Hopefully, most of you experienced writing as a process, often in conjunction with a writing workshop, which has been in schools for several decades. Donald Murray's (1968) seminal work has been echoed and expanded by writing scholars such as Janet Emig (1971), Donald Graves (1983), Lucy Calkins (1986), and Nancie Atwell (1987), offering both a philosophical orientation and a new framework for teaching writing. These scholars provided teachers with new ways of organizing their classrooms with specific instructional strategies that foster success in creating young writers.

As you observe a group of writers at work involved in the process of writing, you will notice that, first and foremost, they are deeply engaged in writing. You will notice that each writer is working at different stages of the writing process. Your student may be revising work as she confers with the teacher while others in the group are editing with peers or gathering information using the internet before drafting begins, all in attempts to ultimately publish and share their work. Teachers, in promoting process writing, must offer time and conditions for students to write. In addition, they must deliver meaningful instruction in the contexts of their students' writing as they serve as guides and writing mentors.

Writing from a Developmental Perspective

A writer's development takes place over time, and practice plays a crucial role in this continued growth. It is a craft that continues to be mastered throughout our lives. Teachers should provide safe places for young writers to explore and hone their writing abilities. Clear guidance, along with the willingness to discuss and negotiate, helps students learn to do the same. When we position ourselves more as guides and less as gatekeepers, young learners strengthen their writing skills (McClay, 2003).

A diverse group of learners, such as students with special needs, English language learners, and struggling writers, require differentiation of instructional tasks. Yet a vital step in assisting students with special needs to become proficient writers is for them to become a member of the classroom community. In a community of writers, the classroom teacher encourages an atmosphere of cooperation rather than competition and teaches their students to support one another's progress. Study groups and cooperative learning environments can strengthen the learning and contribute to a positive classroom environment for all students, including those with special needs.

Explicit instruction and modeling can be especially supportive for writing success. Some students may need to see a sample of the final product in which teachers call attention to the critical elements, such as organizational structure, before completing the writing task. An equally important strategy is developing vocabulary. By providing a list of core words for a particular unit of study, teachers can facilitate a more positive writing experience.

PROMOTING CONCEPTUAL LEARNING

Teaching concepts becomes more complex in the upper grades. The simplicity of teaching a concept such as a "peninsula" using examples and nonexamples clarifies what a peninsula is for most students rather quickly and easily. Middle grade students are beginning to consider more difficult concepts such as "fairness, political stances, and justice." Conceptual knowledge assists students as they organize ideas, see relationships, and synthesize what they knew (or thought they knew). Teaching concepts requires students to manipulate, categorize, see similarities and differences, make predictions, hypothesize, apply, and create. Common Core State Standards (CCSS) calls this *deep conceptual learning* (DCL)). We believe writing helps students to conceptualize understandings and attain deep conceptual learning.

Imagine a sand sifter as a metaphor for students learning concepts. The student's first attempt at understanding the concept—let's consider the concept of "social justice"—includes their own experiences (and in your typical classroom these will be highly varied), what they already know of the topic, and perhaps what they just read in a chapter of a novel. Their bucket of sand represents their past experiences, past knowledge, the instruction you have just shared with them, the texts they have read, and the conversations with peers all around your specific concept. The act of sifting the sand removes small bits of gravel and shells that remain in the sifter as the sand falls through the holes—the students are making connections in much the same way—they are sifting through the information looking for connections, new bits of information that make sense when added to what they know, and if you are lucky, they may experience "a-ha!" moments of clarity. Once the sand is sifted it is free of debris and ready to be used to create a sand sculpture—or to write about what they now know.

Writing in the content areas allows students to think about concepts and ideas that are forming and evolving in their minds and express them *in their own words*. It is meant to provide meaningful opportunities to process and attempt to remember what they are learning or have learned. Students discover connections, describe processes, organize and clarify emerging understandings, raise questions, and acquire new vocabulary in this type of writing in the content areas. Writing can only be learned by writing. Therefore, as students write in the content areas, they write to learn and learn to write: a beautiful cycle with a multitude of benefits. It is for this reason that we claim writing in the content areas is a necessity.

Writing in the content areas can be represented in two equally important categories: writing to organize and clarify concepts (to *learn*) and writing to explain (to *show*) (table 8.1).

Writing to organize and clarify concepts consists of short, informal, unrehearsed, spontaneous, and usually nonevaluative writing techniques. These

Table 8.1 Two types of content area writing

Type	Examples	Traits
Writing to Organize and Clarify	notes, brainstorming, jottings, lists, pro-con lists, to-do lists, sketches, doodles, diagrams, concept mapping, clustering, journaling, response logs, outlines, plans, free/quick writes	✓ Short ✓ Spontaneous ✓ Exploratory ✓ Informal ✓ Personal ✓ One Draft ✓ Unedited ✓ Ungraded
Writing to Explain	research papers, lab reports, mathematical proofs, proposals, biographies, historical accounts, legal analyses, articles, editorials, reviews, essays, literary criticism, speeches, persuasive essays, letters, fiction writing	✓ Substantial ✓ Planned ✓ Authoritative ✓ Conventional ✓ Audience Centered ✓ Composed ✓ Edited ✓ Assessable and Graded

Adapted from Daniels, Zemelman, & Steineke (2007)

techniques reinforce learning by assisting the student to internalize concepts. Writing to explain is done to demonstrate what has been learned. These techniques are more formal, polished, and can be graded or published for an audience other than the writer. Even though much can be learned from a formal, extended, and public writing approach, writing in the content areas is often developed from the following perspectives: (1) opportunity to organize and clarify concepts; (2) the benefits as a diagnostic tool; and (3) an opportunity to clear up misunderstandings. In turn, this feedback can be used to help teachers become more effective (Drake & Amspaugh, 1994).

Writing to Organize and Clarify Concepts

One of the ultimate goals for learning is for students to *remember* what they learn. According to schema theory, knowledge retained in memory is what is accessible for future learning as well as what can be transferred and applied to other situations. Writing can help students to organize and clarify concepts and promotes the ability to refine and expand their evolving ideas and ultimately retain this knowledge. Daniels, Zemelman, and Steinke (2007) claim that in this type of writing, "We are using writing to find out what's inside our heads, to dump ideas down on a page so we can play with them, move them around, make connections, figure out what's important, cross some out, and highlight others. In other words, we are thinking" (p. 21).

Writing to organize and clarify is often in the form of a classroom activity, and it can serve as an informal assessment tool for a quick check for understanding. These initial writing attempts should be considered drafts as they reflect the initial thoughts of the writer on the topic. Frequently, these drafts are never read by anyone other than the writer and the teacher, and there is no need for further development. There are instances when a writer may choose to extend a piece of writing, but generally students do not revise and edit them other than aiding in their learning. While the ultimate goal is for students to develop conceptual understanding and retention of new ideas, we would argue that in these frequent and informal writing opportunities students *learn* to write.

Journal writing is one of the easiest forms of writing to implement in content area classrooms. Fulwiler (2000) has written extensively about the usefulness of student journals as the "heart" of a schoolwide literacy program: "Journal writing works because every time a person writes an entry, instruction is individualized. The significance of journals as records of thought cannot be under-estimated by teachers who value independent thinking. The journal records the student's individual travel through the academic world; at the same time it serves well when formal papers or projects need to be written" (Fulwiler, 2000, pp. 16 & 18).

A word of caution about "overjournaling" students: we recommend orchestrating the amount of time students spend journal writing between all of their other courses in the language arts, science, social studies, and mathematics classrooms. Too much journaling can be overwhelming to students.

Double-entry log is an adaptation of the response journal using a two-column format that allows the student to record double entries that are conceptually related. Double-entry logs can be used in a variety or ways. One way to use a double-entry log is for students to record the main idea from their text and then record findings to support the main ideas (table 8.2). Some content area teachers find that providing students with a double-entry journal helps them by having them list the main headings from their reading on the left and asks students to fill in what they learned from those sections on the right.

Dialectical journals can be written in many ways, but they generally have the same format as double-entry logs. These journals are meant to aid in analysis and encourage metacognitive processes. They are flexible and can be used in any content area. In the left-hand column, students record facts (e.g., this could be a summary of an article, observations about an experiment, historical details, or steps in a mathematical equation). In the right-hand column, students write their reactions, thoughts, questions, and conclusions concerning the factual material in the left column.

Response/prompt journals. Some students will need a word, a picture, a phrase, a question, a short scenario, or open-ended expressions to kick-start, spark, inspire, or motivate their writing. Prompts to promote journal writing include the following: Yesterday I learned . . .; What I am finding hardest right now is . . .; So far in this class . . .; The main idea in today's lesson . . .; and Write all you can about _____.

A seventh-grade student is prompted with "How would you describe mathematics?" Her response is provided below:

Table 8.2 Double-entry log

Main ideas from the text	Ideas that support the main ideas
Matter's physical properties can be explained in terms of its particulate nature.	Described by its measurements of it mass, volume, and density. Made up of tiny particles in constant motion; physical state determined by the arrangement and motion of its particles. State and behavior of matter explained by the nature of its particles and the particles' energy.
Matter can be described and classified as elements, compounds, and mixtures.	

If math were a sound, I think it would be of a stream gurgling.

The reason I do is this. You have your basic math: addition, subtraction, multiplication, and division. This type of math might be represented by the main stream. Now other little streams feed into this which is like the more detailed math which starts off and builds upon your basics.

As the math gets harder and harder, with more and more details, that gets into the sound of rivers, which are louder than basic streams. If you even kept on going further with harder math, sometimes it gets so loud and so many steps that it might even be the sound of the ocean crashing against the beaches; kind of a threatening sound. That is why I think math is the sound of a stream gurgling. (NCTM with J. K. Stenmark, 1991)

Project journal is a valuable tool for documentation of students' work during a particular assignment. These entries can include brainstorming, calculations, notes, internet searches, sketches, data collections, observations, and more. A few examples of project journals include the following: science fair projects, demonstration of a mathematical principle, and a record of place, people, and culture during a particular time period.

Quick writes , they are designed to give students the opportunity to reflect on their learning or to stimulate their thinking with short, open-ended statements. Quick writes can be used at the beginning, middle, or end of a lesson and are intended to take only a few moments. Students are encouraged to let their thoughts flow without concern for mechanics or revisions. This type of writing is one-draft writing for reflecting, generating ideas, asking questions, or to activate prior knowledge. Research (Mason, Kubina, Kostewicz, Cramer, & Datchuk, 2013) supports that students who received instruction in quick writing improved their writing in organizational and persuasive quality. Quick writes can be used for preassessment to gather initial information about the level of skill and/or knowledge students possess prior to instruction.

The *one-minute paper* is a variation of a quick write. It is a short, openended, and flexible form of prewriting or brainstorming, and it works well at the beginning or ending of the class. Also, this strategy can be used as a variation for Think-Pair-Share. An example is asking what was learned in class today, as shown in this example:

Fractions are part of a whole. There are three parts to a fraction—the numerator, denominator, and the dividing bar. One fraction can be named in more than one way, 1/4 = 2/8. Fractions can be added, subtracted, multiplied, and divided. Fractions are related to percentages as they are pieces to a whole.

—Jake, a middle school student

Discussion question generator. Instead of asking students to respond to a prompt or teacher-created question, ask students to write questions to promote classroom participation. The types of questions students generate shows their understanding of the content. As teachers we gain insights from listening to and reading students' questions. This technique can also lead to observing misconceptions and discovering emerging trends in multiple students' perceptions.

Entrance/Exit Slips. This learning-to-write technique eases the students into writing with just a few sentences at the beginning (entrance) or at the end (exit) of the class. Entrance slips help to focus students' attention on the topic for the day and to access prior knowledge. Exit slips help to assess the learning for the day and to determine if there were any misconceptions. Sticky notes, index cards, and half sheets of paper work well as entrance/exit slips.

Note taking requires students to identify what is important about the knowledge they are learning and then state that knowledge in their own words. There is no one correct way to take notes; variations include arrows, bullets, underlining, doodles, and more. Different students will prefer different formats, so presenting a variety of formats is recommended.

Column notes. Recording important points from the class discussion engages the students and forces them to listen actively. Personal notes are more easily remembered than simply reading the text. Writing class notes helps students to remember the content, and the notes are available when it is time to review for a test. Taking good notes is a skill that students will need to be successful in high school and college. Worksheets can be prepared to guide students' note-taking skills, such as column notes (table 8.3).

Outlines. In an outline, students indicate major ideas and their related points (figure 8.1). They can further organize the information by using roman numerals (I, II, III), followed by the next indention with capital letters (A, B, C), then numbers (1, 2, 3) and small-case letters (a, b, c).

Summarizing worksheet. After students have read a section of a text, prompt students to synthesize what they learned (figure 8.2). This is an example from *I Am Regina*, by Sally Keehn (2001).

Table 8.3 Sample column notes

Methods of Traveling	Examples of Seeds	Why do you think the seed travels this way?
Travels with animals and people	Prickly seeds, burrs, or seeds with hooks travel with animals and people (sticklight, burdock, Queen Anne's lace).	They stick to fur or clothes to be carried away and eventually dropped and planted.

Figure 8.1 Outline of chapter.

I. The Changing Earth

A. Position of Earth's continents has changed
  1. Once one large landmass
  2. Earth's crust and upper mantle composed of plates that fit together
  3. Sea floor spreads away from crack in the crust

B. The theory of plate tectonics

1. Moved by convection current in Earth's mantle

Figure 8.2. Summarizing worksheet.

I Am Regina Worksheet

The Indians used sweat lodges. How are they like saunas?
Regina has difficulty retaining her identity. What are the touchstones of her former life?
Explain how the Indians gathered and refined maple syrup.

Writing breaks. In a given interval of time (e.g., five, seven, or ten minutes), the teacher pauses to provide time for students to record their thoughts. What would they like to note and remember? What questions do they have? In table 8.4, the writing breaks have specific prompts to synthesize information.

Numerical autobiography. A unique approach to writing an autobiography is a numerical autobiography, a playful approach to the role numbers can play in our lives. An example of a numeric autobiography (translated from Spanish) written by sixth-grade student Yaneiri Gonzalez, from *Escuela de la Comunidad: Antonio Velez Alvarado in Manatí, Puerto Rico*, follows.

Numbers in My Life

Table 8.4 Writing Breaks

Writing Breaks
Writing Break: In your own words, describe a parabola.
Writing Break: What features do you note in all parabolas?
Writing Break: What question do you have about parabolas?

I was born on August 5, 1984. It was the 8th month of the year, with summer in all its splendor. This means that I am nearly 12 years old, over 6 of which I have spent in school. I can tell you that I weigh 77 pounds, but don't quite reach 5 feet in height.

My immediate family has 4 members. My dad is 30 years old, my mom is 28, and my sister is 6. On my mother's side, I am the oldest of her children. On my father's side, I am the second of 3.

The favorite meal in our house is beef steak with white rice and red kidney beans, but my favorite meal is rice with green peas. My mom, Janet, tells me that when it comes to food, I am like a reptile who can shed its skin a hundred times and that my stomach is infinite.

When I grow up I want to be a judge or a marine biologist in order to see the infinite that is life. Source: www.orillas.org/math/tour/tour/tourdescriptive.html.

Social studies autobiography. Students can write their social studies autobiography in response to such prompts as: What were you doing on a major date in history? What happened in history on your birthday? What happened today in history? There are numerous websites (e.g., http://www.historychannel.com/) where students can enter their birthday and are presented with information such as the top song, headlines, famous people's birthdays, and more. These sites make excellent warm-up writing activities to help open up creative thinking and facilitate students' enthusiasm for history.

Collaborwrites are designed to give students an opportunity to write collectively and to actively move around the classroom. Students at the middle and secondary levels enjoy collaborative opportunities because it provides a bit of physical activity as students work collaboratively. This is the kinesthetic learning style and known as do-ers or tactile learners.

Snowball. Snowball is a cooperative learning strategy that is effective for reviewing information, summarizing and orally expressing facts and information, while providing interaction with peers, physical activity, and motivation. Students are encouraged to take greater responsibility for their own learning and to learn from one another. Students write a key point or brief summary of a key concept and then wad up the paper into a snowball. They form a circle and "toss their snowballs!" Each student picks up a snowball, opens it, and discusses the information on the paper with a neighbor. The above steps can be repeated several times with "no talking," so that the student makes eye contact with a classmate and then tosses the snowball to that person. Snowballing can also be done without throwing the snowball. If the paper gets exchanged between partners, we call this Swap Talk. When circulating the paper to the right or the left at each turn, we call it Pass It On. At the core, these versions all share the spirit of collaborative and collective writing.

Carousel brainstorming. Students rotate around the classroom in small groups, stopping at various stations for a designated amount of time. While at each station, students will activate their prior knowledge of different topics or different aspects of a single topic through discourse and writing with peers. Ideas shared will be posted at each station for all groups to read. Through movement, conversation, and writing, prior knowledge will be activated, providing scaffolding for new information to be learned in the proceeding lesson activity (Lipton & Wellman, 1998).

Cognitive organizers, which are concept organizers, nonlinguistic representations, or concept maps, are graphical representations of relationships between and among terms or concepts. There are many variations for how concept maps can be designed. The benefits for students are the cognitive process of constructing meaning and making sense by consciously or subconsciously integrating these new ideas and their existing knowledge. Concept maps provide students with the opportunity to think about connections, organize their thoughts, and reflect on their understanding (Vanides, Yin, Tomita, & Ruiz-Primo, 2005).

Writing to Explain

Explanatory writing in content area classrooms is typically more formal writing or extended selections of writing. These expository products or informational writings are examples of students' best writing. Often, this type of writing is a "published" piece or one that the student feels he or she is ready to deliver to the public or to the teacher. Published denotes the process of producing a public version of a text and to recognize the importance of developing the sense of pride as part of the process of learning to write.

The general principles that characterize explanatory writing include the following: (1) it focuses on the idea or object being explained rather than on the writer's beliefs and feelings; (2) it often, not always, states its objective early in what might be called an informational thesis; and (3) it presents information systematically and logically (Fulwiler & Hayakawa, 2000).

Students are asked to write essays and papers to show what they have learned. These formal writing activities are expected to be written with care and precision to convey what they have learned in a coherent manner, free of grammatical errors. (Of course, the higher the level of schooling, the fewer grammatical and spelling errors would be expected.) Students should be expected to write for "real-world situations." These types of assignments are motivating to students and provide them some reasons for making sure their manuscripts are neat, orderly, and error free. Bean, Chappell, and Gillam (2003) emphasize the need for students to write for authentic purposes with a specific audience in mind (table 8.5). The audience can be the teacher who will be grading the assignment across the spectrum to an unknown audience that might read a piece of writing in a journal or writing competition. Writing

Table 8.5 Real world writing purposes

Purpose	Explanation	Examples
Express and Reflect	Expresses or reflects on his or her own life and experiences Often looks backward in order to look forward	Memoir, biography, letter, obituary
Inform and Explain	States a main point and purpose Tries to present the information in a surprising way	Brochure, manual, recipe
Evaluate and Judge	Focuses on the worth of person, object, idea, or other phenomenon Usually specifies the criteria to the object being seen as "good" or "bad"	Book or movie review, consumer product review, performance review
Inquire and Explore	Wrestles with a question or problem Hooks with the problem and lets the reader watch the wrestle with it	Letter to the editor, essay exam, letter to a business owner
Analyze and Interpret	Seeks to analyze and interpret phenomena that are difficult to understand or explain	Scientific reports, explaining graphs and pie charts
Take a Stand/ Propose a Solution	Seeks to persuade audiences to accept a particular position on a controversial issue Describes the problem, proposes and solution, and provides justification.	Editorial, Op-ed, proposal, letter to a legislator, speech to run for office, letter to a business

Adapted from Bean, Chappell, and Gillam (2003) as cited in Gallagher (2011)

for real purposes has the added benefit of students seeing that their work has made a difference—even if it is only a response from a member of Congress or a response from a city official to a proposal the students have crafted to solve a local problem.

Often teachers will support this type of writing by providing the students with rubrics outlining the expectations of the assignment when it is assigned. Communicating clear expectations for the students helps students to understand the teacher's expectations and thus turn in better writing materials. Rubrics should also guide the classroom teacher in determining a grade for the writing assignment.

Letters, such as social action letters, provide a purpose, voice, and an audience for writers. In social action or political letter writing, students craft persuasive letters to real audiences outlining problems and proposing solutions. Through this process they learn to incorporate evidence into a written argument about a concern from their own community and then send it to a real person or policymaker. When students are writing letters with a real purpose, they develop a sense of empowerment. Something as simple as having your students write letters to the author of the book they are reading can create an immense amount of excitement.

An *essay* is a piece of writing on any given topic such as an editorial, a feature story, a critical study, even an excerpt from a book. An excellent example of an essay is an eighth-grader responding to a prompt in an application for the Honors, Advanced Placement, or International Baccalaureate in history, English, or mathematics program. The student is engaged in all the stages of the writing process and is clearly aware who will be reading the essay (audience) as the extended selection of writing is prepared. The publication stage is when the teacher in history, English, and mathematics departments read the essay.

RAFT. A writing strategy whose purpose is to make writing feel more authentic in the content areas and to inspire more thoughtful writing is the RAFT writing assignment. Students respond to classroom questions by writing from different viewpoints—Role, focusing on their Audience, making decisions on the Format, and responding to a particular Topic.

THEORY TO PRACTICE

As students attempt to document what they know in their own words, much is required of them. They must gauge what they know and identify what is most important to remember. They must synthesize what they have heard or read into succinct and powerful statements with an economy of words. They must use new words that stand for brand-new concepts they have just learned in ways that demonstrate new understanding. They must catch when their writing does not make sense, then articulate a different statement with clarity. All of these require higher-order, critical-thinking skills. During these thinking processes, their thoughts, insights, and understanding will take on a new form, and these changes will continue to evolve. Writing is both an essential learning tool and a craft that needs cultivation.

REFERENCES

Atwell, N. (1987). *In the middle: Writing, reading, and learning with adolescents.* Portsmouth, NH: Heinemann.

Azzolino, A. (1990). Writing as a tool for teaching mathematics: The silent revolution. In T. J. Cooney & C. R. Hirsh (Eds.). *Teaching and learning mathematics in the 1990s* (pp. 92–100). Reston, VA: NCTM.

Bean, J. C., Chappell, V. A., & Gillam, A. M. (2003) *Reading rhetorically.* New York: Longman.

Benninga, J. S., Tracz, S. M., Sparks, R. K., Jr., Solomon, D., Battistich, V., Delucchi, K. L., Sandoval, R., & Stanley, B. (1991). Effects of two contrasting school tasks and incentive structures on children's social development. *The Elementary School Journal, 92,* 149–68.

Bloom, B. S., Engelhart, M. D., Hill, W. H., Furst, E. J., & Krathwohl, D. R. (1956). *Taxonomy of educational objective: Cognitive domain.* New York: Longman.

Calkins, L. M. (1986). *The art of teaching writing.* Portsmouth, NH: Heinemann.

Daniels, H., Zemelman, S., & Steineke, N. (2007). *Content-area writing every teacher's guide.* Portsmouth, NH: Heinemann.

Drake, B. M., & Amspaugh, L. B. (1994). What writing reveals in mathematics. *Focus on Learning Problems in Mathematics, 16*(3), 43–50.

Emig, J. (1971). *The composing processes of twelfth graders.* Urbana, IL: National Council of Teachers of English.

Fulwiler, T. (Ed.). (2000). *The journal book.* Portsmouth, NH: Boynton/Cook.

Fulwiler, T., & Hayakawa, A. R. (2000). *The Blair handbook* (3rd ed.). Upper Saddle River, NJ: Prentice Hall.

Gallagher, K. (2011). *Write like this: Teaching real-world writing through modeling and mentor texts.* Portland, ME: Stenhouse.

Graves, D. H. (1983). *Writing: Teachers & children at work.* Portsmouth, NH: Heinemann.

Grossman, F. J., Smith, B., & Miller, C. (1993). Did you say "write" in mathematics class? *Journal of Developmental Education, 17*(1), 2–6.

Keehn, S. (2001). *I Am Regina.* New York: Puffin.

Lipton, L., & Wellman, B. (1998). *Pathways to understanding: Patterns and practices in the learning-focused classroom.* Guilford, VT: Pathways Publishing.

Mason, L. H., Kubina Jr., R., Kostewicz, D. E., Cramer, A. M., & Datchuk, S. (2013). Improving quick writing performance of middle-school struggling learners. *Contemporary Educational Psychology, 38,* 236–46.

McClay, J. K. (2003). Engaging reluctant adolescent writers with contemporary literacy: Untangling two knots. In S. Peterson (Ed.), *Untangling some knots in K–8 writing instruction.* Newark, DE: International Reading Association.

Murray, D. M. (1968). *A writer teaches writing: A typical method of teaching composition.* Boston: Houghton Mifflin.

National Council of Teachers of Mathematics. (1991). *Mathematics assessment: Myths, models, good questions, and practical suggestions.* J. K. Stenmark (Ed.). Reston, VA: The Council.

National Institute for Literacy. (2007). *What content-area teachers should know about adolescent literacy.* Retrieved from http://www.nifl.gov.

Oklahoma Writing Project. https://mrbchs.wikispaces.com/Writing+Process+Notes.

Risinger, C. F. (1987). Improving writing skills through social studies. Opinion Paper. (ERIC Document Reproduction Series No. ED285829).

Vanides, J., Yin, Y., Tomita, M., & Ruiz-Primo, M. A. (2005). Using concept maps in the science classroom. *Science Scope, 28*(8), 27–31.

Wolfe, D., & Reising, R. (1983). *Writing for learning in the content areas*. Portland, ME: J. Weston Walch.

Yore, L. D., II. (2003). Quality science and mathematics education research: Considerations of argument, evidence, and generalizability [Guest Editorial]. *School Science and Mathematics, 103*, 1–7.

Engaging with Texts and Peers

Discussion

Discussion is an exchange of knowledge; an argument an exchange of ignorance.

—Robert Quillen

Organized Chaos

I may have been a contender for valedictorian if my teachers had a better understanding of the social aspects of learning in my elementary through high school days. Growing up in the 1960s and 1970s, learning was quiet and individual. Collaborating was cheating, and talking would earn you a detention—I earned plenty!

Even when I was a brand new teacher in 1978, I was told when the principal made his tours around the school he would be most impressed if all my students were sitting quietly at their desks working diligently on a worksheet. When I finally got the courage to allow my classes to be more collaborative and engaged in learning, I was the outlier in my school. One of my accomplishment for which I am most proud is a unit on newspapers I designed for my sixth-grade language arts students.

I clearly remember the moment when I looked up and saw my principal, Mr. Hummel, leaning against my classroom door with a huge smile on his face. My class was not quiet by any stretch of the imagination, and only a few students were working independently. Mr. Hummel saw a group of three students arguing over which article should be the lead article in the next class-produced newspaper, he saw two students charting the temperature and weather conditions in their newspaper folders, he saw students being responsible for grading their peers' completed assignments, and he saw students helping each other to find the different sections of a newspaper to complete their scrapbooks. There was a pile of used and not-very-neat newspapers in the center of the room that had been donated by the Newspapers in Education program. These students were engaged, socially involved, and in a vibrant learning atmosphere.

Mr. Hummel confessed to me later that afternoon that he had come to my classroom to ask me to have the students "hold it down." Because I hadn't seen him when

> he entered my room, he stopped and observed. He told me that he didn't have a clue how I got thirty-two sixth-graders so enthusiastic about newspapers, but he couldn't find a single student "not working."
> That was the moment the smile came across his face.

Decades before the authors of this text became teachers, a visionary educator by the name of John Dewey (1939) described a vastly different approach to teaching. Dewey imagined classroom instruction in a more relaxed atmosphere, where students would work collaboratively to solve problems instead of working in the competitive learning environment that was then the norm. Dewey also suggested that schools should teach subjects relevant to the students' lives and interests. When we began our teaching careers, a quiet classroom, where all students were sitting facing forward in their desks working on worksheets, was often considered to be a well-run class; it was apparent the teacher was in control. While it took decades for Dewey's ideas to filter down into the way we actually teach, Dewey's ideas are the foundation for teaching from a constructivist, sociocultural, and collaborative approach.

Research on the use of book clubs, literature circles, and Socratic seminars was one of the efforts that spawned a renewed interest in discussion-based and collaborative learning groups. Eldredge and Butterfield's (1986) research shows that collaborative learning motivates students, and the social interactions actually have a positive impact on student learning. (Imagine all those years wasted by making sure students did not talk to each other!)

Collaborative learning is not as simple as merely putting students in groups to do work traditionally done individually. Effective group work takes careful planning on the teacher's part. In fact, if group work is not planned, it can have a detrimental effect on some students. According to Blumenfeld, Marx, Soloway, and Krajcik (1996), unplanned group work "can stigmatize low achievers, exacerbate status differences, and create dysfunctional interactions among students" (p. 37). Knowing that no teacher wants to have a negative effect on student learning, we designed this chapter to help you structure learning experiences that embrace the use of social interactions when you teach.

THEORETICAL FOUNDATIONS OF DISCUSSION-BASED LEARNING

In chapter 1, constructivist and sociocultural philosophies of learning were defined, and we explained why we believed they were the foundation for collaborative learning in content areas. You may want to learn more about the theories of Vygotsky, Bruner, Dewey, and Rosenblatt as we are building on their theoretical foundations.

One of the reasons teachers have embraced collaborative learning experiences is the transition that has been taking place over the last few decades. Teaching has gone from the traditional teacher-led instruction, where the teacher was responsible for student learning, to student led, where students take on more responsibility for their own learning. While the teacher is still the director, coach, guide, or facilitator to student learning, they are no longer considered to be the sole person in the room with the knowledge and the answers. Years ago, learning was envisioned as a teacher pouring knowledge through a funnel into the head of a student.

A truly collaborative classroom, in which the teacher guides instruction and encourages students to be more participatory than passive, is an exciting place to teach and to learn. When given the responsibility to read, respond, discuss, and make meaning from texts through discussions with their peers, students read with a different lens: now, they must create the questions and lead the discussions, two skills that are amply appropriate.

Collaborative and discussion-based learning enhances a students' literacy development and understanding of content in three ways: (1) authentic literacy experiences provide opportunities for wide and varied reading; (2) engaged readers are more involved in discussions; and (3) mixed-ability groups are effective and promote communities of learners. In the next sections, we will share common elements in discussion circles that research has shown to be effective. Even though the research stems from a literature circle approach, we believe that the finding also describes the benefits of discussion circles as a collaborative and discussion-based classroom experience.

ELEMENTS OF DISCUSSION CIRCLES

We are confident that what we have learned about literature circles, typically done in elementary and middle grades English or literature classrooms using parts of novels, transfers easily to the secondary content areas. Discussion circles, our broader model of literature circles, use authentic literature, both novels and nonfiction texts, to supplement and support student learning in middle-grade content area classrooms. Maintaining the spirit of literature circles and other similar instructional models that honor student-led, discussion-based collaborative experiences, discussion circles offer rich discourse using a wide variety of texts that support content learning.

Discussion circles can be organized around (1) one nonfiction text; (2) a comparison of two (or more) nonfiction texts; or (3) a paired text set of a nonfiction text with a fiction text. Among the three, the third element—paired text—is the most compelling for supporting learning in the content areas. Examples of paired texts will be presented later in this chapter. If you are using a textbook for your content area, it can serve as the expository text. Pairing that with a novel or short story about the event, discovery, or person involved is a great way to expand upon the topic.

Authentic Experiences

Discussion circles can be used across *all* content areas. At the core, a discussion circle is based on a common authentic text being read and discussed in small groups. A variety of texts may also be provided to the students in one class. Small group discussions using one or more texts can evolve into a whole class discussion that allows students to share interesting ideas and concepts explored in the various books, perhaps from multiple perspectives.

Gaining insight from multiple perspectives is an intellectual practice that must be present in all content area classrooms. This may be especially true in social studies; imagine the richness of teaching about Christopher Columbus from multiple perspectives. One perspective would come from the social studies textbook, and another may be represented by a chapter from Loewen's (1995) *Lies My Teacher Told Me*. Another approach may be a theme-based topic such as World War II, where students are given the opportunity to choose from multiple resources, including informational texts and novels selected by the teacher (for example, Steve Sheinkin's *Bomb: The Race to Build—and Steal—the World's Most Dangerous Weapon* or Graham Salisbury's *Under the Blood-Red Sun*). Students form discussion circles based on the text(s) chosen. Classes can then meet as a whole to discuss the different perspectives of World War II represented in the various texts. Imagine the added dimension to students' understanding of multiple perspectives that will ultimately help them become more critical thinkers. From students' understanding of multiple perspectives, rigorous debate may begin, and their assumptions may be challenged. Authors' biased views on a topic may be revealed. If the multiple perspectives also include a span of time (e.g., similar events from various time periods), students will identify patterns in history.

Texts used in discussion circles can be broadly defined. Rather than traditional texts, consider sharing an artistic interpretation of the event such as a short story, music from the time period, or artwork depicting the historical event. Such additions to your curriculum could be used to ignite a discussion on these topics. Students read or examine the material assigned and reflect on what they have learned. Each student can prepare to share his thoughts, ideas, and questions to show his understanding of the material and the variety of perspectives that are presented. Great discussions do not emerge when everyone is in agreement; differences of opinion help to create great discussions.

Authentic Texts

Fielding, Wilson, and Anderson's (1984) review of primary-grade basals note that their stories had fewer plot complications, less character development, and less conflict among and within characters than authentic texts. It stands to reason that the same kinds of problems might be found in upper-level textbooks. Even though textbooks have improved greatly over the last decades, many still focus on reading passages and completing worksheets. In addition, space limitations in textbooks prevent deeper, expansive presentation of any one topic.

Teachers can supplement the textbooks used in their field with authentic texts such as current news and magazine articles, websites, short stories, novels, and information books. The use of authentic texts, with their focused and substantive treatment of topics, should help to improve student achievement by providing students with engaging texts that are challenging and thought provoking.

Literacy educational researchers have focused attention on the benefits provided to students when they read and discuss real or authentic literature. As discussed in chapter 6, authentic texts are texts that are not superficially created for student instructional purposes and include items such as a magazine article, picture book, short story, brochure, informational text, or novel, to name just a few. Goodman, Freeman, Murphy, and Shannon (1988) describe authentic literature as natural texts that have not been altered to meet grade-level specifications by altering vocabulary words or by modifying the structure of the story. They report that the real literature is richer in vocabulary and in story structure than contrived basals or reading textbooks. Goodman and his colleagues felt it was imperative that students be introduced to authentic vocabulary and story structures (and we would add expository text structures and discipline-specific vocabulary) in order to advance their literacy skills.

Bringing authentic texts into the classroom does not guarantee that students will experience what Dewey (1939) called "educative" experiences. In Wellman's (2000) study of three teachers' first experiences teaching using literature circles, she noted that these teachers "basalized" (Goodman et al., 1988) the authentic texts. As each of them began to implement literature circles with their classes, they turned the authentic literature into the same kinds of traditional reading instruction they were accustomed to in basals, characterized by "strong teacher direction, vocabulary lessons, skill worksheets, and questions at the end of the chapter" (Hill, Johnson, & Noe,

1995, p. 212; Zarillo, 1989). They broke the texts into specific pages to be read, assigned specific vocabulary words to be learned, and developed or borrowed skill sheets to go along with the texts. Although they were using authentic literature, they were not providing students with authentic literacy experiences. Instead, much of the time, they were instituting "collaborative seatwork," a term coined by Nystrand, Gamoran, and Heck (1993) to describe group activities that were in reality the same kinds of questions that came down to the one "right answer" the teacher was expecting students to supply. Authentic literacy experiences require teachers to rethink and reflect on the many ways they can provide students with authentic learning experiences.

Discussion circles should be structured around texts written to support content area instructional purposes. Morrow (1992) shows a link between the texts students read and their own language development. She notes that students exposed to authentic texts "tend to develop sophisticated language structures, including vocabulary and syntax" (p. 251). Echoff's (1983) findings agree with Morrow and show that students who read authentic literature wrote more sophisticated sentences. We recognize the impact of using authentic texts on students' language, literacy, and writing development and support the notion of providing instruction that stretches students' vocabulary, helps them to comprehend sophisticated text structures, and improves their writing abilities.

The key to success using discussion circles is in providing instructional activities to help students prepare to take a more active role in their learning. Students who have only experienced classrooms where they answered the teacher's questions may struggle with developing their own questions for their peers. Students may need assistance in the beginning in learning how to recognize important elements such as new vocabulary, how the information connects to ideas and concepts they have previously learned, how to prepare thoughtful questions, and which graphic organizer is the right one.

Engaged Readers

A second way discussion circles show promise in linking constructivist and sociocultural theory to practical classroom experiences is by developing engaged readers. Wilhelm (1997) describes engaged readers as those students who have "entered a book" (p. 56). He outlines what it means to be able to enter a story, to relate to the problems of the characters, to feel the emotions, and to "project themselves into the story world" (p. 56). Guthrie (1996) states that viewing students as engaged readers is a "shift in perspective" (p. 434) for both teachers and parents. This shift has impacted the way teachers plan instruction for their students who are now more active participants in their learning.

Engaged readers make connections to the text that stay with them longer. Raphael and McMahon (1994) studied fifth-grade students' level of connection to novels they had read in the previous year. The students' ability to recall and describe stories they had read is an indication of the level of engagement students attained with the books. According to their study, "Students remembered 9 of the 16 books they had read the previous year. In contrast, the students who had been in a commercial textbook program could not recall titles, authors, or stories from their pervious year's instruction" (p. 115). This study points to the high level of engagement students realize when they use authentic texts.

The authors of this text believe in the emotional connections we make when we read authentic texts, like historical novels. Important information from the text stays with us because we make connections with the characters, and in essence, the characters become our friends. We, the readers, are able to experience the challenges as the characters are brought to life. Students may read the facts behind World War II in their social studies textbook, but when they are sitting on a fence in Hawaii beside the main character in *Under the Blood-Red Sun* as he describes the planes flying in his direction, students develop a different perspective. The historical events are felt, sometimes with an emotional jolt, not simply read as dates and events on a page.

Rosenblatt's (1978) transactional theory of reading inspired teachers to provide instruction that assisted students in making personal meaning from texts. The author of a text has the responsibility to the reader to describe and explain as clearly as possible, but each reader brings his or her own background knowledge to the reading, which provides varied interpretations of what the author intended the reader to understand. A reader who has never seen snow cannot imagine a scene created by an author in the same way as someone who has experienced the beauty and quiet of freshly fallen snow.

Keene and Zimmermann (1997) found that comprehension improved when students make connections with the texts. They provide three ways students connect to what they read: (1) text-to-self; (2) text-to-text; and (3) text-to-world. Text-to-self are personal connections a student might make with a character, the situation a character finds themselves in, or even a setting. One of our students described herself as a nonreader until she came across *Life on the Mississippi* by Mark Twain. The fact that she lived in a house facing the river was a personal connection that intrigued her to read her first novel. Text-to-text are connections or comparisons between two books or texts. The reader may remember a similar situation or character from another story. Finally, text-to-world are connections made between the text and the reader's worldly experiences, such as from a television program, lesson from another class, or a situation they saw on the news. By the time students reach middle school they should have more text-to-text and text-to-world connections be-cause of their experiences reading a variety of materials.

We would argue that Keene and Zimmermann may need to add one more text connection for students using expository texts in discussion circles. Text-to-schema are connections made by seeing how new information fits with previously learned knowledge. With the guidance of a teacher, sometimes students have to unlearn previously learned information or be helped to see how what they are learning now connects with something they have previ-ously learned.

Mixed-Ability Groups

Discussion circles provide an opportunity for teachers to rely on mixed-ability groups instead of ability groups. While the authors of this text value the use of ability grouping in some situations—it is difficult to teach division to students who still have not mastered adding and subtracting—we also see the benefits to students who experience working with more and less knowledgable peers.

Becoming a Nation of Readers (Anderson, Hiebert, Scott, & Wilkinson, 1985) directed criticism toward the practice of ability grouping and encouraged educators to pursue alternatives to this practice. Studies by Allington and Wamsley (1997) provided insight into the dramatically different styles in which students in different reading groups were being taught to read. Instead of more intense, sustained reading activities for the lower-ability groups, these students were assigned shorter, less complex reading and spent most of their time focused on decoding and oral reading exercises. Students who struggle understanding mathematical, scientific, or historical concepts may find themselves in similar situations. One of the criticisms of content area reading textbooks, like social studies and science, is that the books are sometimes written with vocabulary and reading levels several years above the grade level they are intended to serve. Supplementing authentic literature, both fiction and nonfiction, in content reading areas may provide needed aca-demic support and scaffolding for these students.

Keegan and Shrake (1991) examined their students' responses as they experimented with heterogeneous grouping. When they first began supplementing their basal reading program with authentic literature, they continued to "select each novel for the different ability groups" (p. 543). After exploring Calkins's (1986) idea of a "workshop approach," they implemented a "community of readers" approach and began heterogeneous groups of lit-erature study. Keegan and Shrake (1991) claimed:

> Among all the positive outcomes of our program, images of students' enthu-siasm pop up . . . Alan shouting, "Wow! Where did you find that? Can I read

it next?" . . . Jeff privately reading a book he is afraid his group will not get to before June. That is what reading is all about. (p. 547)

Smith (1988) describes seven characteristics found in classrooms using literature circles. He noted that the learning was always meaningful, useful, continual and effortless, incidental, collaborative, vicarious, and free of risk (p. 11). Even though traditional methods have expected students to work and be evaluated independently, methods supported by the constructivist philosophy encourage collaboration. Through collaborative efforts, students can "share ways of reading and being with text, becoming aware in the process of their own strategies and those of others" (Wilhelm, 1997, p. 11). In this process of discussion, students engage in metacognition and assist each other in making clearer meaning of the text.

Using discussion circles as a way of teaching content and improving reading ability in the middle and secondary grades is an efficacious method. Because discussion circles use authentic literature, these experiences have shown improvements in students' reading and writing abilities. Students in the middle grades are social and desire learning in groups rather than in isolation. Students that are more engaged in the texts, whether they are narrative or expository, take more ownership in their learning. When teachers design classroom instruction to encourage student discourse, they may help students gain the ability to view multiple perspectives and challenge their own preconceived notions of the world. Finally, by eliminating ability grouping, instruction includes the use of peer-to-peer scaffolding techniques. Ideal classrooms today should evolve into communities of learners that provide opportunities for students to support each other's learning through collaborative discussions and projects.

RETHINKING THE TEACHER'S ROLE

The philosophies of Vygotsky (1978), Dewey (1939), and Rosenblatt (1978) build the foundation for a student-centered learning environment. Using discussion circles in classroom instruction changes the role of the traditional teachers from a dominating "in charge" role to a "supporting learning" role. The structure of discussion circles requires a teacher to assume more of a stance as a coach, where the teacher does more directing than controlling. Researchers have assigned a myriad of new titles describing the teacher's role in a literature circle classroom: (1) curator; (2) facilitator (Swafford, 1995); (3) coach from the sidelines; (4) coparticipant (Wiencek, 1996); (5) taking a back seat; (6) supportive; and (7) natural participant (Villaume, Worden, Williams, Hopkins, & Rosenblatt, 1994). For discussion circles, we prefer to stay with the title of teacher that implies careful preparation and planning while maintaining the ability to grasp and expand on teachable moments.

In fact, a teacher has numerous roles to fill while implementing instruction using discussion circles. Gone are the days when the teacher was the center of all the activity and all students were expected to be on the same page and at the same skill level. Through a comparison of the roles of a teacher described by Short and Kauffman's (1999) *"So What Do I Do?" The Role of the Teacher in Literature Circles* with Johnson's (1995) *Time Changes Everything: One Teacher's Story*, we find some commonality and a better understanding of how teachers can support this new approach to teaching (figure 9.1).

A careful comparison of two perspectives identified seven common teacher roles. Even though the author's word choices are not identical, similar themes were connected, revealing the following comparable roles:

1. creating a positive learning environment
2. determining and organizing logistics
3. guiding reading activities
4. choosing themes
5. sharing favorite books
6. introducing ideas through mini lessons
7. learning to "kid watch"

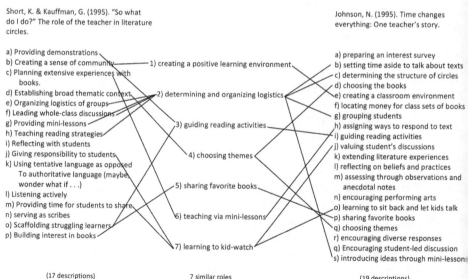

Short, K. & Kauffman, G. (1995). "So what do I do?" The role of the teacher in literature circles.

Johnson, N. (1995). Time changes everything: One teacher's story.

a) Providing demonstrations
b) Creating a sense of community
c) Planning extensive experiences with books.
d) Establishing broad thematic context
e) Organizing logistics of groups
f) Leading whole-class discussions
g) Providing mini-lessons
h) Teaching reading strategies
i) Reflecting with students
j) Giving responsibility to students
k) Using tentative language as opposed To authoritative language (maybe, wonder what if . . .)
l) Listening actively
m) Providing time for students to share
n) serving as scribes
o) Scaffolding struggling learners
p) Building interest in books

1) creating a positive learning environment
2) determining and organizing logistics
3) guiding reading activities
4) choosing themes
5) sharing favorite books
6) teaching via mini-lessons
7) learning to kid-watch

a) preparing an interest survey
b) setting time aside to talk about texts
c) determining the structure of circles
d) choosing the books
e) creating a classroom environment
f) locating money for class sets of books
g) grouping students
h) assigning ways to respond to text
i) guiding reading activities
j) valuing student's discussions
k) extending literature experiences
l) reflecting on beliefs and practices
m) assessing through observations and anecdotal notes
n) encouraging performing arts
o) learning to sit back and let kids talk
p) sharing favorite books
q) choosing themes
r) encouraging diverse responses
q) Encouraging student-led discussion
s) introducing ideas through mini-lesson

(17 descriptions)   7 similar roles   (19 descriptions)

Figure 9.1   Teacher's role in literature circles or book clubs.

A teacher remains a vital and active part of the learning process in a classroom embracing discussion circles. Even though discussion circles are student led, clearly the teacher must attend to many critically important tasks (figure 9.2). As teachers transition from teacher-centered instruction to student-centered instruction (based on student interest and need), the biggest challenge is divorcing themselves from past practices and not simply modifying (or basalizing) what was previously done.

Fullan (1997) describes the process of change as complex and unpredictable. In the early stages of change, teachers must be willing to work under conditions of uncertainty, to learn as they go, to accept anxiety, to work through difficulties, and to not fear the unknown. Fullan (1997) says that changes in the way we teach require us to develop "new skills, behaviors and

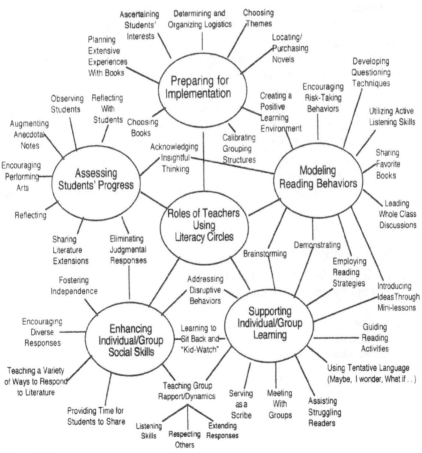

Figure 9.2

beliefs or understandings" (p. 36). While it may seem like a daunting task, this changing role of the teacher is an essential one in creating constructivist and sociocultural learning contexts.

IMPLEMENTING DISCUSSION CIRCLES

How do I get started? Perhaps your professor has given you the assignment to create a two- or three-week unit in your content area. How can you add nonfiction and/or fiction to the content topic you have chosen? With so much quality young adult literature available, bringing authentic literature into all content area classrooms has never been easier.

Many websites will help your efforts to find quality nonfiction and fiction books for use in your classroom. Most national professional organizations provide lists of books that go with specific concepts in your discipline. Refer back to a list of professional organizations in chapter 3 and a list of notable books in various content areas. The American Library Association website also furnishes a variety of lists of adolescent and children's books, including lists of award-winning books.

As we discussed in chapter 3, content area instruction has recently been guided by Common Core State Standards (CCSS). Textbooks have been modified to address these standards and are then adopted by school districts. Many teachers leaving our teacher education programs have taken jobs in districts that mandate certain commercial texts be used in their classrooms. With a little creativity, we believe you can follow your district's required text mandates and incorporate authentic texts as well as collaborative learning environments.

Paired Text Approach

Here are a few ideas to demonstrate how you can incorporate a paired text approach in a social studies unit on the 1960s:

Topic: The 1960s and the civil rights movement
Paired Texts
Informational text: *Time* magazine article describing the Alabama church bombings.
Authentic text: *The Watsons Go to Birmingham—1963* by Christopher Paul Curtis.

Table 9.1 KWL for civil rights movement

What do you Know?	What do you Want to Know?	What have you Learned?
People were tired of being treated badly because of the color of their skin.	Why did people treat people differently?	
	Why was there so much violence in the 1960s?	

Instructional Strategies for Paired Texts and Discussions

KWL. Begin this unit by asking students what they know about the civil rights movement. Students should fill in the *K* section of a KWL chart. Each student should fill in their own charts first, and this will provide ideas for them to share with the whole class later. After students have had time to fill in their individual KWL charts, ask students to share some of their understandings about the civil rights movement and note their comments on a class KWL chart. Keep in mind, the *L* column is the column the students create listing what they "Learned." The list of what they learned serves as a great outline for students to organize for writing an essay on the topic (table 9.1).

You can also modify a KWL to fit the needs of your curriculum. After reading *The Watsons Go to Birmingham—1963*, provide them a copy of the *Time* article written and published about the church bombings. The author of the novel, Christopher Paul Curtis, took some liberties when writing his fictional work, which are clear to see when comparing the novel against the *Time* article.

Anticipation Guide. Create an Anticipation Guide and ask students to complete the form before sharing new information about the time period. Students may benefit from viewing a couple of film clips about the era and some of the racial struggles. Showing the film *Ruby Bridges* may help students to understand the realities of racism in the 1960s (figures 6.8 and 9.3).

About-Point. Provide copies of an About-Point strategy. In the "About" section students are to summarize each chapter in three sentences or less, and in the "Point" section they must reduce their summary to a maximum of three words (figure 9.4).

Multidisciplinary Thematic Approach

On college campuses across the United States, faculty are beginning to tear down the silos of the disciplines and create courses that are interdisciplinary. There is also a growing trend to team-teach across disciplines, showing students how a discipline such as physics is connected to music.

The Watsons Go to Birmingham—1963

Chapter 14 deals with innocent lives lost in acts of violence. Before you read Chapter 14, read the list of issues below and mark the statements you agree with in column A. After reading chapter 14 go back and mark the statement you believe the author agrees in Column B. Be ready to support your stance with documentation from the text.

A (You)	B (Author)		My opinion changed after reading
X	_____	1. The law is always right.	_____
_____	_____	2. Violence is a good way to make a point.	_____
X	_____	3. People who live in the same country usually think alike.	_____

Figure 9.3   Anticipation guide.

About-Point

The Watsons Go to Birmingham—1963

About: (Summarize in three sentences or less)   Point: (3 words or less)

Ch. 1 And you Wonder Why We Get Called the Weird Watsons
Kenny's older brother Byron, a juvenile delinquent, gets stuck   Mean older brother
to the car and the family panics.

Ch. 2 Give my Regards to Clark, Poindexter

Ch. 3 The World's Greatest Dinosaur War Ever

Figure 9.4   About-Point for *The Watsons Go to Birmingham—1963*.

Two teachers in a high school in northwest Ohio joined forces and proposed to their principal an idea—they would like to have the same students in each of their classes. One teacher taught World History and the other taught World Literature. The two teachers created a curriculum combining the two fields of discipline so the students were learning about the historical and literary accomplishment of the time period simultaneously. These innovative teachers also planned periodic visits to a local museum that highlighted the art of the period they were studying as well as providing students with opportunities to listen to music from those same periods.

Perhaps your schools would be interested in designing their curriculum around a theme-based approach to teaching. When students can see how the clearly articulated subjects of math, science, social studies, PE, art, and music are actually interrelated and connected, their motivation to learn across subject lines will most likely be enhanced.

THEORY TO PRACTICE

A socially engaged classroom creates the space for vibrant learning in every content area. Using class time for discussions about your courses' topics help students to make connections with the material that they may not have understood. When a class comes together and helps to create a supportive and collaborative learning environment, the teachers' role can be a delight! Guiding learning instead of trying to coerce students to read and learn the material is every teachers' dream.

Whether you implement book clubs, discussion circles or other collaborative learning activities, we encourage you to teach with enthusiasm and share your excitement for your specific content area. You may be *the one* to ignite a passion for (fill in your passion) in one of your students.

REFERENCES

Allington, R. L., & Wamsley, S. A. (Eds.). (1997). *No quick fix: Rethinking literacy programs in America's elementary schools*. Language and Literacy Series. New York: Teachers College Press.

Anderson, R. C., Hiebert, E. H., Scott, J. A., & Wilkinson, I. (1985). *Becoming a nation of readers: The report of the Commission on Reading*. Washington, DC: US Department of Education.

Blumenfeld, P. C., Marx, R. W., Soloway, E., & Krajcik, J. (1996). Learning with peers: From small group cooperation to collaborative communities. *Educational Researcher, 25*(8), 37–40.

Calkins, L. (1986). *The art of teaching writing*. Portsmouth, NH: Heinemann.

Curtis, C. P. (1995). *The Watsons Go to Birmingham—1963*. New York: Delacorte Books for Young Readers.

Dewey, J. (1939). *Experience and education*. New York: Collier Books.

Eckhoff, B. (1983). How reading affects children's writing. *Language Arts, 60*(5), 607–16.

Eldredge, J., & Butterfield, D. (1986). Alternatives to traditional reading instruction. *The Reading Teacher, 40*(1), 32–37.

Fielding, L., Wilson, P., & Anderson, R. (1984). A new focus on free reading: The role of trade books in reading instruction. In T. Raphael (Ed.), *The contexts of school based literacy*. New York: Random House.

Fullan, M. (1997). The complexity of the change process. In M. Fullan (Ed.), *The challenge of school change.* Arlington Heights, IL: SkyLight Training and Publishing, Inc.

Goodman, K., Freeman, Y., Murphy, S., & Shannon, P. (1988). *Report card on basal readers.* New York: Richard C. Owen.

Guthrie, J. (1996). Educational contexts for engagement in literacy. *The Reading Teacher, 49*(6), 432–45.

Hill, B., Johnson, N., & Noe, K. (Eds.). (1995). *Literature circles and response.* Norwood, MA: Christopher-Gordon Publishers.

Johnson, N. (1995). Time changes everything: One teacher's story. In B. Hill, N. Johnson, & K. Noe (Eds.), *Literature circles and response.* Norwood, MA: Christopher-Gordon Publishers.

Keene, E., & Zimmermann, S. (1997). *Mosaic of thought.* Portsmouth, NH: Heinemann.

Keegan, S., & Shrake, K. (1991). Literature study groups: An alternative to ability grouping. *The Reading Teacher, 44*(8), 542–47.

Loewen, J. W. (1995/2008). *Lies my teacher told me: Everything your American history textbook got wrong.* New York: Touchstone.

Morrow, L. (1992). The impact of a literature-based program on literacy achievement, use of literature, and attitudes toward reading of children from minority backgrounds. *Reading Research Quarterly, 27*(3), 251–75.

Nystrand, M., Gamoran, A., & Heck, M. (1993). Using small groups for response to and thinking about literature. *English Journal 82*(1), 14–22.

Raphael, T., & McMahon, S. (1994). Book club: An alternative framework for reading instruction. *The Reading Teacher 48*(2), 102–16.

Rosenblatt, L. (1978). *The reader, the text, and the poem.* Carbondale, IL: Southern Illinois University Press.

Salisbury, G. (2005). *Under the blood-red sun.* New York: Yearling.

Sheinkin, S. (2012). *Bomb: The race to build—and steal—the world's most dangerous weapon.* New York: Roaring Book Press.

Short, K., & Kauffman, G. (1999). "So what do I do?" The role of the teacher in literature circles. In N. R. M. Martinez (Ed.), *Book talk and beyond: Children and teachers respond to literature.* Newark, DE: International Reading Association.

Smith, F. (1988). *Joining the literacy club: Further essays into education.* Portsmouth, NH: Heineman.

Swafford, J. (1995). "I wish all my groups were like this one": Facilitating peer interaction during group work. *Journal of Reading 38*(8), 626–31.

Villaume, S. K., Worden, T., Williams, S., Hopkins, L., & Rosenblatt, C. (1994). Five teachers in search of a discussion. *Reading Teacher, 47*(6), 480–87.

Vygotsky, L. (1978). *Mind in society: The development of higher psychological processes.* Cambridge, MA: Harvard.

Wellman, D. K. B. (2000). *Implementing literature circles: Three case studies of teachers in transition.* Dissertation, The University of Toledo.

Wiencek, B. J. (1996). Planning, initiating, and sustaining literature discussion groups: The teacher's role. In L. B. Gambrell & J. F. Almasi (Eds.), *Lively discussions!: Fostering engaged reading* (pp. 208–23). Newark, DE: International Reading Association.

Wilhelm, J. (1997). *"You gotta BE the book."* New York: Teachers College Press.

Zarillo, J. (1989). Teachers' interpretations of literature-based reading. *The Reading Teacher 32*(1), 22–28.

Promoting Deep Thinking

Questioning

Judge a man by his questions rather than his answers.

—Voltaire

When Cory was in seventh grade and I was no longer his teacher, he would visit me between classes and stop by after school. He opened doors for me, called me his favorite teacher, and warned other students to behave and pay attention to me. With this about-face in attitude, and the fact that I already knew all of his tricks to evade work, I thought I now had the advantage and I could make a difference in this young man's life. So, I requested to have him again in my eighth-grade language arts class.

Things did not pan out like I had expected. First nine weeks grade—F; second nine weeks grade—D-. When spring rolled around and I was preparing to coach junior high track and field, I convinced Cory to go out for track—he was incredibly fast! The caveat was that he *had* to have a C average to compete. With his spelling test grades averaging five out of twenty, I thought this was an easy place to start. One Thursday night I called his home and asked him to get out a piece of paper and a pencil—we were going to do a pretest and talk about how to spell each word. He couldn't believe I had invaded his home space, and while I was still on the phone he complained to his mother that he didn't think this was fair or that I could legally do this. She met his complaints by handing him the paper and pencil I had told him to get!

Word 1. *Divergent*. We have divergent ideas about school. *Divergent*. Cory wrote something down. Word 2. *Impending*. Do you have a feeling of impending doom? *Impending*. And this process continued for the first ten words. At that point we went back to the first word, and I asked Cory to tell me how he spelled *divergent*. He was, of course, wrong. We talked about the word, and I had him write it correctly three times. We did this for every one of the twenty words on the list. Forty-five minutes later, I wished him luck on the test tomorrow and hung up.

Cory entered language arts with a confidence I had not seen before. When the class took the spelling test, he seemed engaged and eager to write each word. The students held up their papers, and I collected them and graded them while they worked on their creative writing assignments. Cory received a 17/20. I was thrilled; he was devastated. He expected a 20. He stayed after class to talk about his disappointment, and I tried to explain to him what a leap this was for him.

The following Thursday night, Cory received another call from me. This time, I told him I was going to only do ten words with him and he was on his own to work on the other ten. That Friday he received an 18/20. Same results as last time; I was thrilled, he was frustrated. Week three, I called Cory but this time I said that I don't do this for any other student and I know that if he put some time into this he will do fine. After a brief pep talk, I told him I expected him to do as well tomorrow as he had done the last two weeks.

I began the test as I normally did. I said the word, used it in a sentence, and repeated the word. When I got to the fourth word, I thought I saw Cory pull a piece of paper out from his desk, look at it, and slide it back into the desk. I was furious! Followed closely by denial! He wouldn't do that! After all the time and effort I had in this young man he wouldn't dare try something like this. I convinced myself I was seeing things. But then on word seven, he did it again. I was seething! I wanted to go over and just slap him, so I sat on my hands and said, "Number 8. *Accretion*. I can't think of a sentence for accretion. *Accretion*." Again, Cory pulled out the paper, glanced at it, pushed the paper back into his desk and wrote something down. I decided that I would not pick up his test. As I finished with number twenty, the students held up their completed tests and I came around to pick them up. I walked past Cory. He waved it higher, and I returned to my desk.

"Hey, you forgot my test," said Cory.

I replied, "No, I'm not taking it and you know why."

"I wasn't cheating!" Cory said as he puffed up his chest and acted indignant.

"Well, I think you were. I saw you three times pull out a piece of paper, look at it, and put it back."

As he jumps to his feet, he said, "You can check my desk. I didn't cheat!"

I could still see the corner of the crumpled paper so I called his bluff. I walked over to his desk and pulled out the sheet. Across the middle of the page, it said, "Ha, ha, got you Ms. Wellman!"

Questions answered by students unveil what they know. Questions generated by students unveil even more. Questioning is one of the easiest teaching tools to gain access to students' ideas, insights, and understanding. While questioning does require planning, it does not require extensive preparation or a long list of materials. New teachers should prepare a list of questions prior to the lesson, while veteran teachers can often ask questions extemporaneously and naturally. Teachers also need to know when to pose questions, how to respond to students' responses, when to probe for further ideas, and when to redirect with a different question. Although easy to use, there is an art to questioning that maximizes the power to teach and to assess. This chapter explores how questions posed before, during, and after a lesson facilitate and enhance students' understanding. Teacher-generated and student-generated questions open up exciting possibilities for meaningful content learning.

THEORETICAL FOUNDATIONS OF QUESTIONS

Teacher questioning is a prominent feature of classroom talk. Asking questions is the strategy teachers most frequently use to actively engage their students in the learning process. According to Bellack (1975), 45 percent of what teachers say to their students could be characterized as questions that help students focus on the pertinent information. Teachers use questions to serve many purposes in a classroom. Cotton (1988) found a variety of uses, including:

- To develop interest and motivate students to become actively involved in lessons
- To evaluate students' preparation and check on homework or seatwork completion
- To develop critical-thinking skills and inquiring attitudes
- To review and summarize previous lessons
- To nurture insights by exposing new relationships
- To assess achievement of instructional goals and objectives
- To stimulate students to pursue knowledge on their own (p. 2).

Questioning does more than reveal students' knowledge and understanding; it promotes other intellectual practices and habits that are essential for lifelong learning. However, according to classroom research, of the two hundred to three hundred questions asked each school day by a teacher, most are low-level questions: 60 percent factual recall and 20 percent procedural regarding daily routines, leaving only 20 percent that require students to think (Brualdi, 1998). Griffith and Burns (2012) recommend a ratio of 30:70 for teacher talk time versus student talk time. In this chapter, we will explore many ways to transform the recall and procedural questions into substantive ones that facilitate and enhance content area learning.

TYPES OF QUESTIONS

There are many different ways to categorize questions used in classrooms. Most broadly, questions can be *closed*, used to check for understanding or to focus thinking on a particular point, or *open*, used to promote discussion or student interaction (Blosser, 1975). Closed questions often result in dichotomous answers (i.e., yes or no), whereas open questions have the potential to solicit additional information from students. Certainly, to facilitate and enhance learning, open questions are optimal, as they generate the discussion

Table 10.1 Types of Questions

Factual	Answers are simple and straightforward based on fact or knowledge	*When did the Dust Bowl take place?*
Convergent	A limited range of acceptable answers are based on inferences	*What are some reasons the Dust Bowl occurred?*
Divergent	Answers can vary widely based on students' interpretations, analysis, synthesis, and predictions	*Do you think the Dust Bowl can happen again today? Why or why not?*
Evaluative	Answers require sophisticated cognitive or affective judgment	*Do you think the government took appropriate actions to help those affected by the Dust Bowl?*
Combination	A blend of any of the four types	

needed for students to share their own interpretations, expand their ideas, challenge their assumptions, and provide justification for their answers.

Erickson (2007) offers a more specific set of question types for classroom teachers (table 10.1). Students need opportunities to answer all four types of these questions. Each question type necessitates a different set of intellectual skills and strategies in order to answer. Recalling facts, making inferences, analyzing and synthesizing, and making judgments based on reason are all cognitive behaviors that facilitate students to think and to understand. Use a balanced set of questions, including factual when appropriate for a quick check of understanding.

Bloom's Taxonomy

Many different philosophical orientations and instructional theories exist to guide the preparation of quality content area lessons. One of most influential is *Bloom's Taxonomy of the Cognitive Domain* (Bloom, Engelhart, Hill, Furst, & Krathwohl, 1956). Bloom and his colleagues identified six levels of intellectual behaviors within the cognitive domain from the simplest to the most demanding: knowledge, comprehension, application, analysis, synthesis, and evaluation. Often used to inform lesson objectives in observable behavioral language, Bloom's Taxonomy can also serve as another guide for formulating questions to invite and engage students to think in the content areas.

Bloom's Taxonomy was revised by Anderson and Krathwohl in 2001, with the most notable change being that the six levels are expressed as verbs; some of the category names are changed; and the order of the last two levels has been reversed—*evaluate* preceeds *create*. Table 10.2 presents the revised Bloom's Taxonomy (Krathwohl, 2002, p. 215).

Table 10.2 Structure of the cognitive process dimensions of the revised taxonomy

Category	Description	Related Cognitive Processes
Remember (formerly Knowledge)	Retrieving relevant knowledge from long-term memory	Recognizing Recalling
Understand (formerly Comprehension)	Determining the meaning of instructional messages, including oral, written, and graphic communication	Interpreting Exemplifying Classifying Summarizing Inferring Comparing Explaining
Apply	Carrying out or using a procedure in a given situation	Executing Implementing
Analyze	Breaking material into its constituent parts and detecting how the parts relate to one another and to an overall structure or purpose	Differentiating Organizing Attributing
Evaluate	Making judgments based on criteria and standards	Checking Critiquing
Create (formerly Synthesis)	Putting elements together to form a novel, coherent whole or make an original product	Generating Planning Producing

Since one of the goals of questioning is to deepen student understanding of content area concepts, preparing questions that represent a range of cognitive demands is crucial. At a time when differentiation is becoming more important in the classroom, Bloom's Taxonomy offers a framework for teachers and students to generate meaningful questions for content area learning. Table 10.3 presents sample questions using Bloom's Taxonomy in the content areas. You may notice that for some, especially in the higher levels of the taxonomy, the example is not in the form of a question. For example, when a student creates a product, multiple questions had to be thought of, reflected on, and answered without the need for it to be worded in a question.

Engaging Questions

Questioning that engages students in the content area classrooms requires thoughtful preparation. When teachers ask questions that are worth asking, the questioning process promotes thought, allows the teacher the opportunity to probe deeper after an answer is given, and can encourage students to ask more questions than the teacher. In other words, learning becomes dialogic.

Table 10.3 Effective questions to invite students to think by using Bloom's taxonomy

Levels	Definition	Sample Questions		
		Math	Science	Social Studies
Remember	Recall of facts	What is 4 x (9 ÷ 3)?	What are seeds?	What is the Underground Railroad?
Understand	Transfer memorized fact to new situations	Can you use cubes/ counters to create a combination of 4 x (9 ÷ 3)?	Describe how a seed can grow if a person does not plant it.	Compare the Underground Railroad route of Harriet Tubman to the route that Henry traveled.
Apply	Use information in an unfamiliar task	Can you show that 4 x (9 ÷ 3) is the same as (9 ÷ 3) x 4?	How do differences in seeds help them disperse and grow?	Describe some of the hazards the slaves endured as they moved along the Underground Railroad.
Analyze	Breakdown the idea into component parts	What is the communicative property? What is the order of operations?	What is the impact of different methods that seeds travel?	What are some of the risks to the owners of the safe houses on the Underground Railroad?
Evaluate	Suggest well-reasoned decisions	What is the best way to arrive at the answer of 12?	What are the most effective methods seeds use to get from one location to another?	Was the network of people who formed the Underground Railroad justified?
Create	Combine parts to form new solutions to a problem	What are other ways to arrive at the answer of 12?	Show three ways seeds travel to their new locations. (This seems more like a remember question.)	Create a plan of safe escape for runaway slaves.

Rather than following a typical linear exchange—the teacher asks, a student responds, and the teacher affirms or redirects—effective questioning creates a new dynamic among the members of the learning community. Ideally, students generate and maintain meaningful conversations with exchanges of questions and responses among multiple members. Content area learning thrives in such dialogues about worthy concepts. In this way, questioning can also serve as the glue to the *flow* of the lesson. Teachers monitor the student responses not only for understanding of the material but also to stimulate interest and to confirm that the majority of the students are engaged (Hattie, 2012).

Knowledge about different types of questions allows these teachers to pose initial questions that make students think. Effective initial questions make students pause and think, then rethink before expressing their thoughts. Then follow-up questions take students' thinking beyond their initial insights. Students are challenged to explore and expand their understanding, unpack assumptions, and probe deeper into the implications and consequences of their evolving stances. Paul and Elder (2006), fellows at the Foundation for Creative Thinking, advocate the use of Socratic questions to promote critical thinking and discussions (table 10.4).

Probing questions extend students' understanding of a concept beyond their first response. "Why?" questions encourage students to justify and explain their responses and will typically reveal their process of thinking, helping the teacher to understand what he needs to clarify or reteach. A line of subsequent questions are often formed extemporaneously based on the student's initial response. Teachers can ask probing questions to clarify, increase awareness, refocus, and when necessary, redirect.

Written questions can also illustrate a set of skills such as knowledge of proper language conventions, use of specific discipline vocabulary, ability to offer logical justification for an answer, and organization used to present ideas. *Bloom's Taxonomy* (2001) is an excellent tool to guide teachers in creating written questions. Teachers may find other guides for composing complex written questions helpful. We recommend the following:

Table 10.4 Types of Socratic questions

Question Type	Sample Question
Questions of Clarification	*Why do you say that?*
Questions That Probe Purpose	*What is the purpose of...?*
Questions That Probe Assumptions	*How can you verify that assumption?*
Questions That Probe Information, Reasons, Evidence, and Causes	*Can you give an example? Can you tell me why it happened?*
Questions about Viewpoints or Perspectives	*What is another way to look at it?*
Questions That Probe Implications and Consequences	*What are the consequences of that assumption?*
Questions about the Question	*What was the point of this question?*
Questions That Probe Concepts	*Why or how is this idea important?*
Questions That Probe Inferences and Interpretations	*How did you reach that conclusion?*

- Marzano's *Taxonomy* (1993)
- Aschner et al.'s *Taxonomy* (1961)
- Walsh and Sattes's *Taxonomy* (2005)

Hook questions are designed to grab the attention of students or "hook" them. Hook or lead-in questions can be used at the start of each class to activate prior knowledge and to spark a strong reaction for the topic. These lesson starters are thought provoking and a point of entry for the reading, discussion, and/or activities for the day. Introductory questions create excitement for the discussion that leads to deeper learning and readiness to respond to big ideas or essential questions. Starter questions are a direct and meaningful method for introducing the day's lesson or even a unit of study. Here are a few examples:

- Does everyone in America have the same chance to live the "American Dream"?
- When should the needs of a few outweigh the needs of many?
- Should humans interfere with nature?

Voltaire said that we should "judge a man by his questions rather than his answers." *Student-generated questions* are often overlooked as a way to get students to connect with the content being presented. Wonderments that young children have about the world are often in a form of a question, but by the time students get to the middle grades, it feels as though these wonderments have been squelched. In a classroom where risk taking is encouraged and students feel secure no matter their age, they will openly ask questions. Without any prompting by the teacher, they may ask questions to (1) clarify the teacher's or other students' statements; (2) pose new questions that are formed after a learning cycle; and (3) present their ongoing curiosities about the world. Such unprompted and unsolicited questions, of course, should be acknowledged and encouraged. Students will take your lead; questions that you generate naturally in the context of a classroom discourse will serve as models for students to continually offer genuine questions.

Teachers know the questions students ask are many times a better indication of what they understand than the questions they answer. Students should know and be able to create the types of questions that are most useful in your content area. For example, in an English language arts class, the four question types of Question-Answer Relationship (QAR) presented in chapter 6 (Right There, Think and Search, Author and Me, On My Own) may be appropriate (see table 6.4). Using the question types, require students to generate questions for each type to illustrate their learning. Make it a daily challenge; ask your students to generate questions as a way to start a class discussion.

Table 10.5 Questions to Avoid

	Questions to Avoid	
Type	Explanation	Example
Overlaid	Tagging on an additional question	Which two triangles are congruent and also share a common angle?
Multiple	Two related questions in sequence	What tools would you use to measure the mass of your science textbook and what units would you use to record your measurements?
Elliptical	Lacking specificity in what is being asked	How about those two skeletons?
Yes-No	Dead-end of guessing questions with no follow-up	Do you agree with President Obama's decision?
Ambiguous	Fuzzy questions with many potentially different "correct" answers	How does the law of sines differ from the law of cosines?
Choral Response	Provides little value in checking for students' understanding	Which atom has the greatest mass, class?
Whiplash	Ambushing a student with an unexpected question	The slope of this line is, what?
Leading	Pulls the desired responses from the students	Wouldn't you say that you could use a balance and a balloon to show that air is matter?
Teacher-Centered	Can create an invisible barrier between the teacher and the students	Give *me* the mass of the book by using a balance.
Rhetorical	Statement in form of a question that does not require an answer	Who says climate change is a myth?

Adapted from Posamentier and Stepelman (1999).

Question Pitfalls

Not all questions are good questions. Many times a teacher will ask questions that are counterproductive; they may be confusing or they simply do not promote learning. Poor questions will weaken a lesson and may decrease motivation. Posamentier and Stepelman (1999) recommend ten types of questions a teacher should avoid (table 10.5).

One of the most significant problems that arise in classrooms is not allowing time for students to think, or what we call wait time. Don't be afraid of silence! Wait time is the amount of time the teacher allows after a question is posed and before a student begins to speak in response to the question. Research findings state that the average wait time is one second or less. Rowe (1986) identified two important moments for a silent pause: Wait Time 1—after asking a question, before calling on a student to respond;

and Wait Time 2—after a student responds, before the teacher replies or comments. Increasing wait time beyond three seconds is positively related to the following outcomes for students (Cotton, 1988; Rowe, 1986):

- improvements in student achievement
- improvements in student retention, as measured by delayed tests
- increases in the number of higher cognitive responses generated by students
- increases in the length of student responses
- increases in the number of unsolicited responses
- decreases in students failing to respond
- increases in the amount and quality of evidence students offer to support their inferences
- increases in contributions by students who do not participate much when wait time is under three seconds
- expands the variety of responses offered by students
- decreases in student interruptions
- increases in student-student interactions
- increases in the number of questions posed by students.

Walsh and Sattes (2005) call wait time the "miracle pause." As simple as this technique sounds, it often takes effort and practice to implement in the classroom. Students need this time in order to think through their answers and respond at higher cognitive levels (Cotton, 1988). One effective technique is to allow students a few moments to jot down their thoughts before calling on students to respond. This "think time" gives your more reluctant responders a chance to craft their answers. An added benefit to this technique is that students have time to remember their original thoughts and can add to their peers' ideas.

QUESTIONING AS A FOCUS OF INSTRUCTION

Essential questions as described in *Understanding by Design* prioritize content by focusing on "big ideas" about a topic that guide an instructional unit (Wiggins & McTighe, 1998). With an emphasis on inquiry, these types of questions are broad in scope and point to core ideas within a discipline. These key inquiries use multilayered questions that reveal the richness and complexities of a subject. Also called *driving questions*, these questions sustain and hold a unit of study together by linking the concept to the real world (Krajcik, Czerniak, & Berger, 1999). According to Wiggins and McTighe (1998), essential questions may be characterized by what they do (table 10.6).

Table 10.6. Characteristics of essential questions.

Essential Questions		
Characterized by what they do	**Explanation**	**Examples**
Go to the heart of the discipline	Historically important and controversial topics	Which has more influence on development genetics or environment?
Recur naturally throughout one's learning and in the history of a field	Same important questions are asked and reasked	Do animals develop language skills?
Raise other important questions	Open up a subject and its complexities	How does an organism's structure reflect survival of the fittest?
Provide subject- and topic-specific doorways to essential questions	Unit questions frame a set of lesson plans—more subject and topic specific for framing a particular content	Does communism work?
Have no obvious "right" answer	Discussion starters rather than "the" answer the teacher wants	Was arithmetic discovered or created?
Are deliberately framed to provoke and sustain	Designed to be thought-provoking for the students	Do we all possess a "number sense" to help us make sense of numbers?

Essential questions should be referred to frequently throughout the unit. To get at deep content issues, these types of questions cannot be answered in a simple sentence; they are thought-provoking and multilayered.

1. Organize courses and units of study around the questions.
2. Design assessment tasks up front, explicitly linked to the questions.
3. Use a reasonable number of questions per unit (between two and five).
4. Make the questions as provocative and engaging as possible.
5. Make sure every student understands the question.
6. Design specific concrete exploratory activities for each question.
7. Sequence the questions for a natural occurrence.
8. Post the questions in the classroom and arrange resources around them to emphasize their importance.
9. Help students to personalize the questions.
10. Allow sufficient time for "unpacking" the questions.
11. Share your questions and promote essential questions schoolwide.

The following are three strategies that use essential questions as the focus of instruction.

Inquiry-Based Learning

An inquiry-based learning unit may focus on an investigation or a probe that addresses a natural phenomenon requiring repeated attention by the learner over an extended period of time in order to construct deep understanding (Lustick, 2010). One method for promoting learning through sustained inquiry is by implementing questions that can be explored but not answered. These types of questions need to be adapted to meet the varying needs and interests of young adult learners. When students are engaged in an investigation spread over weeks instead of days, they learn the value of patience and perseverance and the joy of discovery that prepares them for a possible career in any field (Lustick, 2010).

Problem-Based Learning

A new commitment to teach critical-thinking skills has ignited interest in involving children in real-life dilemmas within their school, neighborhood, town, state, nation, or world through problem-based learning. Many of the problems our society is currently facing make up the basis for a good question; for example, a unit on environmental issues could ask the questions, "What can a sixth-grader do to make a difference and improve pollution in their school?" "What can a tenth-grader do to make a difference and improve pollution in their community?" As students work with community partners, they are participating in problem solving by learning deeply about an issue and working to find solutions. The potential to help solve real issues facing their communities is an added benefit. Problem-based learning will give students opportunities to

- examine and try out what they know
- discover what they need to learn
- develop their people skills for achieving higher performance in teams
- improve their communications skills
- state and defend positions with evidence and sound argument
- become more flexible in processing information and meeting obligations
- practice skills that they will need after their education (*Study Guides and Strategies*, 2011).

Project-Based Learning

Students' curiosity about their world can be used to enhance curriculum through student-generated questions for investigations and individual and group projects. Research supports students selecting their own projects and integrating knowledge as the need arises, which is motivating and promotes learning (e.g., Blumenfeld et al., 1991; Hmelo-Silver, 2004). A typical framework for a project includes the following: a proposal or outline of the investigation; a research paper; a binder/portfolio with research documentation; and a culminating presentation (oral, written, or both) accompanied by a concrete visual item (poster, skit, diorama, maps, charts, etc.). Many values and purposes are promoted through project-centered learning, such as the following (Kellough & Kellough, 2007):

- Develop skills in cooperation and social interaction
- Develop skills in writing, communication, and in higher-level thinking
- Foster student engagement
- Differentiate students' learning capacities and interests
- Provide an opportunity to add to students' knowledge base
- Provide an opportunity for students to work on projects with personal meaning
- Develop skills in managing time and materials
- Provide an opportunity for students to make an important contribution.

THEORY TO PRACTICE

Questions that teachers ask in class provide students with the cues for what they should be learning. Our role as teachers is to continuously ask questions that invite our students to think and to involve them in the content concepts. Good questions that lead to quality discourse in the classroom do not magically happen. Selecting the right questions, sequencing them in a series designed to build on the answer to the previous question, and probing with just the right amount of nudging are all qualities of skillful questioning.

To observe a master teacher using questions to engage and to teach is truly a sight to behold. Questions used at the right time can stimulate the flow of the lesson and energize the room. In order to answer a well-designed question, students need to both think on their feet and thoughtfully plan out their response. In addition, the way students answer the questions produces meaningful data for the teacher to use to continually inform her teaching.

In this chapter, we have provided many examples of effective questions for a wide variety of purposes. As beginning teachers, you may have to write out a set of questions using our sample questions in your lesson plan. As you gain more experience, you will be able to generate questions with more spontaneity and confidence. Questions will always remain one of the most effective (and easiest) teaching tools you can use.

REFERENCES

Anderson, L. W., & Krathwohl, D. R. (Eds.). (2001). *A taxonomy for learning, teaching, and assessing: A revision of Bloom's Taxonomy of educational objectives.* New York: Addison Wesley Longman's.

Aschner, M., Gallagher, J., Perry, J., Afsar, S., Jenné, W., & Farr, H. (1961). *System for classifying thought processes in the context of classroom verbal interaction.* Urbana, IL: University of Illinois.

Bellack, A. (1975). The language of the classroom. In E. D. Hennigs (Ed.), *Mastering classroom communication.* Pacific Palisades, CA: Goodyear Publishing.

Bloom, B. S., Engelhart, M. D., Hill, W. H., Furst, E. J., & Krathwohl, D. R. (1956). *Taxonomy of educational objective: Cognitive domain.* New York: Longman.

Blosser, P. E. (1975). *How to ask the right questions.* National Science Teachers Association.

Blumenfeld, P. C., Soloway, E., Marx, R. W., Krajcik, J. S., Guzdial, M., & Palincsar, A. (1991). Motivating project-based learning: Sustaining the doing, supporting the learning. *Educational Psychologist, 26*(3–4), 369–98.

Brualdi, A. C. (1998). *Classroom questions: ERIC/AE Digest,* ERIC Digest Series No. EDO-TM-98-02. Los Angeles, CA: ERIC Clearinghouse for Community Colleges, University of California at Los Angeles.

Chin, C. (2007). Teacher questioning in science classrooms: Approaches that stimulate productive thinking. *Journal of Research in Science Teaching, 44*(6), 815–43.

Cotton, K. (1988). *Classroom questioning* (School Improvement Series: Research You Can Use, Close-Up #5). (Contract Number 400-86-0006). Portland, OR: North West Regional Educational Laboratory. http://www..nwrl.org/sepd/sirs/3/cu5/html.

Erickson, H. L. (2007). *Concept-based curriculum and instruction for the thinking classroom.* Thousand Oaks, CA: Corwin Press.

Griffith, A., & Burns, M. (2012). *Outstanding teaching: Engaging learners.* UK: Crown House.

Hattie, J. (2012). *Visible learning for teachers: Maximizing impact on learning.* New York: Routledge.

Hmelo-Silver, C. E. (2004). Problem-based learning: What and how do students learn? *Educational Psychology Review, 16*(3), 235–66.

Kellough, R. D., & Kellough, N. G. (2007). *Secondary school teaching: A guide to methods and resources* (3rd ed.). Upper Saddle River, NJ: Pearson.

Krajcik, J. S., Czerniaik, C. M., & Berger, C. (1999). *Teaching children science: A project-based approach.* New York: McGraw Hill College.

Krathwohl, D. R. (2002). A revision of Bloom's Taxonomy: An overview. *Theory into Practice, (41)*4, 212–18.

Lustick, D. (2010). The priority of the question: Focus questions for sustained reasoning in science. *Journal of Science Teacher Education, 21*(5), 495–511. doi: 10.1007/s1097010-9192-1.

Marzano, R. J. (1993). How classroom teachers approach the teaching of thinking. *Theory into Practice* (3), 154.

McGarvey, L., & Kline, K. (2011). Why "the value of why"? *Teaching Children Mathematics, (13)*3, 132–35.

Paul, R., & Elder, L. (2006). The thinker's guide to the art of Socratic questioning. In *Critical Thinking*. Retrieved July 29, 2013, from http://www.criticalthinking.org/ TGS_files/SocraticQuestioning2006.pdf.

Posamentier, A. S., & Stepelman, J. (1999). *Teaching secondary mathematics: Techniques and enrichment units* (5th ed.). Upper Saddle River, NJ: Merrill.

Rolheiser, C., & Fullan, M. (2003). *Comparing the research on best practices.* Metaire, LA: Center for Development and Learning.

Rowe, M. B. (1986). Wait time: Slowing down may be a way of speeding up! *Journal of Teacher Education, 37*, 43–50.

Study Guides and Strategies. (2011). Problem-based learning. Retrieved from http:// www.studygs.net/pbl.htm.

Walsh, J. A., & Sattes, B. D. (2005). *Quality questioning: Research-based practice to engage every learner.* Thousand Oaks, CA: Corwin Press.

Wiederhold, C. (1995). *Cooperative learning & higher-level thinking: The q-matrix.* San Clemente, CA: Kagan Cooperative Learning.

Wiggins, G., & McTighe, J. (1998). *Understanding by design.* Alexandria, VA: ASCD.

Broadening Capacities for Learning

The Arts

The true sign of intelligence is not knowledge, but imagination.

—Albert Einstein

Real Family versus Foster Family

Ms. Livingston was trying literature circles with her fifth-grade reading class for the first time. She could not imagine how her lower-level and special needs students could possibly handle the complexity of literature circles. However, not allowing them to participate was out of the question. Her ingenious plan to support her struggling students was to separate her five students with special needs so that only one of them was a member of each of the five literature circle groups. The students in the literature circles were assigned one of five roles and given worksheets to help them prepare. Each of the students with special needs was assigned the same role on the same day; each day before literature circles, the special education teacher pulled all five of her students together and helped them complete their role sheet. When the students returned to their groups, they were ready to participate.

On the day that all of these students were assigned the "artful artists" role, Brent entered the classroom with a brown paper bag tucked under his left arm. Ms. Livingston asked him what he had in the bag, and he tucked the bag up tighter under his arm and told her he would show her when it was his turn to be the artist. This made Ms. Livingston quite nervous.

The literature circle book assigned to the whole class was Betsy Byars's *Pinballs*. This story is about three foster children from three different families all placed in the same foster home. The discussion director, vocabulary wizard, passage master, and connector had all taken their turns. The group turned their attention to the artful artist, Brent, who slowly unrolled the end of the brown paper bag and pulled out two baby food jars.

"My artful artist jars show the difference between kids raised in regular families like us and kids raised in foster homes. Can you tell the difference?"

Each jar was turned upside down with the lid serving as the base, similar to a snow globe. On the front of each jar was a label. One said, "Real Family" and the other said "Foster Family." Inside each jar were three balls Brent had made from aluminum foil that he had rolled into perfectly formed spheres.

The four fifth-graders carefully examined both jars but were not allowed to touch them. Other than what was written on the label, the jars looked exactly the same. After careful contemplation, the group concluded that there was no difference.

With a smile, Brent shook the two jars at the same time. In the "Real Family" jar, Brent had glued the spheres to the bottom and the balls remained steady and fixed to the bottom of the jar. But in the jar labeled "Foster Family" the three balls were loose and they bounced all around.

Brent, one of the students his teacher thought couldn't handle the complexity of literature circles, calmly looked at his classmates and said, "In real families, no matter what happens, the kids are secure, they don't get bounced around like they do in foster families."

In the words of Pablo Picasso, "The purpose of art is washing the dust of daily life off our souls." You have experienced it; the moment that your heart begins to flutter, your eyes well up, and your skin comes alive with goosebumps all by consuming something beautiful. The beauty comes from a piece of art, a song, a moment in a live performance, a stanza in a poem, or something else entirely unexpected. For some, something disturbing, bizarre, mysterious, or even grotesque can be a thing of beauty that prompts an emotional response. For most of us, this is an emotional experience that connects with our aesthetic sensibilities and inner selves. And whether such experience is energizing or calming, it is an essential human need.

Some view the arts as fulfilling the task of reality construction or as the balance to our intellect. Yet others argue that art *is* a way of knowing: "an essential form of expression and communication, an expansive and diverse language fundamentally connected to experiencing and engaging in the world around us" (Donahue & Stuart, 2010, p. 19). And there lies the connection between the emotion and the intellect. Our emotional and aesthetic responses allow for curiosities and wonderments, for motivation to dig deeper and to truly understand, and for inspiration to pursue a topic intellectually.

THEORETICAL FOUNDATIONS FOR INTEGRATING THE ARTS

Much has been written about the role of the arts in education. *The Champions of Change* (Fisk, 1999), for example, found astonishing consensus in their findings regarding the benefits of the arts in the lives of our students:

- The arts reach students who are not otherwise being reached.
- The arts reach students in ways that they are not otherwise being reached.
- The arts connect students to themselves and each other.
- The arts transform the environment for learning.
- The arts provide learning opportunities for the adults in the lives of young people.
- The arts provide new challenges for those students already considered successful.
- The arts connect learning experiences to the world of real work (Fisk, 1999, pp. ix–xi).

This list, even at first glance, is humanistic, inclusive, and transformative. Imagine the world in which learning takes in these modes. It is possible through the integration of the arts. The Lincon Center Institute (2008) offers us the following capacities for imaginative learning, meant to be a framework for student learning. As you read this list, think about the capacities for learning in your content area. Which of these do you try to accomplish with your students? Most, if not all, would make our teachers' list of capacities for learning in their own content.

- *Noticing deeply* to identify and articulate layers of detail in a work of art or other object of study through continuous interaction with it over time.
- *Embodying* to experience a work of art or other object of study through your senses, as well as emotionally, and also to physically represent that experience.
- *Questioning* to ask questions throughout your explorations that further your own learning; to ask the question, "What if?"
- *Making connections* to connect what you notice and the patterns you see to your prior knowledge and experiences, to others' knowledge and experiences, and to text and multimedia resources.
- *Identifying patterns* to find relationships among the details that you notice, group them, and recognize patterns.
- *Exhibiting empathy* to respect the diverse perspectives of others in the community; to understand the experiences of others emotionally as well as intellectually.
- *Living with ambiguity* to understand that issues have more than one interpretation, that not all problems have immediate or clear-cut solutions, and to be patient while a resolution becomes clear.
- *Creating meaning* to create your own interpretations based on the previous capacities, see these in the light of others in the community, create a synthesis, and express it in your own voice.

- *Taking action* to try out new ideas, behaviors, or situations in ways that are neither too easy nor too dangerous or difficult, based on the synthesis of what you have learned in your explorations.
- *Reflecting/assessing* to look back on your learning, continually assess what you have learned, assess/identify what challenges remain, and assess/identify what further learning needs to happen. This occurs not only at the end of a learning experience but is part of what happens throughout that experience. It is also not the end of your learning; it is part of beginning to learn something else (https://imaginationnow.files.wordpress.com/2011/03/capacities.pdf).

There is an entire field within the education world (i.e., Arts in Education) in which seminal work is produced and disseminated. The vast resources and professional development opportunities to learn more deeply about the arts integration through agencies, such as the Lincoln Center Institute, and programs are available to teachers. This chapter is not meant to present a comprehensive guide to arts integration. Rather, its purpose is to present possibilities or glimpses for using one of the many art forms (e.g., visual art, music, dance and movement, theater, literary works, movies, etc.) to foster meaningful learning. The tiniest gesture, like playing a piece of music or projecting a photographic image as students walk into your classroom, may lead to the opening of hearts and minds that makes a world of difference.

BROADENING LEARNING CAPACITIES

In recent years, schools have diminished the arts programs for three main reasons. First, the No Child Left Behind Act, with its focus on accountability through high-stakes testing, only tested reading, writing, and mathematics; therefore, schools felt pressured to increase instructional hours devoted to these subjects. Second, school districts, many of which are facing decreased funding, have decided to reduce or even eliminate the arts in schools. Finally, the perception that art is not important in the education of a child and has little impact on test scores makes the decision to cut these types of programs a bit easier. "Something has to go," is the rationale for cutting "artsy" classes that are not directly tested.

The arts survive at the margins of education often as curriculum enrichment, rewards to the good students, or electives for the talented (Manner, 2002). However, Gullat (2007, 2008) links the arts with concrete academic gains; even though not tested, they appear to have a positive effect in students' learning, including "adequate progress" on high-stakes tests. It is due to the many lessons arts teach. Consider Eisner's (2002) list:

- The arts teach children to make good judgments about qualitative relationships. Unlike much of the curriculum in which correct answers and rules prevail, in the arts it is judgment rather than rules that prevail.
- The arts teach children that problems can have more than one solution and that questions can have more than one answer.
- The arts celebrate multiple perspectives. One of their large lessons is that there are many ways to see and interpret the world.
- The arts teach children that in complex forms of problem solving, purposes are seldom fixed but change with circumstance and opportunity. Learning in the arts requires the ability and a willingness to surrender to the unanticipated possibilities of the work as it unfolds.
- The arts make vivid the fact that neither words in their literal form nor numbers exhaust what we can know. The limits of our language do not define the limits of our cognition.
- The arts teach students that small differences can have large effects. The arts traffic in subtleties.
- The arts teach students to think through and within a material. All art forms employ some means through which images become real.
- The arts help children learn to say what cannot be said. When children are invited to disclose what a work of art helps them feel, they must reach into their poetic capacities to find the words that will do the job.
- The arts enable us to have experience we can have from no other source and through such experience to discover the range and variety of what we are capable of feeling.
- The arts' position in the school curriculum symbolizes to the young what adults believe is important (pp. 70–92).

Efland (2002) says when students are interpreting a work of art they are drawing on knowledge from differing domains, which is central to an integrated curriculum. In the classroom, students can use art in a similar way that quick writes are used—as a means of exploring and grappling with ideas. Students may create a drawing, change the words to a favorite or popular song, or create a dance to connect with the content of the lesson. While not necessarily refined works of art; rather, they are tools for thinking. When these alternatives are added to the instructional format, a significantly higher number of students' learning styles are addressed (Zemelman, Daniels, & Hyde, 1998).

When students are asked to create a visual to depict an event or concept, they must review and process the content and recall information in a different way. Processing the material visually and artistically aids in retention (Burgess, 2012). The students' depictions provide insights for the teacher into how they "see" the concepts. Focus can be developed through using a variety of learning styles, such as visual, bodily-kinesthetic, or musical. Through the connection of a personal experience with the subject matter, and with an emphasis on the process of discovery that allows for unexpected outcomes, teachers help students develop more critical-thinking skills (www.aep-arts. org).

Arts for Art's Sake

Before making explicit connections between the arts and the content areas, it is important to state that arts, in and of themselves, have value. This seems like an obvious point to make, especially in this chapter. However, using the arts unapologetically and without rationale for meeting a particular set of "lesson objectives" should be acceptable and even encouraged. The arts have inherent value and purpose in our lives, and classrooms ought to be one of the places where students meet the arts.

Make use of museums, galleries, musical concerts, performances, and exhibitions available in your community. Throughout this book, much is discussed regarding students' prior knowledge and the role of prior knowledge in students' learning. For many students, these experiences of seeing, observing, experiencing, and participating in the arts is not part of their background knowledge. Besides the expanded knowledge about a specific art work or musical production, these experiences also teach process and procedures in how to participate in these experiences.

When actual visits and experiences are not feasible, remember that teachers and teaching artists make great partners. Students need the opportunity to interact with professional artists who have committed their life's work to being a painter, sculptor, actor, director, architect, graphic designer, photographer, writer, singer, dancer, and many others. Typically, this type of partnership occurs in the context of a visiting artist. These programs can be arts focused, teaching elements of one or more art forms, or arts integrated, using the arts to enhance mathematics, science, and social studies (Donahue & Stuart, 2010).

Creating art also aids students' thinking process. Hetland, Winner, Veenema, and Sheridan (2007) provide a framework to capture the kind of thinking nurtured by art and necessary to make art. They believe this framework informs and transforms thinking and knowledge across the content areas beyond art. The studio habits include the following:

- Develop craft—learning artistic conventions
- Engage and persist—working and persevering at art tasks
- Envision—picturing mentally, imagining possible next steps
- Express—creating work that expresses ideas and feelings

- Observe—attending to visual contexts more closely than ordinary
- Reflect—questioning and explaining
- Evaluate—judging one's own work and the work of others by standards in the field
- Stretch and explore—reaching beyond one's capacities, explore playfully
- Understand the art world—knowing about art history and current practices
- Establish communities—interacting as an artist with other artists.

Like literacy skills that cut across the content areas, hence making them a natural connecting agent for integration, the arts can lie at the core of an integrated conception of general education (Efland, 2002).

When students share their artwork in class, they have the opportunity to view a variety of different representations of a single concept. These multiple representations develop more effectively the concepts and specific content, and they guide students in appreciating other students' perspectives and points of view, which is a component of a safe learning community and a supportive audience. Also, students are given the opportunity to collaborate with their classmates to create works of art. When presenting their artwork, it is not meant to be competitive. We encourage teachers to find opportunities to share their students' artwork schoolwide.

The Arts in the Content Areas

Most middle and high schools are compartmentalized into content areas. And yet, as advocated in this book, integration of knowledge and making natural connections among concepts is a way to *fully* educate students in preparation for their active and productive participation in the global society. The integration of the arts in the curriculum will enhance students' learning in the content areas in much the same way. The arts reinforce students' conceptual learning through seeing life representations in art forms that are tied to their learning and experiencing intellectual processes that are inherent in the creation of the arts. In this section, concrete ways in which the arts integrate with content areas are presented.

Arts and Mathematics

At first glance the arts and mathematics may appear to be unrelated, but in actuality it is amazing how many interrelationships exist between the two content areas. There are connections between mathematics and nature, music, dance, sculpture, architecture, pottery, painting, and many others. Mathematics is everywhere around us.

The works of Paul Klee, M. C. Escher, and Wassily Kandinsky are a representative sample of well-known artists who used geometry as the building blocks of their work. Their works can provide a foundational beginning for any geometry unit. In Lynn's classroom, students develop M. C. Escher tessellations to integrate geometric concepts and the arts (figure 11.1). Tessellations are a repeat tiling in which there are no gaps or overlaps. Properties of polygons, interior and exterior angles, and geometric transformations (such as translations, rotation, and reflection) are just a few of the skills that are developed while students construct their tessellations. An ideal integration of geometry and art, the amazing patterns created in the construction of tessellations promote the beauty and wonder of mathematics.

As stated by M. C. Escher, "He who wonders discovers that this in itself is wonder." Students learn many geometric concepts when they participate in a tessellation project. Students may be surprised to learn that mathematics is not just pencil and paper computations. They learn the different attributes of geometric shapes and how those attributes affect its ability to tessellate. Other concepts include the line of symmetry, the number angles and the sum of their measures in a shape, distinguishing between acute and obtuse angles, and estimating angle measurements. However, the most exciting aspect in a tessellation project is students' positive attitude toward mathematics in general. See several examples of tessellations created by Lynn's students.

Origami is the Japanese art of paper folding. This art form uses many concepts in mathematics such as symmetry, right angles, isosceles triangles, parallel lines, pentagons, and the importance of precision and integrating fine art and science. Origami has prompted mathematicians and theoretical

Figure 11.1   Tessellations.

scientists to explore concepts and solve equations in truly unexpected ways. A documentary, *Between the Folds* (available through *Independent Lens*, a PBS program), is often used in upper-level mathematics courses (even in college) as an introduction to this beautiful and sophisticated integration.

One entry point for using origami in a mathematics class is through folding a paper frog (figure 11.2). After folding their paper frog, students experience making lines of symmetry, angles, and other shapes; next, they can make their origami frog jump. Students can measure and collect the length the frog leaps, which becomes an authentic data set. The students can rank the data from the shortest leap to the longest leap and determine the *range* of their data. Then the students can determine the *mode*, *median*, and *mean* of the data set (figure 11.3).

A possible graphical representation of the data collected using the origami frogs is a box and whisker plot (or box plot) (figure 11.4), which is a method for visually displaying the range and spread of the data. This graphical representation can assist the students in analyzing the data. In a box and whisker plot the ends of the box are the upper and lower quartiles, so the box spans the interquartile range. The median is marked by a vertical line inside the box, and the two lines outside the box extend to the highest (maximum) and lowest (minimum) data points. When the student interprets the box plot, they might choose to create a different data display to get a different look at the data. For more information, see the Khan Academy tutorial: https://www.khanacademy.org/math/probability/data-distributions-a1/box--whisker-plots-a1/v/constructing-a-box-and-whisker-plot.

Other graphical representations include stem-and-leaf plots, circle graphs, scattergrams, and double bar graphs. Instruction today recommends an abundance of problems drawn from data presented in tables, charts, and graphs so

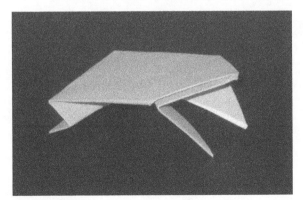

Figure 11.2   Origami frog.

Name _____   Date_____

Frog leaps	Rank from shortest to longest
54 cm	22 cm
37 cm	31 cm
92 cm	32 cm
33 cm	33 cm
69 cm	37 cm
45 cm	37 cm
32 cm	40 cm
22 cm	41 cm
109 cm	45 cm
31 cm	54 cm
37 cm	68 cm
40 cm	69 cm
83 cm	83 cm
41 cm	92 cm
68 cm	109 cm

1. Subtract the shortest frog leap from the longest frog leap. This is the range of your data set. 87 cm
2. What distance appears most frequently? This is your mode. 37 cm
3. What is the middle frog leap in your data set? This is your median? 41 cm
4. Looking at the 15 frog leaps, what is an estimate of the average leap of your frog? About 43 cm
5. What is the average or mean of your data set? Add up all 15 leaps and divide by   15 to determine the mean. 52.8 cm

Figure 11.3   Frog leap recording sheet.

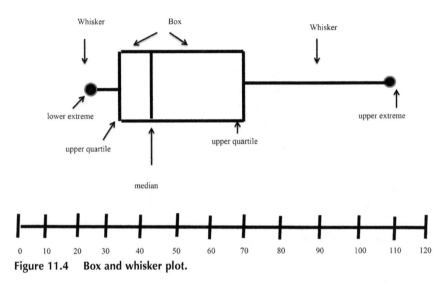

Figure 11.4   Box and whisker plot.

that students have the opportunity to make conjectures and to convert data into charts and graphs, with and without technology.

Arts and Science

As the saying goes, a picture is worth a thousand words. Using images in a content area can provide extra support to students learning challenging concepts. These visual images taken from the internet, from the teacher's travels, or observed in virtual museum trips can stimulate new views of the world. Visual images, not verbal explanations, are often more effective in displaying multiple relationships and processes that are difficult to describe (Cook, 2011). However, visual images with verbal explanations are the best approach to increase student learning (Nilson, 2017).

To the delight of many teachers, art in the form of photos and drawings is available for free through a range of government and professional organizations. Did you know that NASA posts "Image of the Day" and "Astronomy Pic of the Day" on its website? On the day that this paragraph was written, "Dreamy Swirls on Saturn" was featured with the caption: "NASA's *Cassini* spacecraft gazed toward the northern hemisphere of Saturn to spy subtle, multihued bands in the clouds there" (https://www.nasa.gov/multimedia/imagegallery/index.html). U.S. Geological Survey and the National Institute of Health offer similar access to public domain images teachers can readily use in the classroom. Imagine greeting each day with an image of a natural wonder or magnified body part invisible to the naked eye, like neurons created by scientists and artists. Or think about how your lesson on a challenging topic will be enhanced by one or two brilliant images that will say so much more than you can describe.

When science is viewed as inquiry and highlighted as a human endeavor, the arts can be used as a tool for artistic expression to (1) communicate science explanations, (2) engage in science as a means for explanation, and (3) communicate their ideas to the public and to their classmates (NRC, 1996). No wonder so many scientists were also artists! Beatrix Potter, Ansel Adams, and Leonardo da Vinci are just three of countless many who have merged scientific pursuits and artistic endeavors. Their desire to capture and document their own scientific discovery is understandable. As scientists and artists use drawings or photographs to closely observe and document ideas, students can use drawings and other art forms as a tool to develop and document more complex understandings (Stein, McNair, & Butcher, 2001).

Arts and Social Studies

Many of the most important events in history, like the Revolutionary War, are documented by artwork, music, and literature. Hearing about George Washington crossing the Delaware with his troops does not have the same impact as seeing a painting depicting the event. Paintings are primary resources that provide images that are difficult to describe in textbooks. Historical context and realities of that time period can be portrayed through the use of paintings. One selection of a work of art is a more recent rendition of *Washington Crossing the Delaware* illustrated by Cheryl Harness (figure 11.5) from her picture book, *George Washington* (2006).

A social studies unit on the civil rights movement could be enhanced with a lesson about the artists known as the Florida Highwaymen. During the difficult time of racial unrest, a group of entrepreneurial young black artists in Florida found a way to make an honest living by painting Florida landscapes on scraps of wood tossed out from home construction sites. The artists sold many of their paintings door to door but received their name from setting up stands along the side of the Florida highways. Originally the artwork sold for a few dollars, but the values have escalated and the paintings today are considered quite collectible. Many arts advocates argue that using artwork like the pictures painted by the Florida Highwaymen is a method for intellectually and emotionally engaging students in issues of the individual and society.

Introducing students to the arts of different cultures as primary sources of learning history introduces students to the "feel" of a culture in addition to the "facts" of a culture (Goldberg, 2006). Fowler (1996) states, "Human beings invented each of the arts as a way of representing particular aspects of reality

Figure 11.5 *Washington Crossing the Delaware.* **By Cheryl Harness.**

in order to understand and make sense of the world, manage life better, and to be able to share these perceptions with others" (p. 55).

Other iconic photographs and paintings that capture historical moments are *Raising the Flag on Iwo Jima* during World War II (figure 11.6) and Dr. Martin Luther King Jr. as he delivers his "I Have a Dream" speech during the civil rights movement (figure 11.7). Hearing Dr. King deliver his famous speech can be a moving experience for students instead of just reading a few of his most famous lines. These are only a few of the many examples that can help to bring history to life and impact the way students grasp past historical events. Period photographs and other primary source documents are engaging historical tools that should be part of students' educational experiences.

Music is another form of art with tremendous impact on learning. According to Jäncke (2008), "Autobiographical information associated with musical melodies is evoked when we hear relevant music or when we are engaged in conversation about music or episodes and events in our life in which music has been important. Hearing music associated with our past often evokes a strong 'feeling of knowing'" (p. 21). And other prominent neuroscientists have documented the connection between music and memory. So why not use music, not simply to remember moments in our autobiography, but to recall moments in history? Music captures moments in time in a way that no other art form can. Some will tell the story of the moment purely in sounds, like a jazz tune, or in words, like "Dust Bowl Blues" by Woody

Figure 11.6   *Raising the American Flag at Iwo Jima.* **Library of Congress photo and print archives.**

Guthrie. But all will recreate the tone and the mood of the time in ways that elicit our own emotional responses.

Arts and English Language Arts

The arts are often defined as a language of expression and communication. They act as a language of expression for people and cultures throughout the world and provide humankind with modes for reflecting on, expressing, and documenting experiences while serving as a unique document of cultures and history (Goldberg, 2006).

> For both teachers and students, the arts can be a form of expression, communication, imagination, observation, perception and thought. The arts are integral to the development of cognitive skills such as listening, thinking, problem solving, matching form to function, and decision-making. They inspire discipline, dedication and creativity. (Goldberg & Phillips, 1992, p. v)

In a classroom where the students are English language learners, the arts can serve as the unifying language. The student who just arrived from Egypt

Figure 11.7   Dr. Martin Luther King Jr. gives his "I Have a Dream" speech. Library of Congress photo and print archives.

or China may not be able to use language to communicate, but a creative teacher can provide students access to expressing themselves through the arts as an alternative to a typical assessment. For example, allow students to draw a concept instead of a written response. The arts provide students with a range of opportunities to express themselves in a variety of ways that are beyond what is found in most traditional classrooms.

Mix
Chants with sand paintings
Mysteries with a shadow show
Biographies with portraits
Value statements with totem poles
Spooky tales with black crayon resists
Snow poetry with soap bubble paintings
Color words or phrases with batik
Monster tales with squished paint blobs
Character sketches with cartoon sketches
Wind poems with pinwheels or wind chimes
Haiku with silkscreens or bamboo painting

Picturesque phrases with torn paper scenes
Earth poetry with rock painting or mud painting
Descriptions of scenes with wet watercolor paintings
Lies or tall tales with oversized, exaggerated creatures
Limericks with crazy gourd characters or vegetable people
Poems about feelings with melted crayon or wet chalk designs
Proverbs with clay plaques or wood collages or stained glass designs
Tales about people with paper-mâché or clay-sculpted masks
City poems or observations on city life with skyline paintings
Impressionistic poetry with paper mosaics or crayoned pointillism
Autobiographies or me-poems with body outlines or face silhouettes
Ecology posters or ecological bumper stickers with junk sculpture

(Frank, 1979, 1995, p. 230).

Integrating the arts in the content areas is the basis for this chapter, but it is equally important if your content area is in the arts to integrate other content areas with your subjects as well. To illustrate this idea, two faculty members at a small college, an art professor and a history professor, created a new course for first-year students that integrated "drawing" with "environmental issues" and a dose of "superhero." Students in this course studied the historical impact of global warming while creating artwork depicting Future Bear, a superhero polar bear that takes the initiative to protect his environment from global warming (see Future Bear @ http://futurebear.strikingly.com). Creative ideas like this one can be achieved in your own school when you sit down with colleagues to see where your interests intersect.

THEORY TO PRACTICE

Real life is integrated. During the art class, which is a separate content area, the art teacher and the content area teacher can plan for more extended art projects together that are connected to the curriculum being developed in the classroom and implemented during the scheduled art class time. The art teacher has a variety of art tools and media that may not be as readily available to the content area teacher. An art specialist can ensure that students are actively engaged with *all* the art forms. The ideal goal would be to balance between the art-integrated curriculum in the content areas and arts as a separate content discipline. Zemelman, Daniels, and Hyde (1998) recommend that art be brought to students in its "full-strength formula: robust, powerful, idiosyncratic, critical, and more than a bit dangerous" (p. 163).

All teachers should enhance their curriculum by engaging in the arts. Our students view their teachers as writers when they observe us writing, as mathematicians when we problem solve, and as scientists when we observe our surroundings. Equally important is for our students to observe us as artists and to participate in our own creative process along with our students. As teachers we can model for our students how to use the tools of art to explore and express content area concepts.

When students explore their ideas through art, they have the opportunity to develop cognitive and creative skills and most importantly their imaginations. Paul Ostergard, vice president of Citicorp, stated, "A broad education in the arts helps give children a better understanding of their world. . . . We need students who are culturally literate as well as math and science literate" (http://www.brandbelieving.com/paul-ostergard-vice-president-citicorp/). We argue that imagining is at the core of creating, and creating is an action process. Many art forms involve working with others and creating new ideas, two areas we want to enhance for the twenty-first-century student (Sprenger, 2010). The arts foster creativity and provide a safe place for students to explore and communicate ideas while enhancing problem solving and critical-thinking skills. In the arts there are multiple representations and interpretations that are correct and valid responses. The arts are not just a decorative extra to support the content areas; they are essential and fundamental to learning.

REFERENCES

Burgess, D. (2012). *Teach like a pirate*. San Diego, CA: Dave Burgess Consulting.

Cook, M. (2011). Teachers' use of visual representations in the classroom. *Science Education International, 22*(3), 175–84.

Donahue, D. M., & Stuart, J. (Eds.). (2010). *Artful teaching: Integrating the arts for understanding across the curriculum, K–8*. New York: Teachers College Press.

Efland, A. D. (2002). *Art and cognition: Integrating the visual arts in the curriculum*. New York: Teachers College Press.

Eisner, E. (2002). *The arts and the creation of mind*. In chapter 4, What the arts teach and how it shows (pp. 70–92). New Haven, CT: Yale University Press. Retrieved from www.arteducators.org › Advocacy.

Fiske, E. B. (Ed.). (1999). *Champions of change: The impact of the arts on learning*. Committee on the Arts and the Humanities: The John D. and Catherine T. MacArthur Foundation.

Fowler, C. (1996). *Can we rescue the arts for America's children?* New York: American Council for the Arts.

Frank, M. (1979, 1995). *If your're tyring to teach kids how to write, you've got to have this book*. Nashville, TN: Incentive Publications.

Goldberg, M. (2006). *Integrating the arts: An approach to teaching and learning in multicultural and multilingual settings*. New York: Pearson.

Goldberg, M., & Phillips, A. (Eds.). (1992). *Arts as education*. Cambridge, MA: Harvard Educational Review.

Gullatt, D. E. (2007). Research links the arts with student academic gains. *The Educational Forum*, *70*(3), 211–20.

Gullatt, D. E. (2008). Enhancing student learning through arts integration: Implications for the profession. *The High School Journal*, *91*(4), 12–25.

Harness, C. (2006). *George Washington*. National Geographic Children's Books.

Hetland, L., Winner, E., Veenema, S., & Sheridan, K. (2007). *Studio thinking: The real benefits of visual arts education*. New York: Teachers College Press.

Jäncke, L. (2008). Music, memory and emotion. *Journal of Biology*, *7*(6), 21. doi:10.1186/jbiol82

Lincoln Center Institute. (2008). The capacities for imaginative learning. Retrieved from https://imaginationnow.files.wordpress.com/2011/03/capacities.pdf.

Manner, J. (2002). Arts throughout the curriculum. *Kappa Delta Pi Record*, *39*(1), 17–19.

National Aeronautics and Space Administration. (2017). Image galleries. Retrieved from https://www.nasa.gov/multimedia/imagegallery/index.html.

National Research Council. (1996). *National science education standards*. Washington, DC: National Academy Press.

Nilson, L. B. (2016). Teaching at its best: A research-based resource for college instructors (Fourth ed.). San Francisco, CA: Jossey-Bass.

Sprenger, M. B. (2010). *Brain-based teaching in the digital age*. Alexandria, VA: Association of Supervision and Curriculum Development.

Stein, M., McNair, S., & Butcher, J. (2001). Drawing on student understanding: Using illustrations to invoke deeper thinking about animals. *Science and Children*, *38*(4), 18–22.

Zemelman, S., Daniels, H., & Hyde, A. (1998). *Best practice: New standards for teaching and learning in America's schools* (Second ed.). Portsmouth, NH: Heinemann.

12

Creating Lifelong, Vibrant Learners
Motivation

People often say that motivation doesn't last. Well, neither does bathing—that's why we recommend it daily.

—Zig Ziglar

Pac-Man

Pac-Man was all the rage in the early 1980s. I was in my third year of teaching sixth grade and had been quite successful at using fun, motivational games to get my students to complete homework and be on their best behavior. Each season brought a new motivational bulletin board; October had thirty-two footballs making progress toward the goal posts, and each day each student earned or didn't earn another inch toward their goal. During parent-teacher conferences in early November I met with one very frustrated mother. Her son was doing poorly in every class and did not seem to care. When the mother mentioned that he wanted a Pac-Mac game, I had an idea. I asked the mother if she would support buying her son that game if he was able to play a version of it to get his work done.

Here is how I imagined it:

I would create a game board similar to what Pac-Man looked like. I would use a paper punch and punch out over 250 paper "dots" and meticulously glue each dot in place. I would make three ghosts for each teacher and inform them that when Mike did not get his work completed for class, they were to give him a ghost and tell me they had given him one. Just like the game, when he got three ghosts, the game would be over and he would not get the Pac-Man game from his mother. Mike would be inspired, and his grades would shoot up!

Here is what happened:

I spent the entire weekend creating the board just as I described. It was adorable. I put the three ghosts in four envelopes and delivered them to each of his teachers before school on Monday morning. I explained the game to them and invited them to come by my classroom to see Mike's personalized Pac-Man game. I was so proud!

215

In homeroom that day, Mike seemed upbeat and excited to get started on his very own Pac-Man game. He assured me he had completed his homework in every class. He left for his first class at 8:00 a.m. At 10:08 a.m., when the bell rang to dismiss students from second period, two teachers appeared at my door with three ghosts in hand.

The game was over. It took him less time to "lose" the game that it had taken me to create it! I learned two lessons that day: (1) never work harder than your students; and (2) the ultimate goal is "intrinsic" motivation.

His mom bought him the Pac-Man game anyway—that week.

One of the most, if not *the* most, important role of a teacher is that of a coach with just the right amount of nudging with an appropriate amount of support. This mix is what creates and sustains motivation. Several education scholars have referred to motivation as a key "pillar" of effective instruction. Malloy, Marinak, and Gambrell (2010) note, "Motivation refers to the likelihood of choosing one activity over another, as well as the persistence and effort exerted when participating in the chosen activity" (p. 1). Considering choice, persistence, effort, and participation are all ingredients for learning, skills in motivating students seems imperative to teacher effectiveness (Good & Brophy, 1991).

Some critics of public education assert that schools have a tendency to take the enjoyment out of the learning process. Perhaps this criticism is a fair one in that learning in middle and high schools has remained virtually unchanged in decades. The principles of learning presented in this text—sociocultural and constructivist perspectives, role of prior knowledge in the meaning-making process, integration within and among the disciplines, use of authentic texts and authentic learning contexts, and more—are meant to challenge that status quo. Many of these principles transform the role of the student in the learning process, and this transformation hinges on the intentionality of the teacher in creating the most desirable learning environments.

THEORETICAL FOUNDATIONS OF MOTIVATION

Motivation is referred to as the "*personal* investment that an *individual* has in reaching a *desired* state or outcome [emphasis added]" (Ambrose, Lovett, Bridges, DiPietro, Lovett & Norman, 2010, p. 68). According to this definition, the desire must stem from the individual, and the investment to want to accomplish the goals has to be personal. It seems logical, then, to begin the conversation about motivation with defining (1) the individual (i.e., middle and high school students) and (2) what a desired state or outcome is for that individual.

First, let us focus on the individual. Teachers must grapple with the developmental stage of preteen and teenage students; these students are highly attuned to what their peers are doing and what those peers perceive as acceptable behavior. During these years, many students have trouble staying focused on academics with the exciting and ever-changing social life exploding around them. Sometimes, a teacher feels like a miracle worker just getting their attention for a few moments, let alone finding a topic that will sustain their interest. In addition, reading levels tend to fall off during these years (Klein, 1997), and often students are deterred from showing any interest in learning. These are the kinds of students that need a supportive teacher to encourage continued school achievement and success. For these and other reasons, teaching this age group has unique challenges.

Considering the challenge of working with students at this age, the second factor—desired state or outcome—may be the key to motivation. Keeping in mind what the teacher is expected to teach, they may offer students opportunities to set personal goals that are valuable and important. Create possibilities for students' curiosities about a particular topic to play a role in their work, and have them reflect and assess their learning in ways that are personally meaningful. After completing a unit on a particular topic, could you offer a mini-inquiry project based on their remaining questions? Is there a task that mirrors real-life situations that students can use to demonstrate mastery? Can students take a social action approach or tackle problem-based projects that would deepen their learning? The smallest ideas that you may have about these and other questions may be the seed to motivate your students to learn.

FACTORS THAT CONTRIBUTE TO MOTIVATION

Entire college courses are taught on motivating students, and we encourage you to take one of these courses for a better understanding of how you can help students achieve their potential. For the purposes of this book, we will highlight five important factors that contribute to motivating high levels of achievement and satisfaction in students—and you, their teacher.

1. Organization of learning experiences around themes or big questions.
2. Importance of establishing a community of learners.
3. Creating opportunities for students to learn in social situations—even with their friends.
4. Necessity of teachers to model and encourage literate behaviors.
5. Allowing students to become active participants in self-reflection and assessment of their learning.

Organization of Learning Experiences

One of the most thrilling aspects of teaching is organizing a unit of instruction that builds on previous student knowledge, takes into account students' abilities, and challenges students while at the same time providing support to those students. Many researchers have noted the importance of organization on students' learning experiences (Strong, Silver, Perini & Tuculescu, 2003; Strickland, Ganske & Monroe, 2002). Organizing effective units of instruction, or even daily lesson plans, take a great deal of experience. Most teachers have experienced well-planned lessons that did not live up to expectations, and sometimes a "teachable moment" or lesson has surprised us by the enthusiasm of our students' response to a lesson. We are confident you will experience a "teaching high": an exuberant feeling when learning is clicking and students are immersed in the topic, seemingly unable to get enough information. Organizing effective learning experiences will do a great deal toward motivating your students and in turn good classroom management. Students engaged in a topic are less likely to be looking for ways to be disruptive.

However, we understand the realities of today's curricular demands and understand that many may be required to follow the district or state adopted textbook of your discipline. You may not have many opportunities to "create" a unit based on a theme or novel. Integrating authentic literature into your content area instruction along with finding ways to integrate subjects by bringing mathematics into your social studies class or art into your mathematics class will provide motivation to your students. Using a variety of "texts" that are readily available on the internet can help establish connections between content area subjects. The integration of genres such as fiction, entertainment, sports, and music that are not commonly included in a school's curriculum may be the spark that grabs a student's attention. Popular culture and young adult literature are easily woven into an already established curriculum. Keep in mind your gifted students will be clamoring to learn more or learn more deeply about topics that interest them.

The following is a checklist of items for guidance when planning learning experiences for your students:

- Make your curriculum relevant—match content area requirements with what students want to learn.
- Answer the question "Why do we have to learn this?" by creating an enthusiastic learning environment.
- Organize units that stimulate and provoke students' interests.
- Provide access to interesting and challenging reading materials, not just books.
- Allow students to self-select their reading materials.

- Provide explicit instruction, when needed.
- Work challenging tasks into your assignments but provide support.
- Research skills should be developed even in middle school; teach them the steps to investigating a question.
- Allow them to work in groups and with their friends.
- Be aware of opportunities and work to build their intrinsic motivation.
- Model and show examples of good reading, writing, listening, speaking, and viewing,
- If you can make it a "hands-on" experience—do so!
- Discussion should be often and deep.
- Ask yourself, "Would I be interested in this unit taught in this manner?"

Establishing a Community of Learners

Middle and high school students are living some of the most challenging years of their lives. More than a few times we have heard people joke that they would not want to relive those years. It is during this time that students begin to question and challenge the notions and beliefs they learned at home. Many times students will encounter cognitive dissonance as they try to make sense of this new information. The process of restructuring this new information so that it fits with what they already know can be scary and confusing. Sometimes they have to let go of an earlier belief, and that can be uncomfortable. Helping students to negotiate this terrain is one of the reasons these students are so exciting to teach!

It is also a challenging age to teach. One of the most important aspects of working with students is providing them with learning experiences that challenge, push them to consider new ideas, and support them as they explore and question (Strong et al., 2003). Teachers must create a strong community of learners where all students feel safe to take learning risks without fear of being teased or ridiculed (Gambrell & Marinak, 1997). This goes for teachers as well! A teacher who makes a flippant comment can at the least embarrass a student, and at the worst, devastate a student and turn her sour on school. This does not mean a teacher should not have a sense of humor with her students, but the student should never be the punch line or be held up as an example of poor work. This is a tough age, and it is our responsibility to encourage and support our students.

Equaly important is to identify and help students to develop their strengths. The strengths you are able to recognize may not even be visible to the student with the strength. How you treat your special needs or struggling students should be the model of inclusiveness. Do not separate your struggling students away from the class; help them discover ways to work together. Keep in mind methods to engage students with Asperger's or autism, whose strength may not lie in the discussion but may lie in artistic representation or locating and keeping track of details. Encourage and guide your students to be supportive of classmates instead of a typical reaction of separating from students who are different from them. Students at this age can turn into "agents of change," as demonstrated by a class of seventh-graders that came to the defense of one of their peers with Tourette's when a substitute teacher began to discipline a student for an outburst. Several students calmly came to their friend's aid and explained to the substitute what Tourette's was and that she could not discipline him for the outburst; "it is just the way he is."

Keep the following checklist in mind when examining yourself to see if you have created a vibrant community of learners:

- Do you connect the required curriculum with current issues and topics?
- Do you find ways for students to take ownership of their learning?
- Do you search for relevant books, magazines, and web pages that will excite student learning?
- Are you cognizant of the emotions your students are experiencing?
- Do you avoid confrontations with a student where they feel threatened or a "need to save face" among their peers?
- Have you provided field trips or other opportunities so students can see how what they are learning in school is used in real-world situations?

Learning in Social Situations

One common practice that needs to be revisited is the insistence by teachers that students should not be allowed to work in groups with their friends. As you think back to your last experience working in a group of peers that were not your friends, you can probably remember the amount of time negotiating roles and deciding who would serve as the leader. On top of the task in which you were asked to engage, you also had to learn to negotiate how to work together. According to Sandmann (2006), adult writers would not choose to work with strangers, so why do we insist that our students work with strangers? A group of already established friends could get to the work of the task quicker because role negotiations need not take place (Rosenblatt, 2004). Sandmann (1990) noted, "Friendship appears to support the writing process. These students created their own best work environment given the opportunity to do so" (p. 203). As learning in social situations becomes more prominent in classrooms (Gambrell, 2001; Strong et al., 2003; Rosenblatt, 2004; Strickland et al., 2002), teachers should consider allowing the students' already formed relationships the opportunity to enhance collaborative learning. As Sandmann (2006) encourages us, "With relationships in place, the work becomes central. Students readily learn from one another in this supportive environment" (p. 23).

One of the most common mistakes we have seen is the assumption by a teacher that his students know how to work in groups. Teamwork is one of the important skills students need to be explicitly taught. Experience will provide students with a great deal of knowledge, but a teacher that can help students negotiate the pros and the cons of group work will most likely have students that enjoy working in learning teams.

When incorporating teamwork in classrooms, encourage students to participate by sharing ideas and showing respect for others' opinions. The following list of additional items is important to keep in mind when using teamwork as part of social learning in the classroom.

- Teach students how to have respectful disagreements.
- Teach students how to play on each other's strengths; this is a great way to show how diverse individuals can actually support one another.
- Promote learning conversations, including how to embrace a variety of ideas.
- Allow students to choose a cause or topic and allow them to form groups by their interest.
- Monitor students' social growth and provide feedback and time for them to self-reflect on how they are doing and what they could do better.

Imagine your role more as a coach, and try not to participate in your students' discussions. When students realize their learning does not *always* have to be teacher directed, they learn to think for themselves.

Model and Encourage Literate Behaviors

Most students want to make their teachers and parents proud. Your enthusiasm for learning will be contagious to your students. As content area teachers, we find our specific areas fascinating, and we need to share our excitement with our students (Jensen, 2005; Ivey & Broaddus, 2001; Strickland et al., 2002). A secondary mathematics teacher turns March 14 into a schoolwide "Happy Pi Day" event. While some teachers may be less than enthusiastic about politics, we also know a social studies teacher who is able to engage her students in the election process with great success. The biggest debate from her students—who she is voting for!

The ability to think critically and broadly is essential to being a responsible leader in the twenty-first century. A teacher that models the importance of lifelong learning will do a great deal toward creating future lifelong learners out of his students. Include your students in your scholarly interests by sharing books you have enjoyed or news items you have found interesting. According to Kragler and Nolley (1996), the most common reason students give for selecting a particular book is that someone made a recommendation; that someone is often their teacher. Following is a list of examples for teachers to model and encourage literate behaviors:

- Serve as an enthusiastic reading/writing role model.
- Provide time to read in school.
- Read to your students; hearing a great reader helps them in the area of fluency.
- Share your scholarly interests with your students.
- Take time to have a "teachable moment" sparked by a news item.
- Embrace and encourage self-expression, including providing multiple ways for students to show you what they have learned.

Active Participants in Reflection and Assessment of Learning

At the end of the learning process, students' reflections and assessment about what they have accomplished and internalized may be more important than grades given to them by the teacher. Consider asking students to reflect on the following questions:

- What did you learn?
- How did that connect to what you already know?
- Does that new knowledge fuel additional questions?
- What is still unknown?
- Did you think you met the learning goals?
- If not, what could you do?

Engage students in talking about their accomplishments or aspirations using their insights. What they share with you might uncover the paths for future learning in your classroom.

ENCOURAGING GUYS

Teaching remains a predominantly female occupation. For the past twenty years, females have made up 82 to 84 percent of elementary teachers, and men are even scarcer in preschool and kindergarten, making up only 2 percent of those teaching that age. With evidence showing that males are lagging behind females in performance, many believe adolescent boys are being shortchanged (Whitmire & Bailey, 2010; Taylor, 2004; Young & Brozo, 2001).

As teachers, we must address this issue and make changes to incorporate activities and topics that engage boys in academics. According to Brozo (2002), "Reading often conflicts with boys' sense of masculinity" (p. 13). In 1999, a reading campaign called "Get Caught Reading" produced a variety of posters showing celebrities and athletes reading. Teachers should find ways to promote reading to both genders, including the use of a few of the free posters available through http://www.getcaughtreading.org/ showing men as reading models (figure 12.1). The Association of American Publishers (AAP) sponsors this site, and the posters are free.

Teachers also need to be aware that what we find fascinating might not be what our students find interesting. "Evidence abounds that language teachers are more likely to select and use narrative fiction that may be less appealing to boys" (Brozo, 2002, p. 77). Adolescent boys usually prefer expository texts, which are defined as nonfiction and informational books (Herz & Gallo, 1996), which should be encouraging news to content area teachers. "Teachers will never make significant progress eradicating boys' difficulty with reading and learning unless they dedicate themselves to discovering boys' interests and acquainting boys with quality books related to those interests" (Brozo, 2002, p. 78). Helping adolescent boys find entry points into active literacy

Figure 12.1   Get caught reading. Stock photo ID: 153714878.

must be a high priority for teachers, because it is from young men's early interests in books that a lifestyle of habitual reading can be nurtured (Young & Brozo, 2001). Furthermore, we know that reading ability is correlated with overall academic success (Donahue, Voelkl, Campbell & Mazzeao, 1999). Following is a checklist of ideas for promoting literate behaviors with guys/boys in mind:

- Promote reading as gender neutral; it is for both genders.
- Provide suggestions for books and articles you think boys will enjoy.
- Avoid stereotypical assumptions that align with a specific gender.
- Allow same-sex book clubs or group work.
- Use male literate examples; bring in men to read aloud to students.
- Engage boys through drama and art.
- Encourage boys to participate in making book choices.
- Expect students to set their own reading expectations; for example, tell them the book needs to be read by next Friday and let them decide how to chunk the book into reading assignments—you may be surprised that chapters are *not* the way they will divide the text.
- Do not get hung up on reading levels; interest in the topic should be the deciding factor.
- Respect what they *are* reading. A student choosing a comic book or a joke book is still reading.
- Introduce them to "Guys Read," a web page launched by author Jon Sciescka that recommends books for guys by guys.

THEORY TO PRACTICE

Teachers are responsible for the atmosphere of learning by setting the tone and mood of their classrooms. Adolescent students need an environment that provides opportunities to engage in literate behaviors, including exploring a topic more thoroughly if they develop an enthusiasm for a subject they find particularly interesting. Through the guidance of a great teacher, students learn to become independent thinkers and vibrant, lifelong learners.

REFERENCES

Ambrose, S., Lovett, M., Bridges, M., DiPietro, M., & Norman, M. (2010). *How learning works: Seven research-based principles for smart teaching.* San Francisco, CA: Jossey-Bass.

Brozo, W. G. (2002/2010). *To be a boy, to be a reader*. Newark, DE: International Reading Association.

Donahue, P. L., Voelkl, K. E., Campbell, J. R., & Mazzeo, J. (1999). NAEP 1998 Reading Report Card for the Nation and the States.

Gambrell, L. B. (2001). What we know about motivation to read. In R. F. Flippos (Ed.), *Reading researchers in search of common ground* (pp. 129–43). Newark, DE: International Reading Association.

Gambrell, L. B., & Marinak, B. A. (1997). Incentives and intrinsic motivation to read. In J. Guthrie. *Reading engagement: Motivating readers through integrated instruction*, 205–17. International Literacy Association.

Get caught reading. www.getcaughtreading.org.

Good, T., & Brophy, J. (1991). *Looking in classrooms* (5th ed.). New York: Harper & Row.

Herz, S. K., & Gallo, D. R. (1996). What is young adult literature anyway? Can it be any good if students like it? *From Hinton to Hamlet: Building bridges between young adult literature and the classics*, 7–12. Westport, CT: Greenwood Publishing.

Ivey, G., & Broaddus, K. (2001). "Just plain reading": A survey of what makes students want to read in middle school classrooms. *Reading Research Quarterly*, 36(4), 350–77.

Jensen, E. (2005). Motivation and engagement. In E. Jensen, *Teaching with the brain in mind* (2nd ed.) (pp. 102–11). Alexandria, VA: Association for Supervision and Curriculum Development.

Klein, G. (1997). *The recognition-primed decision (RPD) model: Looking back, looking forward*. Mahwah, NJ: Lawrence Erlbaum Associates, Inc.

Kragler, S., & Nolley, C. (1996). Student choices: Book selection strategies of fourth graders. *Reading Horizons*, 36(4), 5.

Malloy, J. A., Marinak, B. A., & Gambrell, L. B. (Eds.). (2010). *Essential readings on motivation*. Newark, DE: International Reading Association.

National Reading Panel. (2000). *Teaching children to read: An evidenced-based assessment of the scientific research literature on reading and its implications for reading instruction*. Washington, DC: National Institute of Child Health and Human Development.

Reeves, A. R. (2004). *Adolescents talk about reading: Exploring resistance to and engagement with text*. Newark, DE: International Reading Association.

Rosenblatt, L. (1938). *Literature as exploration*. New York: Appleton-Century.

Rosenblatt, L. (1978). *The reader, the text, and the poem*. Carbondale, IL: Southern Illinois University Press.

Rosenblatt, A. F. (2004). Preventing urban learners from becoming struggling readers: Can brain research be a foundation for good literacy teaching? In D. Lapp, C. C. Block, E. J. Cooper, J. Flood, N. Roser & J. V. Tinajero (Eds.), *Teaching ALL the children: Strategies for developing literacy in an urban setting* (pp. 202–19). New York: Guilford Press.

Sandmann, A. L. (1990). The effects of social interaction on variously skilled fourth graders' writing processes and products. Unpublished doctoral dissertation, University of Cincinnati.

Sandmann, A. L. (2006). Nurturing throughtful revision using the focused question card strategy. *Journal of Adolescent and Adult Literacy, 50*(1), 20–28.

Strickland, D. S., Ganske, K., & Monroe, J. K. (2002). *Supporting struggling readers and writers: Strategies for classroom interventions.* Newark, DE: International Reading Association.

Strong, R., Silver, H., Perini, H., & Tuculescu, G. (2003). Boredom and its opposite. *Educational Leadership, 61*(1), 24–29.

Taylor, D. L. (2004). "Not just boring stories": Reconsidering the gender gap for boys. *Journal of Adolescent and Adult Literacy, 36*(4), 290–98.

Whitmire, R., & Bailey, S. M. (2010). Gender gap. *Education Next 10,* 2. (Retrieved November 4, 2014, http://educationnext.org/gender-gap/).

Young, J. P., & Brozo, W. G. (2001). Boys will be boys, or will they? Literacy and masculinities. *Reading Research Quarterly, 36*(3), 316–25.

Index

About the Authors

Lynn Columba is an associate professor at Lehigh University's College of Education, where she teaches future mathematics educators to embrace an interdisciplinary mathematics classroom. Her research focuses on the integration of literacy and technology into mathematics. Lynn taught for fourteen years in Jefferson County Public Schools in Louisville, Kentucky. She received her EdD from the University of Louisville, where she taught in the Early and Middle Childhood Department in the School of Education for three years. She joined the College of Education at Lehigh University in 1989, where she has served as the program director of the Teaching, Learning, and Technology Program for ten years. Her scholarly interests include promoting the integration of literature, discourse, and writing in the mathematics classroom.

Cathy Y. Kim joined the Education Department at Muhlenberg College in 1998 as the literacy specialist. She also serves as the coordinator of Professional Programs, overseeing Muhlenberg's certification programs. She holds a BS in Education with a concentration in mathematics from the University of Illinois at Urbana–Champaign, and she taught third and sixth grades in the Chicago Public Schools while completing her MA in Linguistics with an area of concentration in second language acquisition at Northeastern Illinois University. In 1993, she enrolled in the PhD program in Curriculum and Instruction in Language and Literacy at the University of Illinois at Urbana-Champaign, where she completed all of the required coursework in the program. Since her arrival in Allentown, she has established herself as one of the most sought after literacy specialists and educational consultants in the region. Her book, *The Power of Picture Books in Teaching Math, Science, and Social Studies*, is in its second edition.

Alden J. Moe, professor emeritus from Rollins College and Lehigh University, has taught elementary, middle, and secondary grades before completing his PhD in Literacy Education, Educational Psychology, and Child Development at the University of Minnesota. Throughout his illustrious career, he held various faculty and administrative positions at Purdue University, Louisiana State University, Lehigh University, and Rollins College. Alden's research has focused on reading diagnosis, children's literature, and vocabulary development. He has authored, coauthored, or edited over 150 publications, and this book will be Alden's fifteenth book.

Debra Wellman taught middle-grade students at two districts before coming to Mary Miller Jr. High in Georgetown, Illinois, for twelve years. She received her PhD from the University of Toledo and joined the education department at Rollins College in 2000. She has served Rollins in several administrative capacities, including as the director of the Christian A. Johnson Center for Effective Teaching, various interim dean roles, and dean of the College of Professional Studies. Her scholarly interests include the examination of the duration and value of preservice field placements, book clubs as a means for teaching reading and content areas, and effective ways to support new teachers, including new college professors.

CPSIA information can be obtained
at www.ICGtesting.com
Printed in the USA
BVHW08s2345260618
520127BV00003B/3/P

9 781475 842364